INTERCULTURAL COUPLES

INTERCULTURAL COUPLES

Exploring Diversity in Intimate Relationships

Edited by

TERRI A.KARIS AND KYLE D. KILLIAN

 Routledge
Taylor & Francis Group
New York   London

306.845
In8

Routledge
Taylor & Francis Group
270 Madison Avenue
New York, NY 10016

Routledge
Taylor & Francis Group
2 Park Square
Milton Park, Abingdon
Oxon OX14 4RN

© 2009 by Taylor & Francis Group, LLC
Routledge is an imprint of Taylor & Francis Group, an Informa business

Printed in the United States of America on acid-free paper
10 9 8 7 6 5 4 3 2 1

International Standard Book Number-13: 978-0-7890-2940-9 (Softcover) 978-0-7890-2939-3 (Hardcover)

Library of Congress Cataloging-in-Publication Data

Intercultural couples : exploring diversity in intimate relationships / edited by Terri A.
Karis, Kyle D. Killian.
p. cm.
Includes bibliographical references and index.
ISBN 978-0-7890-2939-3 (hardbound : alk. paper) -- ISBN 978-0-7890-2940-9 (pbk.
: alk. paper)
1. Interethnic marriage. 2. Intercountry marriage I. Karis, Terri A. II. Killian, Kyle
D.

HQ1032.I58 2008
306.84'5--dc22   2008024924

Visit the Taylor & Francis Web site at
http://www.taylorandfrancis.com

and the Routledge Web site at
http://www.routledge.com

Contents

Contents

SECTION III   Particular Cultural Combinations

Acknowledgments

This book would not have been possible without the creative work of the contributing authors. I appreciate their heartfelt engagement with the topic of how partners navigate cultures, and their patience with the process of bringing this project to completion. In particular I want to acknowledge Paul Rosenblatt for many years of mentorship and friendship; without his support and guidance, this book would not exist. Thanks to Dr. Stella Ting-Toomey for kind words of encouragement, reminding me that life balance is important, regardless of work demands. Special thanks to my collaborator, Kyle D. Killian. Working together on this project deepened my appreciation for his good mind and good heart. Thanks also to Jennifer Kropidlowski McCarten for conscientious and creative editorial assistance.

Terri A. Karis

I, too, would like to express my deep appreciation of the creativity, and persistence, of our exceptional colleagues who contributed to this volume. A special note of thanks to Terri A. Karis, who was pivotal in bringing our contributors to the table, and kept the project on track when the path seemed daunting. I also thank my parents, David and Sallie Killian, for their nurturance and their active support of my intellectual development and academic pursuits. Finally, I must thank Anna M. Agathangelou—colleague, partner, and the mother of our two sons, Mikael Lawrence and Aleksi Christos. Her intelligence, compassion, commitment to social justice, and daily praxis are truly inspiring. She is one of those rare persons whose energy and passion really makes a difference to all who know her.

Kyle D. Killian

Contributors

Anna M. Agathangelou
Department of Political Science
   and Women's Studies Program
York University
Toronto, Canada

Gonzalo Bacigalupe
Department of Counseling and
   School Psychology
University of Massachusetts
Boston, Massachusetts

Manijeh Daneshpour
Marriage and Family Therapy
   Program
St. Cloud State University
St. Cloud, Minnesota

Stanley O. Gaines, Jr.
School of Social Sciences and Law
Brunel University
London, United Kingdom

Jessie Grearson
Freelance Writer
Falmouth, Maine

Terri A. Karis
Department of Psychology
University of Wisconsin-Stout
Menomonie, Wisconsin

Kyle D. Killian
Faculty of Health and Centre for
   Refugee Studies
York University
Toronto, Canada

Wendy Leeds-Hurwitz
Department of Communication
University of Wisconsin-Parkside
Kenosha, Wisconsin

Roxana Llerena-Quinn
Department of Outpatient
   Psychiatry
Harvard University Children's
   Hospital
Boston, Massachusetts

Ingrid Piller
AMEP (Adult Migrant English
   Program) Research Center
Macquarie University
Sydney, Australia

Marina W. Ramkissoon
Department of Sociology,
   Psychology and Social Work
University of the West Indies
   (UWI)
Mona Campus Jamaica
Mona, Jamaica

Mudita Rastogi
Clinical Psychology Program
Argosy University
Schaumburg, Illinois

Paul C. Rosenblatt
Department of Family Social
   Science
University of Minnesota
St. Paul, Minnesota

Lauren Smith
Department of Women's Studies
University of Wisconsin-
   Whitewater
Whitewater, Wisconsin

Stella Ting-Toomey
Department of Human
   Communication Studies
California State University
Fullerton, California

Lynn Visson
Monterey Institute of
   International Studies
Monterey, California

Introduction

Kyle D. Killian

Attend to how couples deal with cultural differences, by maximizing or minimizing them, using them as reality, mask or metaphor for their relationship issues.—Celia Jaes Falicov

Marriage does not change people; it merely unmasks them.—Sydney Harris

In this era of globalization, when high-speed travel and communication technologies allow us to quickly bridge physical distances, we see unprecedented increases in movement across national and cultural borders, with greater numbers of people leaving their motherlands to visit, study, find employment, and establish relationships. In the United States, 11.7% of the population, or 35 million people, are immigrants (Shibusawa, 2007), with over 9 million immigrants entering the United States between 1991 and 2000. Adding to the burgeoning diversity already evident in the United States, the number of cross-cultural couples has also increased rapidly in the past three decades (Estrada, 2005; Hernandez, 2003; Laird, 2000). Yet, scant few articles (e.g., McGoldrick & Preto, 1984), chapters (Falicov, 1995), and texts (Grearson & Smith, 1995) have provided readers with helpful ways of understanding the diverse experiences and dilemmas of this growing population.

How does one go about defining the scope, or terrain, of this book? Borrowing from Bateson (1979), Keeney (1982) tells us that the fundamental act of epistemology is drawing *distinctions*:

distinguishing an "it" from the background that is not "it"; We do this when we demarcate or draw a boundary around an individual as different from a family, or use the difference between you and me in order to engage in a conversation. All that we know, or can know, rests upon the distinctions we draw (p. 156).

Cultures vary in regard to how the world of experience is punctuated, and particular punctuations organize or pattern events in particular ways.

People have distinctive ways of making meaning and creating frames of reference, and cross-cultural couples are distinguished by looking at the *distinctive borders* that partners cross in establishing a relationship together; such borders, or *ecosystemic* distinctions, include nationality, race, ethnicity, mother tongue, and religion. Punctuating this text and its accompanying terrain, I define *cross-cultural couples* as consisting of partners from different countries, nationalities, ethnicities, and religions who may possess quite divergent beliefs, assumptions, and values as a result of their socialization in different sociocultural spaces. While all relationships are complex, cross-cultural or intercultural couples experience another level of complexity because both overt and subtle cultural "differences making a difference" (Bateson, 1979, p. 6) are part of the couple dynamics. Since social locations on multiple ecosystemic axes of power inform and organize relational dynamics, with or without our awareness, concerted efforts to recognize how privilege and power intersect with ecosystems of culture, nationality, gender, and class are crucial to advancing our understanding of cross-cultural couples.

Many of the prevailing theories of couple and family development have fallen short in their attempts to recognize and elucidate the unique experiences of partners within their particular sociohistorical and politico-economic milieus. When cultural difference is viewed as an opportunity for meaningful discussion, rather than a problem or burden, cross-cultural partners can more readily acknowledge and process a host of social locations, cultural selves, and differentials in privilege (Ho, Rasheed, & Rasheed, 2004; Killian, 2001, 2002). Racial and ethnicity status, language, biculturalism and level of acculturation, social class, and cultural narratives are just a few sources of difference that may be experienced as crisis or opportunity; culturally based misunderstandings represent an ever-present potential pitfall, while a willingness to work at recognizing and talking about such differences creates the chance to deepen one's understanding and acceptance of an alternative point of view. Thus, while they often experience the same types of relationship conflicts as couples comprised of partners from the same cultural backgrounds (Biever, Bobele, & North, 1998; Ho, 2005), cross-cultural couples, like interracial couples (Killian, 2001, 2003; Rosenblatt, Karis, & Powell, 1995), frequently face distinct challenges and situations that require additional reflection, consideration, and negotiation by partners, especially in contexts that problematize the forging of such connections. For example, what languages will be spoken in the home? If the partners choose to marry, which religious traditions and rituals are featured in the ceremony? And, as the couple forms a new family system, which parenting and disciplinary practices and cultural customs will be retained into the next generation, and which will be abandoned? These are just a few of the questions addressed in this volume.

The literature is replete with cautionary tales and bleak predictions regarding the chances of cross-cultural couples achieving dyadic bliss and stability. Specifically, researchers have pointed to the higher risks of communication difficulties, marital dissatisfaction, divorce, and child abduction, if the relationship fails (Bratter & King, 2008; Chin, 1994; Fu, Tora, & Kendall, 2001; Hegar & Greif, 1994; Usita & Poulsen, 2003). Joanides, Mayhew, and Mamalakis (2002) discussed how differences in religion and ethnicity can cause difficulties, and Softas-Nall and Baldo (2000) highlighted how even a shared ethnic origin does not always trump differences in national origin. In underscoring how such differences contribute to couples' distress (even misery), such work, albeit indirectly and unintentionally, tends to support attitudes and notions rooted in the principle of *homogamy*. A dominant discourse in mate selection literature (Surra, 1990) and Western society (Killian, 2003), homogamy holds that people are initially attracted to one another, and later achieve relationship success and satisfaction, because of similarities in background. Heterogamous mate selection practices run counter to this discourse of homogamy, and various notions or "rationales" of why persons do not, or *should* not, select partners across cultural, national, and/or linguistic borders continue to be prevalent. Thus, while some researchers claim that respectful exploration and negotiation of differences in social location and accompanying power can produce strong intimacy and mutual understanding (e.g., Heller & Wood, 2000), others seem resigned to the inevitable hard work required to push through the "innate hostility" present in intercultural relationships (McFadden & Moore, 2001). Rather than invoking visions of potential synergy and complementarity, such studies seem to assume ontological fear and loathing for persons who choose to cross cultural borders.

While cross-cultural relations and, more specifically, the formation of cross-cultural couplehood were once assumed to be inherently problematic, in recent years cross-cultural couples have increased in both numbers and social acceptance, and there is now a growing awareness of how little we really know about them. Addressing this gap in our knowledge, this volume presents 12 chapters focusing on cross-cultural couple formations (i.e., a partner from the United States and another from abroad). The chapters tackle a broad range of topics and issues, including systemic considerations of the phenomenon of cross-cultural couples, bilingual couples, interfaith relationships, struggles in such couple formations (e.g., differential acculturation) and different methods of approaching solutions, and the use of the Internet to meet partners from diverse backgrounds.

This book is organized into three sections. Section 1 features three chapters that offer epistemological lenses through which to view the phenomenon of persons coming together from radically divergent social locations and occupying different axes of power. In chapter 1, Paul Rosenblatt offers a systemic theoretical analysis of some of the factors that make a difference in intercultural relationships, noting the importance of race, gender, and class in determining relative power and privilege in the relationship. In developing their own intricate, multilayered systems, intercultural couples are affected by the other systems in which they are embedded, including their families, cultures of origin, and economic, legal, and political systems. Paul Rosenblatt focuses on three key areas of system dynamics: (a) major aspects of the ecosystem in which the couple lives; (b) interpersonal power in the couple relationship; and (c) changes in couple system dynamics as the relationship evolves over time.

In chapter 2, entitled "Ambiguity as a Solution to the 'Problem' of Intercultural Weddings," Wendy Leeds-Hurwitz engages the negotiations/ challenges that emerge in processes such as planning an intercultural wedding. Weddings are an instantiation of ongoing struggles of self-formation and ritualized cultural expressions. When partners from diverse backgrounds decide to come together to form a relationship, boundaries already in place (e.g., what is a normative family? what kinds of ontologies are presumed? what are the implied processes of negotiating/contesting power dynamics?) are challenged, reaffirmed, and/or disrupted. Leeds-Hurwitz examines ambiguity as an interactional resource. She argues how crucial it is to draw on familiar practices, albeit contradictory at times, to design an inclusive, yet "proper" wedding. A case study describes the specifics of how ambiguity worked for a particular couple. A detailed description of how two couples infused a canopy, often used in Jewish weddings, with African influences, invites readers to consider the layered and multiple identity statements embedded within a single ritual.

In chapter 3, "A Mindful Approach to Managing Conflict in Intercultural Intimate Couples," Stella Ting-Toomey discusses a mindful approach to relationship conflicts, including cultural/ethnic value clashes, communication decoding problems, identity insensitivity issues, family and network pressures, and the process of raising bicultural children. Ting-Toomey examines the value dimension of individualism-collectivism and its impact on intimate relationship expectations and the importance of understanding a partner's cultural/ethnic identity development stage. She then explores issues of raising secure, bicultural children, concluding with some guidelines for dealing mindfully with intercultural-intimate relationship conflicts.

Taking off from the general frameworks for conceptualizing cross-cultural relations presented in section 1, section 2 features four chapters that analyze and reflect on specific assumptions regarding intercultural couples with one partner from the United States, drawing from the diverse disciplines of linguistics, English, family therapy, and women's studies and politics. In chapter 4, linguist Ingrid Piller engages the circulating discourses about Western partners and desire; in this case, literally the Wild West, in "I Always Wanted to Marry a Cowboy." Federico Fellini is credited for saying "A different language is a different vision of life," and the impact of language on partner expectations and couple formation is explored in Piller's contribution to the volume.

Next, in chapter 5, entitled "The Luckiest Girls in the World," Jessie Grearson and Lauren Smith address what it's like to live and love in the West, in what is constituted as the land of individualism and romance. The authors express the hope that their daughters, having grown up in international families, will be able to "see marriage as a compelling and beautiful fable that varies from culture to culture, then maybe they will be able to write their own stories," making them truly the "luckiest girls in the world." In chapter 6, entitled "'We're Just a Couple of People': An Exploration of Why Some Black–White Couples Reject the Terms *Cross-Cultural* and *Interracial*," Terri Karis draws on Lakoff and Johnson's (1987) theory of metaphor to explore what is highlighted and obscured by the terms *cross-cultural* and *interracial* when they are applied to Black–White heterosexual couples. While these terms are often used interchangeably, looking at the social function each serves offers one way to make sense of why some Black–White couples choose, at least in certain situations, not to label themselves as cross-cultural and/or interracial couples.

Chapter 7 engages the question "What happens when East and West meet via the Internet marital trade?" In "Electronic Attachments: Desire, the Other, and the Internet Marital Trade in the 21st Century," Anna M. Agathangelou and Kyle Killian discuss seduction, desire, and power in an era where cyberspace is fertile ground for fantasy, and marital trade Web sites promise wish fulfillment for Western males seeking "good wives." Gender, economics, and the idea of bodies as borders intersect in this chapter, with the authors questioning the assumption that the Internet is a liberatory medium, offering the promise of freedom, where persons' social locations on axes of power somehow no longer matter. Agathangelou and Killian suggest that persons initiating transborder relationships via the Internet would do well to recognize that their virtual expectations and desires do not evade power relations, including the power to access resources and people's bodies, like those purchased in such technological transactions.

Section 3 of the volume offers five chapters that introduce readers to particular cross-cultural formations. Chapters draw on these particular different couple combinations to highlight significant questions that otherwise might fall off our theoretical tables. In chapter 8, "Russian–American Marriages," Lynn Visson places in sociohistorical and politicoeconomic context a range of factors that have played a role in the attraction between Russians and Americans. Tracing the phenomenon to the present day, Visson explores cultural constructions of "real men" and "feminine women," ideal Russian–American combinations, and disasters/disappointments. What is the significance for the development of cross-cultural relations? How does knowing about these constructions enable us to think of other possibilities?

In chapter 9, entitled "Constructions of Difference Among Latino/Latina Immigrant and Non-Hispanic White Couples," Roxana Llerena-Quinn and Gonzalo Bacigalupe address how power and privilege permeate the construction of identity and the dynamics of intercultural couples. Llerena-Quinn and Bacigalupe suggest that a more productive relational stance is found in couples that are explicit about the mutual value of interacting across their cultural divide.

In chapter 10, "Asian Indians in Intercultural Marriages: Intersections of Acculturation, Gender, and Exogamy," Mudita Rastogi details how acculturation impacts individuals' values, family structure, relational expectations, and gender schemas and the effects these have on the way intercultural relationships form and develop. Because members of the Asian Indian community in the United States range widely in their level of acculturation, Rastogi focuses on intercultural marriages of two types: (a) Both the wife and the husband identify as Asian Indian but differ in their levels of acculturation; and (b) one partner is of Asian Indian heritage and the other is not. She discusses potential challenges faced by couples where one partner comes from outside the Asian Indian community and provides case vignettes to illustrate these issues.

In chapter 11, "Bridges Crossed, Paths Traveled," Manijeh Daneshpour discusses how Christian–Muslim couples deal with strong reactions and fear great disapproval from their families, ethnic group, and/or society at large. Daneshpour describes what makes these marriages unique and special, potential challenges for interfaith couples, and suggestions for engaging those socially constituted differences and making them work *for*, rather than against, the marriage.

In chapter 12, Stanley Gaines and Marina Ramkissoon provide an overview of research done in the Caribbean on interpersonal relationships, with specific emphasis on Jamaica. Comparisons between Black Jamaicans, at home and abroad, and Black and White Americans are made to demonstrate challenges for interpersonal relationships and to suggest areas for further research. The roles of slavery and alterity are highlighted as significant factors in interpersonal relationships between Blacks in Jamaica and White Americans. Drawing upon interdependence theory, Gaines and Ramkissoon examine the concept of accommodation, particularly as influenced by personal differences in cultural values, and address differences in cultural value-accommodation links as potential sources of conflict in U.S./Caribbean relationships.

The crossing of different borders/boundaries by intercultural couples may result in social resistances and/or disruptions from the families of origin and society. Since intercultural mate selection is many times not sanctioned by dominant mainstream practices and value systems, families may resist the selection of a person from outside of their religion, social class, and culture, and larger communities may be reticent to accept a partner of a "foreign" background. Yet, many individuals disrupt these dominant practices and value systems, braving barriers and risking alienation to form their couplehood and their lives with each other. Highlighting both the struggles and productive practices that cross-cultural partners experience in their relationships and lives, this book was not written to make these couple formations into a spectacle. Instead, it intervenes to challenge and disrupt the principle of homogamy, opening up space for partners to establish deeper understanding and respect for one another as they (a) experience personal, structural, and cultural differences that make a difference; (b) negotiate familiar codes and values; and (c) hopefully, allow room for practices and ways of relating that are inclusive and integrative.

References

Bateson, G. (1979). *Mind and nature.* New York: Dutton.

Biever, J. L., Bobele, M., & North, M. W. (1998). Therapy with intercultural couples: A postmodern approach. *Counseling Psychology Quarterly, 11*, 181–188.

Bratter, J. L., & King, R. B. (2008). "But will it last?": Marital instability among interracial and same-race couples. *Family Relations*, 57, 2, 160–171.

Chin, K. (1994). Out-of-town brides: International marriage and wife abuse among Chinese immigrants. *Journal of Comparative Family Studies*, 25, 53–70.

Estrada, D. (2005). Supervision of cross-cultural couples therapy: Giving voice to the code of silence in the supervision and therapy room. *Journal of Family Psychotherapy*, 16, 17–30.

Falicov, C. J. (1995). Cross-cultural marriages. In N. S. Jacobson & A. S. Gurman (Eds.), *Clinical handbook of couples therapy* (pp. 231–246). New York: Guilford.

Fu, X., Tora, J., & Kendall, H. (2001). Marital happiness and inter-racial marriage: A study in a multi-ethnic community in Hawaii. *Journal of Comparative Family Studies*, 32, 47–60.

Grearson, J. C., & Smith, L. B. (1995). *Swaying: Essays on intercultural love*. Iowa City, IA: University of Iowa Press.

Hegar, R. L., & Greif, G. L. (1994). Parental abduction of children from interracial and cross-cultural marriages. *Journal of Comparative Family Studies*, 25, 135–138.

Heller, P., & Wood, B. (2000). The influence of religious and ethnic differences on marital intimacy: Intermarriage versus intramarriage. *Journal of Marital and Family Therapy*, 26, 241–252.

Hernandez, M. (2003, March). *The crucible of intermarriage*. Workshop conducted at the annual Psychotherapy Networker Symposium, Washington, DC.

Ho, M. K., Matthews Rasheed, J., & Rasheed, M. N. (2004). *Family therapy with ethnic minorities*. San Francisco: Sage.

Joanides, C., Mayfew, M., & Mamalakis, P. M. (2002). Investigating inter-Christian and intercultural couples associated with the Greek Orthodox Archdiocese of America: A qualitative research project. *American Journal of Family Therapy*, 30, 373–383.

Keeney, B. (1982). *Aesthetics of change*. New York: Guilford.

Killian, K. D. (2001). Reconstituting racial histories and identities: The narratives of interracial couples. *Journal of Marital and Family Therapy*, 27, 27–42.

Killian, K. D. (2002). Dominant and marginalized discourses in interracial couples: Narratives: Implications for family therapists. *Family Process*, 41, 603–619.

Killian, K. D. (2003). Homogamy outlaws: Interracial couples' strategic responses to racism and to partner differences. *Journal of Couple & Relationship Therapy*, 2(2/3), 3–21.

Laird, J. (2000). Culture and narrative as central metaphors for clinical practice with families. In D. H. Demo, K. R. Allen, & M. A. Fine (Eds.), *Handbook of family diversity* (pp. 335–358). New York: Guilford.

Lakoff, G., & Johnson, M. (1980). *Metaphors we live by*. Chicago: University of Chicago Press.

McFadden, J., & Moore, J. L. (2001). Intercultural marriage and intimacy: Beyond the continental divide. *International Journal for the Advancement of Counseling*, 23, 261–268.

McGoldrick, M., & Preto, N. (1984). Ethnic intermarriage: Implications for therapy. *Familv Process*, 23, 3, 347–364.

Rosenblatt, P. C., Karis, T. A., & Powell, R. D. (1995). *Multiracial couples: Black and White voices*. Thousand Oaks, CA: Sage.

Shibusawa, T. (2007, April). Rethinking the family: The complexities of intergenerational families and migration. Invited presentation at the annual Culture Conference of the Multicultural Family Institute, Piscataway, New Jersey.

Softas-Nall, B. C., & Baldo, T. D. (2000). Dialogues within a Greek family: Multicultural stories of a couple revisited. *The Family Journal: Counseling and Therapy for Couples and Families, 8*, 396–398.

Surra, C. (1990). Research and theory on mate selection and premarital relationships in the 1980s. *Journal of Marriage and the Family, 52*(4), 844–865.

Usita, P., & Poulsen, S. (2003). Interracial relationships in Hawaii: Issues, benefits, and therapeutic interventions. *Journal of Couple and Relationship Therapy, 5*, 73–83.

Section I

Theoretical Frameworks for Understanding Intercultural Couples

1

A Systems Theory Analysis of Intercultural Couple Relationships

Paul C. Rosenblatt

Intercultural couples develop their own intricate, multilayered systems, and they are affected by the many other systems in which they are embedded, including their families and cultures of origin and an assortment of other economic, legal, political, and social systems. The systemic complexities in the life of any particular intercultural couple are so great that to try to identify and analyze the full range of systemic issues for intercultural couples is nearly impossible. But there are some key areas of system dynamics that are of great importance to many intercultural couples and, in this chapter, I focus on three such areas that are central to the lives of large numbers of intercultural couples: (a) key aspects of the ecosystem in which the couple lives; (b) interpersonal power in the couple relationship; and (c) changes in couple system dynamics as the relationship evolves over time.

Each particular combination of cultures, social class, location where the couple lives, and so on creates a set of challenges, issues, and themes that might be quite different from what couples with other combinations of characteristics experience (Cottrell, 1990). In this sense, every intercultural couple needs its own theory. For example, is there much in common between a heterosexual couple in which one partner is Yoruba from Nigeria and the other is middle-class Mexican and a same-sex couple in which one partner is Hong Kong Chinese and the other is from rural Greece? Maybe not, but a systems theory analysis can give us a sense of significant questions to ask and of the dynamics that may be present across most combinations of intercultural couples.

The Diversity of Intercultural Couple Systems

Couples come together in many different situations, and those situations have cultural meanings, social arrangements, and systems demands. Thus, each couple is embedded within a complex array of shoulds, limits, interactions, competing pressures, expectations, and models of how to be a couple. For example, what it means for a Chinese student from Taiwan who is attending a U.S. university to marry a Euro-American student from the United States is very different from what it means for a poor Taiwanese farmer to go to Viet Nam and pay a wife-finding service to provide him with a bride whom he then brings back to Taiwan. In both cases, a marriage has occurred, but what the marriage means to the participants and how they and their families of origin make sense of it might be quite different. So in looking at cross-cultural couples, it is not simply that they have come together from two different cultures. It is also that the circumstances of their coming together may have differing meanings. The circumstances, and the differing contexts that the circumstances provide in the two cultures, mean that one couple deals with issues quite differently from another from the beginning.

For example, consider the two cross-cultural marriages involving Chinese from Taiwan. In one, a young Taiwanese woman who is a student in the United States marries a Euro-American man. In the other, a middle-aged Taiwanese man who is a poor farmer goes to Viet Nam and pays $8000 in order to come home with a Vietnamese bride. For the Taiwanese partners, both marriages may be practical and desirable. In a simplification of motivations and feelings, it might be part of what seems to be true to the Taiwanese woman to say that she may, by marrying an American, free herself from certain difficulties that she fears if she married a Taiwanese man (perhaps obligations to care for his elderly parents or perhaps an explicit patriarchal control that is uncomfortable for her). She may also be gaining an economic foothold in a country where she can earn a reasonable amount of money to send back to her family in Taiwan. In a simplification of motivations and feelings for the Taiwanese man, it might be part of what seems to be true to him that he may have found himself too low in status to marry a Taiwanese woman, so to have a wife (helpmate, bearer of his children, sexual partner, and person who will help care for his elderly parents), he has had to go out of the country (Wang & Chang, 2002). In effect, he moves from a marriage market where nobody (who is acceptable to him) wants what he has to sell to a marriage market where his comparative wealth makes him sufficiently attractive to a large number of women (cf., Cohen, 2003). The Euro-American marrying a woman from Taiwan may be attracted by a different culture and a partner whose slight build and cultural background may seem to him to allow more control, freedom from being threatened, and erotic satisfaction than he might have in a marriage to a Euro-American woman. The Vietnamese woman marrying a man from Taiwan may bring a substantial economic benefit to her parents, more than she could provide by working in nearby sweatshops for years and then marrying a Vietnamese man. Perhaps these would not be the cultural understandings any of these people would have. But the cultural understandings will almost certainly not be identical for the two marriages and, whatever they are, they need to be taken into account by anyone who wants to understand the dynamics of these versions of intercultural marriage.

In the two examples of couples in which one partner is Chinese from Taiwan, the cultural systems manifest themselves in many ways. These include (a) cultural understandings of the economic context and economic transactions in acquiring a spouse; (b) variations in forms of patriarchy; (c) local and international marriage "markets;" (d) cultural standards for an appropriate spouse; (e) degree of obligation to provide care or financial support for spouse's parents; (f) filial obligations to one's own parents and how marriage relates to that; (g) what it takes to achieve economic well-being by the standards of one's culture; (h) cultural shoulds about having children; (i) cultural standards of sexuality and erotic satisfaction; and (j) the practical help a spouse provides in one's socioeconomic niche.

To further explore the diversity of intercultural couple systems, consider couples in which a male soldier from the United States marries a woman from a country where he was stationed. Will people from her culture of origin or her husband's assume that she had been a sex worker? And what if the two partners do not share a language in which they can communicate more than the most superficial information? What will their cultures of origin make of that? Can they achieve what their culture considers a good marriage despite limited ability for marital communication? Or consider a picture bride from an Asian country who marries a man in the United States whose ancestors came from her country, but he has grown up in the United States and does not understand her culture or language. What will people in her culture and his make of that relationship? Or consider women who cross national boundaries as labor migrants and then become wives in the country to which they migrate, or women who marry cross-nationally in order to become labor migrants in the country of their husband. These examples point to the possible importance of such cultural systems phenomena as the way that individual and couple status are linked to the premarital pasts of the partners, the cultural meanings given to the communication challenges faced by an intercultural couple, the importance of communication in achieving cultural standards of a good marriage, what the standards for a good marriage are in their two different cultures, and the often blurry line between labor migration and intercultural marriage (Piper & Roces, 2003).

Then there is the matter of the form of marriage. A number of marriage forms may be available to couples. For example, a marriage between a Thai woman and a foreigner may involve a Buddhist ceremony at her home village, a formal registration with government authorities, or long-term cohabitation without formal recognition (Cohen, 2003). And they may choose to live in Thailand or the man's home country or somewhere else, any of which has the potential to have a strong differential influence on the couple relationship. Understanding what might go on in the couple's relationship is further complicated when we consider that it may not be the first marriage for either, and they may already have children from a former marriage.

The Value of a Comparative Approach

This chapter uses examples of intercultural couples in which one partner is from the United States and examples where neither is from the United States. With a comparative approach it is easier to identify dynamics that are not unique to the United States context but are basic to intercultural couples in general. In this way we can better distinguish whether a particular couple's issues are linked to aspects of U.S. culture(s), to the comparative wealth of the United States, to U.S. ideas about "race," or the mere fact of the partners coming from different cultures.

This chapter also uses examples where the two partners come from cultures that seem quite different. In reality, many intercultural couples come from cultures that overlap considerably in values and ways of making sense of the world. While focusing on couples who differ markedly in culture makes it easier to see the dynamics of cultural difference at work, many of the same dynamics may operate for couples who come from cultures that are only subtly different.

Ecosystems

Cultural Differences about Many Things

Any two cultures may differ in numerous ways, so even if a couple finds much to attract them, including many similarities, they may differ in ways that can be a source of conflict and stress. Often an intercultural couple must struggle with different ideas of what marriage involves. One partner may be rooted in a culture where marriage is a relationship between two individuals who live in comparative isolation from their families of origin, whereas the other comes from a culture where marriage is a uniting of two families, at least one of which will be intimately involved in the couple's daily life (Breger & Hill, 1998). For example, in years past, a Western woman married to a Thai man might be horrified to discover that his idea of marriage includes the possibility that he will take several additional wives (Cohen, 2003). Or a German man married to a Thai woman might be surprised to learn that her idea of marriage is that it is fundamentally about not love or sex but economic security for herself and her family of origin (Mix & Piper, 2003).

It may be rare that both partners start out ignorant of each other's culture. Indeed, many people who enter an intercultural relationship have had long-term contact with the partner's culture—perhaps as a student, a soldier, or a citizen of a colonized or economically dominated society. The contact can provide resources of information, but that information can also be accompanied by stereotypes and expectations that get in the way of the couple getting to know each other (cf., Tseng, 1977; Yuh, 2002). These stereotypes and expectations may fuel struggles that will go on for many years in the couple relationship (e.g., Yuh, 2002). For example, a Euro-American man may continue to expect his "petite bride" from Asia to be docile and sexually interested, and a woman from Asia may continue to expect her American groom to be egalitarian and interested in her inner thoughts. In a sense, the fundamental basis of the relationship, at least in early contact, may have been established decades or even centuries before the couple ever met. For example, colonization of one partner's country by the other partner's may have established power relationships between individuals from the cultures involved, undermined self-esteem of many citizens of the colonized country, and set precedents for patterns of couple relationship (e.g., that the person from the colonizing country is a man who does not learn the partner's language).

On the other hand, stereotypes may work for the couple, seem accurate to the partners, and help them to have a marriage that feels good to them (Wieling, 2003). From this perspective, stereotypes are not a hazard to the couple relationship but a building block, a set of promises, and the terms of a desired, implicit marital contract.

Families of Origin in the Couple System

Even if both partners in a committed intercultural relationship are thousands of miles from their families of origin, those families may still be very much a part of their lives. There may be considerable communication, flow of resources and information, visits, and constant renewal via family contacts. There may also be clearly communicated expectations for how the couple should live and for what each partner should do. In that sense, each partner may have not only married an individual. He may have married a family and a culture.

Families of origin may oppose and resent the establishment of an intercultural relationship (Barbara, 1985/1989). Such opposition may be effective at ending a potential relationship or undermining a relationship that has already been established. Even if a family of origin lacks the power to stop or end a relationship, they may feel that a social contract has been violated by the marriage, perhaps because their family member will no longer be near to provide assistance and connection. They may feel deep loss at the reduction or ending of face-to-face contact. They may feel embarrassed in relationship to their community and extended family and may face unpleasant sanctions from those people as a result of the couple relationship. All of this may be communicated to the intermarried offspring and her partner, which may put considerable pressure on the couple. Perhaps the pressure is on the "foreign" partner to assimilate to the other's culture as quickly as possible (Yuh, 2002). This may involve her communicating only in the language of the partner, avoiding conationals, and observing no customs of her culture of origin.

Families of origin can be burdened by the attributions others make about an intercultural marriage. For example, in Thailand people may assume (often erroneously) that a Thai woman who is married to a foreigner must have been a prostitute (Cohen, 2003). Such attributions, which might often be made on the basis of the comparative age of the two partners or whether they seem able to converse fluently in a shared language, may cause great discomfort to members of a family of origin. Even if they know that the attribution is false, they may feel on the defensive or not want to be seen in public with the couple.

Just as the couple's relationship patterns unfold over time, the ways in which families of origin relate to the intercultural couple also develop over time. There is likely to be a long period of time for a family of origin to figure out what the couple relationship involves and does not involve (Barbara, 1985/1989). Parents may assume that things will be better or worse, by their standards, than they turn out to be. Their child may change religion, change to a less modest way of dressing, change to culturally inappropriate involvement in the economy where he is now living, and so on. Or, by contrast, their child may continue to adhere to all crucial cultural standards.

Gender Relations and Patriarchy in Cultures of Origin

Gender is one of the most challenging areas for intercultural couples to negotiate. Expectations for men and women can be quite different from culture to culture. Cultures may differ not only in how they define women and men but even in assumptions about the space they are to occupy (Barbara, 1985/1989). In one partner's culture, a woman's place may be the kitchen and the back of the house, while in the other partner's culture, her place may be just as much in the public sphere as her partner. Each partner also may expect gender patterns from the other that do not fit the other's dispositions, beliefs, and ways of acting. The Euro-American man who expects a love relationship with a submissive woman from southeast Asia may be shocked to find that the relationship he has with her is something quite different, perhaps a mixture of resignation by her to his patriarchal domination and assertions of her right to have her spheres of power and autonomy in relating to her family of origin, practicing her religion, and raising children. He may even find that she is powerfully assertive and can and will hold her own in power battles.

Although some women in intercultural marriages can be seen as victims of exploitation and abuse, the women in such relationships may see their experiences in a more complex and nuanced way. Despite what seems to an observer to be exploitation and abuse, a woman may experience her marriage as of great value, and her identities may be multiple and evolving, not simply the identity of a victim (Nakamatsu, 2003). She may, for example, feel that she and her family of origin are well compensated for the costs she is incurring, that she is bringing honor to herself and her family of origin by being a proper wife to her husband, and that she is making progress toward economic and educational goals of great importance. In fact, it would be a diminishment of the agency of women who choose to enter an intercultural marriage to ignore that they may be experiencing things they value and doing what they want to do (Nakamatsu, 2003).

To understand how gender and patriarchy may operate in a cross-cultural couple, it is important to examine issues relating to violence. Partners may differ in their views about how much male use of violence and the threat of violence is considered part of the ordinary couple relationship. A man who courts a woman from another culture with charm, gifts, compliments, and professions of love may at the same time think it is not out of line to physically hurt her if she does something he would rather she did not do. In one culture it might be inconceivable that love is associated with violence, while in another the two go together as an ordinary, not to be contested or even questioned part of married life.

A final aspect of gender relations concerns assumptions about to whom a couple's children belong. In some cultures a couple's children are both of theirs for purposes of loyalty to family of origin or in case of divorce. But in many cultures, the children belong to the man's family of origin, and in the case of divorce the children would be legally and morally his.

Being Different from Most or All Surrounding Couples

Many intercultural couples differ from most or all of the surrounding couples in their community. One result might be more couple cohesion than is true for most couples in the community (Barbara, 1985/1989), perhaps more than is good for them. Many relationships are more comfortable and/or allow more room for growth when they strike a balance of togetherness and apartness.

Not infrequently, a partner who is a cultural outsider where the couple is living must face racism, ethnocentrism, and other forms of bigotry (e.g., Korean military brides in the United States; Yuh, 2002). Bigotry may be directed primarily at the partner who is from far away, but it may also be reflected onto the partner who is not, and if they have children it will almost certainly be directed at the couple's children. This is not to say that being the target of bigotry is necessarily shared. In fact, one of the challenges of being non-White in the United States and partnered with someone who is White is that the White partner might not understand and sympathize with the bigotry directed at his non-White partner (Killian, 2002; Rosenblatt, Karis, & Powell, 1995; Yuh, 2003).

Power in the Couple System

Wealth Differences

Some cross-cultural marriages involve a substantial wealth difference. Wealth differences have cultural meanings; they are also a basis for power and privilege. Somebody from an economically poor country may be glad to buy into the greater privilege that comes with greater wealth. Gaining access to greater financial resources may even be a primary motive for their contracting an intercultural marriage (Cohen, 2003; Spickard, 1989; Woelz-Stirling, Manderson, Kelaher, & Gordon, 2000). But they also may find it a matter of discomfort and guilt to live with so much wealth when most people in their home culture do not. And the wealth difference may mean that the partner with greater wealth uses that wealth as a foundation for power in the relationship. On the other hand, to the extent that wealth is a factor in the couple coming together and one way that the partner with greater wealth maintains power in the relationship, it may of necessity be a continuing part of the couple relationship that the wealthier partner gives wealth, or what wealth can buy, to the other. One cannot maintain wealth as a basis of relationship power by hoarding it. Person A cannot maintain a relationship with person B that rests in part on A giving B wealth if that never occurs (see Cohen, 2003, on such dynamics in couples where one partner is Thai and the other a foreigner).

The interest in wealth and the effort to acquire wealth on the part of the partner who is less wealthy often involves debts and obligations to family of origin (see Cohen, 2003, talking about Thai women married to foreigners; Woelz-Stirling et al., 2000, talking about Filipina women married to Australians). As these dynamics often play out, the less wealthy partner is in the middle, supplicated by or receiving demands from her family of origin (and feeling strong responsibility to provide for them financially) and supplicating or putting demands on her wealthier partner.

This does not mean that the wealth dynamics necessarily remain a permanent part of the couple relationship. The need to transfer wealth to a family of origin may diminish. Or wealth may move so much from control of the wealthier partner to the control of the one who is not wealthy that the wealth difference disappears or is even reversed. This may happen because the laws of the country in which they reside block the wealthier partner from being able to own houses, land, and other assets, so the partner who is less wealthy may ultimately have assets of great value registered in her name (as is the case with some Thai women married to foreigners; Cohen, 2003). Also, wealth may become less important as a basis of power as things shift in the couple relationship. For example, if they share children, connections to the children may become more important as a power issue. Or if the partner with greater wealth becomes frail of health, that may change couple power dynamics.

Despite wealth differences, the chemistry and power issues in the couple relationship may have to do with matters other than wealth. For example, the attraction and the power dynamics may have to do with the person from the less wealthy country seeking adventure, freedom from constraints of the home culture; escape from something dangerous, painful, or stigmatizing from the home culture; or love (Mix & Piper, 2003).

Whose Cultural Territory Are They in?

The cultural territory a couple is in can make an enormous difference in the resources available to the partners. Living where one partner's language, preferred foods, religion, modes of dressing, holidays, types of recreation, etc., are dominant provides enormous resources to one partner and makes him the more competent person in getting around in all sorts of ways (Rosenblatt & Stewart, 2004). Perhaps that is one reason why intercultural couples tend to fit their practices and patterns to the surrounding environment (Cottrell, 1990). And by doing so, they add to the power of the person whose home territory they are in and to the marginalization, insecurity, homesickness, anxiety, and incompetence of the partner who is a stranger. In one's home country, one can feel that one belongs, but as an immigrant, one will not easily feel a sense of familiarity, security, or belonging (Yuh, 2002). Furthermore, one's partner and in-laws may exert continuing pressure to abandon one's culture and to try to become just like people in the partner's culture (Yuh, 2002). Related to this, it is probably a rare bicultural, bilingual couple whose children are equally fluent in the language and culture of both parents (cf., Rosenblatt & Stewart, 2004; Yuh, 2002). Rather, the children's language practices (and because of that their values and thought patterns) come to fit the country in which they are living, which further marginalizes and undermines the parent who is a cultural and linguistic outsider.

Couples are not, however, randomly assigned to environments. In fact, the environment in which they live may be predetermined by the conditions that brought them together—for example, relations of power and wealth among nations, their sexual and financial chemistry, situations in one partner's society of origin that make it more interesting, necessary, safe, or acceptable to seek a partner from another culture. And it is not as though one partner made the other come to his country. Quite often people may end up living in a country they thought they wanted to live in. However, they eventually may be disappointed by the discrepancy between what they hoped for and what they experience. For example, the Korean woman who hoped to leave the sexism of Korean society behind may find a different and no more benign sexism in the United States (Yuh, 2002).

From another angle, countries are not neutral about residents from elsewhere. Power in a couple's relationship, the possibility of various remedies to couple problems, and the experiences of their children (if they have children) are affected by the laws of the country in which they live. If, for example, one partner is not granted the rights that the other is, or if the law requires children to be embedded primarily in the culture of one of the partners, that may have a profound effect on the couple relationship.

Whose Language Is the Language of the Couple's Life?

It is not uncommon for intercultural couples to start out not being able to communicate much. They may not be fluent in a shared language (for example, couples in which she is Chinese and from Asia and he is Euro-American; Rosenblatt & Stewart, 2004). Over time, they are likely to come to have more shared fluency in a common language, but whose language is it? If it is the language in which one of the partners is quite fluent, that gives that partner a power base in dealing with any issue that requires mutual communication. It is probably no accident that the language that comes to be the couple language is more likely to be the language of the partner who has more power (often older men who have more economic resources than their women partners). It is perhaps a rare person who can feel as much at home in a second language as in his mother tongue. Thus, if a couple's arguments, decision-making, planning, self-disclosure, love making, and so on are in the first language of one partner and not of the other, the one for whom it is a first language will gain in many ways. Problems of communication may be a challenge for any intercultural couple (Markoff, 1977), and they are compounded by the links between who has more power in the relationship and the language in which the couple communicates. At another level, the choice to become fluent in the partner's language is a symbol of willingness to give up one's own culture and language-based self in order to get along with one's partner (Breger & Hill, 1998). But many people never become fluent in their partner's language. And if they are living in their partner's country they will not only be marginalized outsiders in the larger society, they will also be so in their own families (Yuh, 2002), where their partner, bicultural children, and in-laws will all be much more fluent in the local language. Such marginalization can be an issue for the entire family, because whatever the outsider is feeling as a result of marginalization—sorrow, loneliness, low self-esteem, etc.—will be played out in system dynamics. For example, if the marginalization leads to conflict, processes of mutual lowering of self-esteem, or processes of emotional distance, interactions involving all family members will reflect and suffer from the marginalization.

Insulation from a Partner's Power

In some couples, the less powerful partner is insulated from the power of the more powerful partner a great deal of the time. This can be because what they do each day occurs in separate spheres or because the partners have separate groups of associates with whom they spend considerable time (Cohen, 2003). They may never go together to functions and ceremonies that are part of only one partner's culture (cf., Sung, 1990). Additionally, if their social contacts are segregated by gender, culture, religions, or something else, each partner has a venue for complaining about and letting off steam about the other (Cohen, 2003).

There is also the power of passive, covert resistance. Yuh (2002), for example, describes how Korean military brides may mask their strong oppositional feelings in dealing with their much more powerful American husbands and in-laws. But these brides continue to hold covertly to their values and opinions. So on the outside, the Korean bride may seem politely accepting of her mother-in-law's ideas about cooking and household decoration, but inside she may have a richly critical, even scornful view of those standards and may constantly renew her sense that Korean ways are better. Although on the surface the power imbalance will seem to have conquered the Korean bride, on the inside, she is still fighting a war of resistance.

Failures of communication can also be about insulation from power. If one cannot understand one's partner very well, one cannot be influenced by one's partner. Although we might typically think of a partner who is living in the spouse's home society and who lacks fluency in the language of that society as being in a less powerful place, it is possible that at times the lack of language skills is a counter to the power of the spouse. One cannot be swayed by what one does not understand.

The Evolving Couple System

A Lifetime of Unfolding Challenges and Systemic Change

A great many of the cultural and family-of-origin differences a couple will have to deal with are present at the beginning of their relationship, but most of those differences are probably not known by the couple at first. It is only when they must actually deal with each emerging real-life issue that they find out how they differ and what kinds of challenges those differences create (Tseng, 1977). Firsts are a challenge for any couple but they may be greater challenges for intercultural couples—e.g., first intense disagreement, first serious illness, first pregnancy, first childbirth, first death of a parent or sibling, perhaps the first instance of what might be experienced as emotional or physical abuse. Lacking some of the shared footing of a monocultural couple, an intercultural couple will have more to struggle with. And because many of those firsts are inherently difficult, energy draining, and make thinking clearly difficult, those struggles can be harsh and unpleasant. For example, a first pregnancy is demanding in itself, without the added burden of struggling with different cultural understandings about what pregnancy means and what should or should not go on during and immediately following a pregnancy.

A common challenge faced by intercultural couples is that one partner often comes from a more individualist culture and the other from a more family-oriented one (see, for example, Sung, 1990). That difference plays out at many levels. One level is how much their life will center on service to the family of origin of the partner from a more family-oriented culture. The partner from the more family-oriented culture will expect to devote more income and time to the family of origin and will be more inclined to live with parents or others in the family of origin or to bring the parents into the couple household. At another level, the partner from a more individualist culture may expect to travel, spend leisure time, and make decisions more as an individual. Whereas a partner from a more family-oriented couple may be more comfortable with and have a strong sense of obligation about doing things collectively (with partner and family), a partner from an individualist culture may have ambivalent feelings about couple or family time together or at least expect and want to have a substantial amount of personal time and space.

Couples who have children will face a set of problems that couples who do not have children will avoid (see, for example, Sung, 1990). Children can be a wonderful source of connection for an intercultural couple and can facilitate processes of developing mutual understanding, but their presence can also create difficult conflicts between the partners—including whose culture and language counts, how much one partner's acceptance of the other is superficial and how much it is deep, and what to do about aspects of the other's culture that are rather intolerable. For example, if by one's cultural standards the partner's table manners are unacceptable, that will be more of a problem if the couple is raising children together. If there are big cultural differences concerning child rearing, that area of conflict can be avoided by avoiding having children together. People who are interculturally married may not realize this at first or, at a conscious level, perhaps ever, but intercultural couples who continue to put off having children may have concerns about the difficulty of resolving key cultural differences that would be salient if they were raising a child.

All this is not to say that differences are necessarily the bane of an intercultural couple relationship (Falicov, 1995). It is not that simple. Some of the differences that people experience in an intercultural couple attract them, please them, make life easier for them, help to glue the couple together, or free them from aspects of their own culture of origin that they experience as constraining or unpleasant (Fong & Yung, 1995–1996). In an intercultural relationship the differences may enable one to transform one's sense of self in ways that delight one and may make parenting fascinating, joyous, and enormously satisfying.

And couples do not necessarily experience their differences the way an observer might see them. An outsider may perceive, for example, that a woman from a small town in Iowa is very different in cultural background from her husband who is from a big city in Senegal. But the couple themselves may focus on how alike their backgrounds are. For example, they may both have grown up valuing education, curious about the world, Roman Catholic, and loving sports. Alternatively, consider couples who seem to be from the same culture. An observer may see great similarity between a U.S. citizen who is Polish Catholic and one who is Italian Catholic, but the partners may feel that there is cultural chasm between them.

A central challenge for intercultural couples is finding ways to deal with their differences that are adaptive, flexible, and constructive (Falicov, 1995). Falicov suggests that this involves accepting and even nurturing some degree of separateness in which each partner can be cultural in her own way. It also means learning how to deal with and negotiate difficult areas of difference. And it probably means changing in ways that integrate parts of their separate cultures. But it is not that simple, because couples have to deal with their other differences, too, differences that may not be considered cultural in the conventional sense of the term, such as gender, age, physical vitality, extroversion-introversion, or self-confidence. And any particular situation may be dealt with differently, so in one situation the cultural differences matter not at all, whereas in another they matter enormously. For example, a couple might not be bothered by their cultural differences while entertaining guests but may have tremendous difficulty dealing with the fact that one partner comes from a culture in which it is important to perform certain rituals to protect loved ones from dangerous spirits that are believed to be everywhere, while the other partner comes from a culture where such notions are dismissed as superstitious nonsense.

At another level, how a couple deals with their differences probably has much to do with power differences, if the partner with greater power can force the other to accommodate to his cultural values and ways. This is not to say that the couple experiences what is going on between them as a matter of power. They may frame their processes of dealing with difference in terms of mutual respect, accommodation, religious morality, common sense, or in any of a number of other ways.

Life Cycle Events

Life cycle events such as pregnancy, childbirth, acquiring a home, and deaths are key times at which a couple's fundamental differences about what is important emerge (Tseng, 1977). These can also be difficult times to find the energy, time, patience, and focus to try to come to terms with differences. Couples may be surprised at how different their basic orientations are. For example, heterosexual couples in which the woman partner is Chinese and from Asia and the man is Euro-American may be startled to find out how differently they feel about what is appropriate in the weeks immediately after the woman gives birth (Rosenblatt & Stewart, 2004). She may desire and even need a 30-day ritual in which she is nurtured and greatly limits what she does, while he is likely to want her to return quickly to a busy, high-activity life.

Intercultural Couples as Ecosystem for Others around Them

From an ecosystemic perspective (Maddock, 1993), intercultural couples are not only in an ecosystem of their families of origin and community, they are also part of the ecosystem for these people. On one level that means that they have an impact on others, that the fact of their existence as a couple and the ways they play out their differences may make things happen in the lives of people around them. On another level, some of what has been described in this chapter as though it goes on in the intercultural couple may also be understood as going on at the interface of the couple system with the systems in which they are in contact. For example, tensions over sending economic resources to one partner's family of origin can be understood as happening at the interface of the couple with that family of origin or at the interface of both couples with their communities of origin. From that perspective, the dynamics of power in the couple are entangled with power dynamics in families of origin and community. In fact, the couple is separate from these larger systems only from a particular frame of reference. From another, she never left her family of origin and home community and he never left his (Rosenblatt, 1994). This implies that to understand intercultural couples we must always pay attention to their links with other systems.

Conclusion

Intercultural couples can be usefully understood in systemic terms. This chapter has explored three systemic areas: (a) key aspects of the ecosystem in which the couple lives; (b) interpersonal power in the couple relationship; and (c) changes in couple system dynamics as the relationship evolves over time. Although each particular intercultural couple is in its own unique systemic niche, paying attention to these three systemic areas will provide a window into much that may go on in that couple. There is a vast amount yet to be learned about intercultural couples, but we already have useful analytic tools for understanding and, if appropriate, helping intercultural couples.

References

Barbara, A. (1989). *Marriage across frontiers*. (D. E. Kennard, Trans.). Philadelphia: Multilingual Matters. (Original work published 1985)

Breger, R., & Hill, R. (1998). Introducing mixed marriages. In R. Breger & R. Hill (Eds.), *Cross-cultural marriage: Identity and choice* (pp. 1–31). New York: Berg.

Cohen, E. (2003). Transnational marriage in Thailand: The dynamics of extreme heterogeneity. In T. G. Bauer & B. McKercher (Eds.), *Sex and tourism: Journeys of romance, love, and lust* (pp. 57–81). New York: Haworth Hospitality Press.

Cottrell, A. B. (1990). Cross-national marriages: A review of the literature. *Journal of Comparative Family Studies, 21*, 151–169.

Falicov, C. J. (1995). Cross-cultural marriage. In N. S. Jacobson & A. S. Gurman (Eds.), *Clinical handbook of couple therapy* (pp. 231–246). New York: Guilford.

Fong, C., & Yung, J. (1995–1996). In search of the right spouse: Interracial marriages among Chinese and Japanese Americans. *Amerasia Journal, 21*(3), 77–98.

Killian, K. D. (2002). Dominant and marginalized discourses in interracial couples' narratives: Implications for family therapists. *Family Process, 41*, 603–618.

Killian, K. D. (2003). Homogamy outlaws: Interracial couples' strategic responses to racism and partner differences. In V. Thomas, T. Karis, & J. Wechtler, (Eds.), *Clinical issues with interracial couples* (pp. 3–21). New York: Haworth Press.

Maddock, J. W. (1993). Ecological dialectics: An approach to family theory construction. *Family Science Review, 6*, 137–161.

Markoff, R. (1977). Intercultural marriage: Problem areas. In W. Tseng, J. F. McDermott, Jr., & T. W. Maretzki (Eds.), *Adjustment in intercultural marriage* (pp. 51–61). Honolulu: Department of Psychiatry, University of Hawaii.

Mix, P. R., & Piper, N. (2003). Does marriage "liberate" women from sex work? Thai women in Germany. In N. Piper & M. Roces (Eds.), *Wife or worker? Asian women and migration* (pp. 53–71). Lanham, MD: Rowman & Littlefield.

Nakamatsu, T. (2003). International marriage through introduction agencies: Social and legal realities of "Asian" wives of Japanese men. In N. Piper & M. Roces (Eds.), *Wife or worker? Asian women and migration* (pp. 181–201). Lanham, MD: Rowman & Littlefield.

Piper, N., & Roces, M. (2003). Introduction: Marriage and migration in an age of globalization. In N. Piper & M. Roces (Eds.), *Wife or worker? Asian women and migration* (pp. 1–21). Lanham, MD: Rowman & Littlefield.

Rosenblatt, P. C. (1994). *Metaphors of family systems theory*. New York: Guilford.

Rosenblatt, P. C., Karis, T. A., & Powell, R. D. (1995). *Multiracial couples: Black and White voices*. Beverly Hills, CA: Sage.

Rosenblatt, P. C., & Stewart, C. C. (2004). Challenges in cross-cultural marriage: When she is Chinese and he Euro-American. *Sociological Focus, 37*, 43–58.

Spickard, P. R. (1989). *Mixed blood: Intermarriage and ethnic identity in twentieth-century America*. Madison: University of Wisconsin Press.

Sung, B. L. (1990). *Chinese American intermarriage*. New York: Center for Migration Studies.

Tseng, W. (1977). Adjustment in intercultural marriage. In W. Tseng, J. F. McDermott, Jr., & T. W. Maretzki (Eds.), *Adjustment in intercultural marriage* (pp. 93–103). Honolulu: Department of Psychiatry, University of Hawaii.

Wang, H., & Chang, S. (2002). The commodification of international marriages: Cross-border marriage business in Taiwan and Viet Nam. *International Migration, 40*, 93–116.

Wieling, E. (2003). Latino/a and White marriages: A pilot study investigating the experiences of interethnic couples in the United States. In V. Thomas, T. A. Karis, & J. L. Wetchler (Eds.), *Clinical issues with interracial couples: Theories and research* (pp. 41–55). Binghamton, NY: Haworth.

Woelz-Stirling, N., Manderson, L., Kelaher, M., & Gordon, S. (2000). Marital conflict and finances among Filipinas in Australia. *International Journal of Intercultural Relations, 24*, 791–805.

Yuh, J. (2002). *Beyond the shadow of camptown: Korean military brides in America*. New York: New York University Press.

2

Ambiguity as a Solution to the "Problem" of Intercultural Weddings

Wendy Leeds-Hurwitz

Often it is assumed that the goal of interaction is for all participants to accurately and completely understand one another; this has led to comments about the need for "good" or "more" communication. Despite this, there are times when "it is to the interests of both parties to leave the situation as fuzzy, amorphous and undefined as possible" (Kursh, 1971, p. 190). I explore in this chapter a situation in which not understanding one another is actually the best resolution to matters, specifically an intercultural wedding. Hendry and Watson (2001) provide a list of ends that are best served by ambiguity (their term is *indirection*); of these, the case study described here most clearly fits their category of strengthening group ties as well as membership boundaries. In this case, as in others, "the toleration of ambiguity can be productive if it is taken not as a warrant for sloppy thinking but as an invitation to deal responsibly with issues of great complexity" (Levine, 1985, p. 17). In other words, since human social interaction is complicated, with each interaction potentially having multiple functions or goals, effort should be made to understand that complexity and appreciate the methods people have devised for coping with it, rather than assuming that simplicity is always best. It is likely that, once scholars recognize ambiguity as a solution to complex social interactions, it will be discovered as an appropriate resolution to potential conflicts in other contexts beyond this one example, especially other intercultural interactions.[1] As Weiser (1974) suggests, ambiguity occurs primarily during "socially tricky situations" (p. 724), and that is a good description of the majority of intercultural interactions.[2]

Intercultural Weddings

I have spent about a decade studying intercultural weddings (Leeds-Hurwitz, 2002, 2004). Intercultural, as used here, includes several different types of weddings: interracial, interethnic, international, interfaith, and interclass. These were put into one category because the central problem in all cases is really the same: how to do two different things simultaneously. Any wedding brings together two people and their families, who carry with them different sets of expectations. If they are similar in terms of race, ethnicity, nationality, religious beliefs, and class backgrounds, then they are likely to have experienced many similar weddings, and so their assumptions will be similar about what the wedding they are planning should look like. However, if their family backgrounds diverge in any one of these ways (and certainly if they diverge in more than one way), then family members are likely to bring differing expectations to the planning of the event, and conflicts can easily result. Mary Catherine Bateson (1994) points out that:

> A certain amount of friction is inevitable whenever people with different customs and assumptions meet. It is familiar enough between genders or across class lines in a single society. What is miraculous is how often it is possible to work together to sustain joint performances in spite of disparate codes, evoking different belief systems to affirm that possibility. (p. 23)[3]

This, briefly, is why intercultural weddings pose a problem for those who would satisfy all participants and why it is valuable to study examples of successful resolutions to this problem.

There are several obvious and easy solutions that avoid the problem altogether. The most common are these: the couple can choose to emphasize only one of the two backgrounds to the exclusion of the other or highlight neither background (by eloping, having a courthouse ceremony, or having a mainstream ceremony; that is, one that fits White, upper-middle-class, Christian expectations, even if this does not describe both families, since this variant is familiar by now to most people via popular culture representations). It is also possible to organize two entirely different weddings, one for each side (an especially common choice of international couples).[4] As it turns out, only a small percentage of intercultural couples even attempt to reference both family backgrounds in the event, and some of these events are unsuccessful. In this case, lack of success means one or the other side is not entirely pleased with the resulting ceremony. Even so, success is possible, if infrequent. Of those couples who successfully designed ceremonies honoring both families, one resolution involved combining old symbols in a new way. Essentially, they used ambiguity as an interactional resource. An example of this is described in the following pages.

Before presenting a specific case study, it may be helpful to provide a summary of the research, which began with my interests in both ritual and intercultural communication. There are a few major types of rituals common to most cultures, those called rites of passage. These include birth, coming of age, marriage, and death. Most Americans today have minimal personal experience with birth or death, and there is no single coming-of-age ceremony followed in the United States (although specific cultural groups often have their own rituals for this, such as the quinceañera, the Mexican American celebration of a girl's 15th birthday). That left marriage as the obvious ritual to examine. The entire marriage is, or at least can be, quite long and therefore difficult to study. But a wedding is the beginning marker of a marriage, and in the United States weddings are highly elaborate events. People spend a lot of money on weddings, and they spend a lot of time planning every detail. Another advantage to studying weddings was that, because the wedding ceremony is so carefully designed, my presence as an observer did not change what occurred, as it might have at another, smaller event.

Whenever possible, I attended weddings. But many interesting weddings occurred before I met the participants, or at times and places where I was unable to attend, so I also interviewed couples. When possible, these interviews included additional family members (usually one or more of the parents) because the bride and groom do not make all of the decisions by themselves but obtain opinions from their relatives (especially from parents, and especially if they pay the costs). Since most couples have photographs and/or videotapes of their weddings, in addition to interviewing them about the wedding I was usually able to also review these records. As background, my students and I also attended to the popular culture materials readily available to couples (films, television shows, newspapers, magazines) and interviewed wedding specialists (those who perform weddings, as well as those with supporting roles: florists, dressmakers, caterers, photographers, wedding planners, etc.).

The focus of my study was on the material culture elements of the weddings: the clothing worn by major participants, the objects integrated into the ceremony (such as rings or candles or flowers), and the food at the reception that most often followed the main event (including the wedding cake). Material culture items most often serve not only a functional role but also a symbolic one.[5] As a result, they convey information silently, and so they were a perfect topic to study. A symbol is anything that stands for something else: a white wedding dress originally was intended to signify virginity and innocence, and even if this is not literally accurate for a particular bride today, wearing a white gown is now traditional as a symbol of a formal wedding in the United States.[6] Participants who share wedding traditions (such as all the family members on the bride's side) have seen the same sorts of clothing, objects, and foods before and know how to interpret them without lengthy explanations. Those who do not share traditions also often do not share the same interpretations of the material culture and other symbols integrated into the ceremony.

This study expanded until it included 112 couples. At that point, feeling that I understood the patterns available to couples designing intercultural weddings, I stopped conducting new research and wrote up my findings. Of the 112 couples, most did something of great value to them but did not find ways to combine traditions into a single ceremony. Six couples did and, as a result, their stories are important examples of successful intercultural communication applied to real-life situations. One of those stories will be presented here as a case study and analyzed to show how ambiguity served as an interactional resource to the couple.

Case Study

This is a wedding between a groom who primarily identifies as African American and a bride who primarily identifies as Jewish, but their identities are actually a lot more complicated than that brief summary implies.[7] The groom's mother is African American and Christian; his father is White and Quaker. Of these possibilities, the groom views himself as African American and Quaker "sometimes." The bride's mother is Hungarian and Jewish; her father is Italian and Catholic. She grew up with her mother and views herself as primarily Jewish in keeping with the traditional matrilineal transmission of Jewish identity. Her family had primarily a cultural rather than religious affiliation in that they celebrated major holidays at home but were not active in a synagogue. Since both the bride and groom came from multicultural families themselves, they were already accustomed to managing (and observing their parents manage) cultural differences. In fact, most of the couples that succeeded in combining multiple cultural identities into a single ceremony came from multicultural families, implying that successful intercultural negotiation is a learned skill. This is important because it means that anyone should be able to learn it if it becomes relevant to their lives.

The officiant (person who performed the ceremony) was also experienced in managing intercultural weddings. She provided the basic outline of the ceremony, working with the bride and groom to tailor it to their own needs. For example, the bride wanted to include two of the standard elements of Jewish weddings, use of a *huppah* (canopy) and breaking a glass, and the groom was comfortable with these choices. As it turned out, they modified both traditions. In a typical Jewish wedding, the groom breaks a glass by stepping on it (actually, a lightbulb is normally used to represent the glass, being far easier to break, and it is wrapped in a cloth so that no one has to contend with broken shards of glass). In this case, they stepped together on the lightbulb representing a glass. As with other old symbols, breaking the glass has acquired several different meanings over the years: it has a religious connotation (it stands for the destruction of the Temple, a major historical event) and a secular one (representing the loss of the bride's virginity). This couple revised the tradition to represent the importance of equality in their relationship, an unusual but not unique change. As they stepped on the "glass" together, the pastor explained to the audience, "We cannot create a new world without bringing forward traditions that have shaped our histories. Where those traditions are beloved, but incorporate actions which exclude or demean, we must remake those traditions so that they continue to inform, but not limit, our lives."[8]

This couple incorporated many other symbols into their wedding ceremony, but the *huppah* will be my focus here. The *huppah* serves as a canopy over the bride, groom, and officiant, marking them as visually distinct from the crowd. Traditionally, the *huppah* represents the larger Jewish community accepting the new couple, so close friends or family members representing different elements of that community hold the four poles. In this case, equality was again highlighted by the fact that the *huppah* poles were held by two of the groom's friends and two of the bride's cousins. As is often the case when traditions are followed that only one side of the audience will understand, the pastor explicitly described the significance of breaking the glass, as well as the *huppah* and the poles, so that those who were not accustomed to these traditions would understand them. She specifically referred to those holding the poles as representing the larger community of the bride's and groom's family and friends (rather than the traditional Jewish community) by saying, "their presence today signifies the support of their community."

But explaining one element does not preclude leaving another unexplained. At no point did the pastor explain the meaning of the specific elements used in this *huppah*, and that is where ambiguity crept in. Originally, a *tallis*, or prayer shawl, would have been used as the *huppah*, although today that is not so often the choice. As a *tallis* specifically represents the community of those who pray together, obviously it would be inappropriate for an interfaith marriage. A traditional *huppah* will most often be blue and white (the colors of the Israeli flag and of a traditional tallis), although again that would clearly have conveyed inappropriate connotations in this case. This particular *huppah* was made of fabric from Kenya, bought by the bride and groom on a trip there exploring his family's roots. The fabric was mainly orange and black, patterned with a saying that translates essentially to "all that glitters is not gold." In addition to the African fabric, this *huppah* was unusual in another way: the four poles used to hold it up were made from manzanita trees taken from property owned by the groom's family, a clear statement of social class identity (for one cannot have a more obvious indication of middle-class status than owning property). Thus, connections to a particular family, as well as to social class, race, and religion, were all incorporated into the same symbol.[9]

After the wedding, this *huppah* was made into a shade for the window in the couple's bedroom, where it serves as an index they see every day, a reminder of their wedding and the multiple identities incorporated into it. The manzanita sticks now lean against the same window (Figure 2.1).

An index is a symbol that literally was part of what it now represents. In the same way that wearing a wedding ring on a daily basis serves as a reminder of the commitment made in a wedding, so do these parts of the *huppah* in the bedroom serve to remind this bride and groom of the solution they found to the problem of bridging their intercultural differences. The *huppah* worked, not despite but because of the different assumptions guests brought to the wedding. Members of the bride's Jewish community recognized the canopy being used as an unusual variant of *huppah*, but one nonetheless. It functioned in the traditional manner, marking off the couple as simultaneously distinct from the crowd and a new unit within the community, even if it did not resemble a *huppah* any of the participants had ever seen before. Members of the groom's African American community recognized the cloth as associated with Africa and as a symbol of African American identity. They were unaccustomed to having African cloth held over the heads of the bride and groom, but since they

Figure 2.1 *Huppah* as a window shade.

at least knew what the cloth was, a new use was not completely bizarre.[10] Essentially, each group saw what they expected to see and could adequately interpret and ignored what they did not understand. Since there was at least one meaning everyone understood for the symbol, they did not look for a possible second meaning. Not knowing how to interpret the second meaning, therefore, did not cause any distress—not even knowing it was there, no one could be unhappy that they did not understand it. In this way, the ambiguity of this symbol was its strength: each person saw something they could understand, and no one felt confused or left out as a result of what was beyond their awareness.

Conclusion

This wedding is unique yet also representative of what intercultural couples can create when they wish to design a ceremony that will publicly mark their union. The *huppah* made with fabric from Africa stands as the most visible symbol of how one particular couple succeeded in combining their multiple identities into a complex new whole. It works as a *huppah* because it has the same component elements and use that a *huppah* always has: a piece of cloth, held up by four poles over the bride and groom. Yet it marks this as an uncommon union, for instead of continuing the Jewish symbolism, African American and social class symbolism substitute: the cloth purchased on a trip to Kenya, the poles made of trees from the groom's family's land. This *huppah* differs from all other *huppot*[11] yet remains functionally recognizable to the Jewish guests of the wedding. Simultaneously, it is recognizable to African American guests as a link to Africa and a common history of slavery and to family members as a link to the land they now own. The creativity shown by the bride and groom in inventing something to meet all their requirements speaks well for their ability to adapt traditional symbols of one culture to their unique needs and their multiple identities. Its transformation into a window shade speaks to the importance of their marriage for their daily lives. In making it, they created a visible link from the past to the present and future that says: we found a way to mesh our identities once; we can and will continue to do so throughout our lives together.

The lesson of this case study is that ambiguity can be a solution to a problem rather than a problem on its own. If everyone is happy with what occurs, then it is appropriate. Everyone present at an event will never understand all the meanings of all the symbols; that is the nature of symbols. By taking advantage of this ability of symbols to be polysemic (to convey multiple meanings simultaneously), this example demonstrates the value of ambiguity as an interactional resource. As Bateson (1994) suggests, "Ambiguity is the warp of life, not something to be eliminated" (p. 9). It would be appropriate to look for other examples of ambiguity (whether intercultural or not) to see if this is a common solution or an infrequent one. Since it has already been suggested that skill in intercultural negotiation was most likely learned by this bride and groom as a result of their multicultural backgrounds, it should be possible to teach this sort of graceful solution to others who sometimes believe their problems are insoluble.

Notes

1. See Mandelbaum (1990) for elaboration on the concept of interactional problems.
2. Of course, not all contexts where ambiguity serves as an appropriate resolution to a problem will be intercultural. For discussion of ambiguity in organizational contexts, see Eisenberg (1984), Leeds-Hurwitz (1989), or Putnam and Sorenson (1982). Black (2001) describes ambiguity as a resource in diplomacy.
3. See Fitch (2003) for comments about the taken-for-granteds in intercultural interactions.
4. For examples of all of these forms, see Leeds-Hurwitz (2002).
5. See Leeds-Hurwitz (1993) for further discussion of the relevance of material culture to communication, and for further discussion of food, clothing, and objects as those aspects of material culture worthy of particular attention.
6. See Leeds-Hurwitz (1993) for elaboration of the concept of symbol, its history and its use.
7. Further details about this couple and their wedding can be found in Leeds-Hurwitz (2002) in the descriptions of couple 74. What is provided here are only a few elements necessary to this reanalysis of the data. My thanks to the couple for taking the time to review this chapter for accuracy.
8. All quotes from the ceremony are taken from the text provided by the bride and groom.
9. For further discussion of the idea that symbols can convey multiple meanings, see Babcock (1978) and Leeds-Hurwitz (2002).
10. Members of the bride's community who were not Jewish would have been to at least some prior Jewish weddings and thus gained some familiarity with the *huppah* as symbol; similarly, members of the groom's community who were not African American would have learned to recognize the connotations of African fabric.
11. *Huppot* is the plural form of *huppah*. Many American Jews actually use a more casual form, *huppahs*, combining the Hebrew word with the English plural form.

References

Babcock, B. A. (1978). Too many, too few: Ritual modes of signification. *Semiotica, 23*(3–4), 291–302.
Bateson, M. C. (1994). *Peripheral visions: Learning along the way.* New York: Harper Collins.
Black, A. (2001). Ambiguity and verbal disguise within diplomatic culture. In J. Hendry & C. W. Watson (Eds.), *An anthropology of indirect communication* (pp. 255–270). London: Routledge.

Eisenberg, E. (1984). Ambiguity as a strategy in organizational communication. *Communication Monographs, 51,* 227–242.

Fitch, K. L. (2003). Taken-for-granteds in (an) intercultural communication. In P. J. Glenn, C. D. LeBaron, & J. Mandelbaum (Eds.), *Studies in language and social interaction in honor of Robert Hopper* (pp. 91–102). Mahwah, NJ: Lawrence Erlbaum.

Hendry, J., & Watson, C. W. (2001). Introduction. In J. Hendry & C. W. Watson (Eds.), *An anthropology of indirect communication* (pp. 1–15). London: Routledge.

Kursh, C. O. (1971). The benefits of poor communication. *Psychoanalytic Review, 58,* 189–208.

Leeds-Hurwitz, W. (1989). *Communication in everyday life: A social interpretation.* Hillsdale, NJ: Ablex.

Leeds-Hurwitz, W. (1993). *Semiotics and communication: Signs, codes, cultures.* Hillsdale, NJ: Lawrence Erlbaum.

Leeds-Hurwitz, W. (2002). *Wedding as text: Communicating cultural identities through ritual.* Hillsdale, NJ: Lawrence Erlbaum.

Leeds-Hurwitz, W. (2004). Intercultural weddings and the simultaneous display of multiple identities. In R. Chuang & M. Fong (Eds.), *Communicating ethnic and cultural identity* (pp. 135–148). Boulder, CO: Rowman & Littlefield.

Levine, D. (1985). *The flight from ambiguity: Essays in social and cultural theory.* Chicago: University of Chicago Press.

Mandelbaum, J. (1990). Communication phenomena as solutions to interactional problems. *Communication Yearbook, 13,* 255–267.

Putnam, L. L., & Sorenson, R. L. (1982). Equivocal messages in organizations. *Human Communication Research, 8,* 114–132.

Weiser, A. (1974). Deliberate ambiguity. *Chicago Linguistic Society Papers, 10,* 723–731.

3

A Mindful Approach to Managing Conflict in Intercultural Intimate Couples

Stella Ting-Toomey

Intercultural-intimate conflict can be defined as any antagonistic friction or disagreement between two romantic partners due, in part, to cultural or ethnic group membership differences. Beyond cultural or ethnic group membership differences, differences in relationship expectations, goals, and conflict styles and perceived scarce resources (e.g., time, attention, or money as scarce resources) may further complicate an already complex conflict situation.

Some prominent sources of intercultural-intimate conflict may include cultural/ethnic value clashes, communication decoding problems, identity insensitivity issues, family and network pressures, and raising bicultural children. The chapter is organized in four sections. First, a mindful approach to intercultural-intimate relationship conflicts will serve as a starting point for discussion. Second, the value dimension of individualism-collectivism and its impact on intimate relationship expectations will be examined. Third, the importance of understanding a partner's cultural/ethnic identity development stage will be addressed. The chapter then concludes with some general guidelines to communicate mindfully in intercultural-intimate relationship conflicts.

A Mindful Approach: Conceptual Bases

In any intercultural-intimate conflict, it is difficult to pursue all "my needs" or all "your needs" and come up with a neat conflict resolution package. In most intimate conflicts, couples who engage in constructive conflict tend to cultivate multiple paths in arriving at a mutually satisfying common ground. They are committed to understanding their partners' cultural value lenses and their underlying relationship expectations. Committed relationship couples learn to listen mindfully to their partners' viewpoints with patience and with cultural openness and sensitivity. They are willing to adapt some of their culture-based conflict styles and modify some of their conflict positions to come to acceptance and common ground compromises. They also make time to dialogue with their children and adolescents in their quests for cultural and personal identity validation. Committed intercultural couples who are constructive conflict partners practice mindful attendance, listening, reframing, and collaborative dialogue skills on a daily basis (Ting-Toomey & Oetzel, 2001).

Mindfulness: A Starting Point

To be a mindful observer, interpreter, or counselor of intercultural conflict, one must develop a holistic view of the essential factors that frame the interactive process of an intercultural-intimate conflict. According to Langer's (1989) concept of mindfulness, mindfulness can include the following characteristics: (a) learning to see behavior or information presented in the conflict situation as novel or fresh; (b) learning to view a conflict situation from several vantage points or perspectives; (c) learning to attend to the conflict context and the person in whom we are perceiving the behavior; and (d) learning to create new categories through which conflict behavior may be understood (Langer, 1989, 1997). Applying this Western mindfulness orientation to intercultural conflict, the perspective suggests a readiness to shift one's frame of reference from an ethnocentric lens to an ethnorelative lens and the possibility to see things from the other person's cultural frame of reference. Mindfulness also can support the use of new categories (e.g., different cultural value dimensions) to understand cultural or ethnic membership differences and the commitment to experiment with creative avenues of conflict problem-solving.

On the other side of the spectrum, *mindfulness*, from an Eastern Buddhist orientation, means "emptying our mindset" and learning to listen deeply without preconceived notions, judgments, and assumptions. Through an Eastern philosophical lens (Chogyam, 1976; Kabat-Zinn, 1994; Thich, 1975, 1998), mindfulness means learning to observe an unfolding conflict episode with one-pointed wakefulness and watchfulness. It means being fully present—attending fully to our own and our partner's desires, interests, and arising emotions. It also means listening deeply with all our senses open and all our perceptual filters unclogged.

In fact, the Chinese character for "listening" refers to the term "ting," which means "listening with one-pointed attention with our ears, eyes, and a focused heart." Thus, mindful listening in any conflict situation means listening to the words, tones, nonverbal nuances, and multilayered meanings and contexts that underlie the words. This nuanced way of listening is of great benefit in an intercultural tug-and-pull conflict episode. It slows down the antagonistic, polarized conflict process. It increases the chance of mutual, authentic understanding. It essentially involves a gradual shift of worldview or cultural perspective as viewed from an alternative lens. It means taking into account not only how things look from a person's own cultural identity perspective but how they look and feel from his intimate partner's identity perspective. It also displays respect that allows the conflict storyteller to tell a complete conflict story without interruptions and judgments.

Mindfulness: An Integrative Viewpoint

The roots of mindfulness practice are in the contemplative practices common to both Eastern and Western spiritual traditions (Robins, Schmidt, & Linehan, 2004). It is, at once, a spiritual, meditative, reflective, and an applied way of conscious living. The same authors note that mindfulness, as a set of skills, is the "intentional process of observing, describing, and participating in reality nonjudgmentally, in the moment, and with effectiveness" (p. 37). Thus, from an integrative viewpoint, mindfulness means attending to one's own internal assumptions, arising emotions, intentions, cognitions, and conflict behaviors and, at the same time, becoming attuned to the other's conflict assumptions, emergent or reactive emotions, intentions, cognitions, and conflict styles, as the conflict process unfolds (Ting-Toomey, 1999). Mindful reflexivity requires us to tune in to our own cultural and personal habitual assumptions in scanning a conflict interaction scene. Concurrently, mindfulness also means stretching our imagination and making a commitment to really understand the conflict lens from our intimate partner's cultural worldviews and experiences.

In fact, in the interpersonal and intercultural conflict communication literature (Cupach & Canary, 1997; Ting-Toomey, 1997), researchers have identified the three components of knowledge, motivation, and constructive conflict skills as prerequisites to competently managing a wide range of conflicts. In the context of intercultural-intimate conflicts, knowledge of our partner's cultural value patterns, cultural/ethnic identity issues, conflict styles, and rituals can help us to be more mindful in dealing with our partner's anger, jealousies, resentments, or hurts in times of conflict crisis. Paying mindful attention to the process of conflict rather than merely to the outcome and understanding deeply what different verbal and nonverbal messages mean through our partner's cultural lens can help us to use appropriate and effective responses in dealing with the intimate conflict situation. *Motivation* refers to the emotional energy and commitment that a person has and his readiness to integrate newfound intercultural conflict knowledge with culture-sensitive practice. *Skill* refers to the operational performance of appropriate and effective conflict behaviors. *Appropriateness* is the degree to which behaviors are regarded as proper and match the expectations generated by the culture. *Effectiveness* is the degree to which communicators achieve conjoint personal and interpersonal conflict goals in a given conflict situation. Of course, major problems often arise when both intimate partners hold different definitions and interpretations of appropriate and effective practices in a conflict situation.

Thus, to be mindful of intercultural differences, we have to learn to see unfamiliar behavior from a nonjudgmental or nonreactive angle. We also have to acquire the necessary knowledge, motivation, and skills, including being alert to different cultural value patterns, different relationship expectation issues, different communication decoding processes, and being sensitive to different cultural and ethnic identity struggles in our intimate partners.

Approaching Intercultural-Intimate Conflicts: Invisible Obstacles

The role of the individualism-collectivism value dimension and its impact on intercultural relationship expectations and interaction decoding processes are often like a hidden tsunami that stirs up tremendous intercultural-intimate conflict problems. Cultural value patterns form the basic criteria through which we evaluate our own behaviors and the behaviors of others. They cue our expectations of how we should act and how others should act during the course of an intimate relationship development process. Cultural value orientations serve as implicit guidelines for our motivations, expectations, perceptions, interpretations, meaning formations, and communicative actions. By being mindful of how different value patterns can create unintentional clashes in our relationship lives, we may be able to deal with these undercurrent dimensions intentionally rather than reactively with unconscious incompetence.

Individualism-Collectivism Value Dimension

If one partner in an intimate relationship comes from an individualistic cultural system, and another partner comes from a group-orientation cultural system, this cultural gap may be a major factor underlying an existing relationship conflict. Because of its importance, the individualism-collectivism value dimension has received consistent attention from both intercultural researchers and cross-cultural psychologists (Gudykunst, 2003, 2004; Gudykunst & Ting-Toomey, 1988; Hofstede, 1991, 2001; Triandis, 1995) from around the world. Intercultural scholars have provided evidence that the value patterns of individualism and collectivism are pervasive in a wide range of cultures. Individualism and collectivism can explain some of the basic differences and similarities concerning relationship development processes between cultures.

Basically, *individualism* refers to the broad value tendencies of a culture in emphasizing the importance of individual identity over group identity, individual rights over group rights, and individual needs over group needs. Individualism promotes self-efficiency, individual responsibility and accountability, and personal autonomy and privacy. In contrast, *collectivism* refers to the broad value tendencies of a culture in emphasizing the importance of the "we" identity over the "I" identity, group rights over individual rights, and ingroup needs over individual wants and desires. Collectivism promotes relational interdependence, a relational self, group harmony, ingroup network conformity, and a mutual face-saving conflict tendency (Ting-Toomey, 1988, 1994, 1999).

Individualistic and collectivistic value tendencies are manifested in everyday family, school, and workplace interaction. *Individualism* pertains to societies in which ties between individuals are loosely linked and everyone is expected to look after himself and his immediate family. For individualists, unique personal qualities, taking individual initiative, and a strong "doing" orientation are important assets in the ebb and flow of a developing interpersonal relationship. Comparatively, *collectivism* refers to societies in which ties between individuals in the community are tightly intertwined. Group members view their fate as interdependent with one another. While they will look after the welfare of ingroup members, they also expect their ingroup members to look after their interests via long-term reciprocal obligations. Collectivists also tend to draw a clear boundary between ingroup (i.e., "one of us") and outgroup (i.e., "one of them"). For collectivists, demonstrated loyalty, long-term trust, and carrying out prescribed role responsibilities and relational obligations are key in developing quality interpersonal relationships. Gender role expectations and relational role obligations (i.e., the meaning of being a "good" husband or a "good" wife or the meaning of being an "ideal" father or an "ideal" mother) are closely tied to the fundamental beliefs and worldviews of a culture. Hofstede's (1991, 2001) research reveals that factors such as national wealth, geographic spread, population growth and density, immigration patterns, and historical roots affect the development of individualistic and collectivistic value tendencies.

Overall, individualism is a cultural pattern that is found in most northern and western regions of Europe and in North America. More specifically, high individualism has been found in the United States, Australia, Great Britain, Canada, The Netherlands, New Zealand, Italy, Belgium, Denmark, and Sweden. Collectivism is a cultural pattern common in Asia, Africa, the Middle East, Central and South America, and the Pacific islands. Less than one third of the world population resides in cultures with high individualistic value tendencies, while a little more than two thirds of the people live in cultures with high collectivistic value tendencies (Triandis, 1995). High collectivistic value tendencies have been found in Guatemala, Ecuador, Panama, Venezuela, Colombia, Indonesia, Pakistan, Costa Rica, and Peru (Hofstede, 2001). The top individualist values emphasized are freedom, honesty, social recognition, comfort, hedonism, and personal equity. The top collectivist values are harmony, face-saving, filial piety (being sensitive and pleasing to the parents' wishes), equality in the distribution of rewards among peers (for the sake of group harmony), and fulfillment of others' needs (Triandis, 1995).

It has also been found that different layers of individualism (e.g., emphasizing personal need in the U.K. or immediate family need in Sweden) and collectivism (e.g., emphasizing work group need in Singapore or caste need in India) exist in different cultures. For each culture, it is important to determine the group with which individuals have the closest identification (e.g., their family, their corporation, their religion, etc.). For example, for the Vietnamese, it is the extended family; for the Japanese, it is the corporation; and for the Irish, it is the Roman Catholic Church.

In addition, gender differences exist in adherence to individualistic or communal-oriented values. U.S. males generally have been found to adhere more to individualistic values than to communal or relational-oriented values. U.S. females, on the other hand, generally have been found to subscribe to relational-oriented values more than U.S. males (Tannen, 1990, 1994; Wood, 1997). However, compared to females in collectivistic societies such as Greece, Italy, Japan, and Mexico, U.S. females still hold reasonably high levels of individualistic-oriented values.

Cultural membership values such as individualism and collectivism shape our interpretations of concepts such as "autonomy" and "connection" in a close relationship. The "I" identity cultural members (e.g., Germans, Swiss, British, Danes, and "mainstream" U.S. Americans) tend to emphasize personal privacy and relationship exclusiveness. They tend to draw a clear boundary between their intimate romantic relationship and the social world around them. They also tend to assert and defend their viewpoints more directly during an interpersonal conflict episode in comparison to the "we" identity cultural folks. In comparison, the "we" identity cultural members (e.g., Chinese, Japanese, Iranians, Egyptians, and Mexicans) tend to emphasize family reaction and ingroup network connection. They also tend to emphasize ingroup "facework" issues more than individualists.

Facework is the specific verbal and nonverbal behaviors that people engage in to maintain or restore face loss and to uphold and maintain face gain (Ting-Toomey, 1988). *Face* is a claimed sense of positive social self-worth or social self-value that a person wants others to have of him. It is how a person wants to be seen as a certain type of individual in a given interaction episode. While individualists tend to emphasize self-oriented face-saving and face-defensive moves in a conflict encounter situation, collectivists tend to emphasize other face-saving and mutual face-saving in a conflict negotiation process (Ting-Toomey, 2004; Ting-Toomey & Kurogi, 1998).

It is also important to note that tremendous individual, gender, ethnic, social class, and regional variations exist within the broad label of a national culture. Thus, on the personality trait level, terms such as *independent self-construal* and *interdependent self-construal* (Markus & Kitayama, 1991) are equivalent to cultural group membership systems terms such as *individualists* and *collectivists*. Being mindful about both cultural membership differences and unique personality distinctions within and between cultures is critical in any intercultural-intimate relationship bonding process.

Different Expectations on Love

While passionate love is treasured where kinship ties are weak (e.g., in the larger U.S. culture), passionate love is diluted where kinship ties are strong (e.g., in Korea and India). Romantic passionate love has been found to be a critical component in the "falling in love" stage of many individualists. This is one of the reasons why individualists believe that getting married without love is a disastrous action. However, research indicates that many collectivists value companionate love (i.e., long-term companion comfort and support) more than passionate love relationships (Gao, 1991).

In individualistic cultures, most individuals typically fall in love first (which sometimes involves intensive dating procedures) and then either get married or move on to another dating partner. For example, empirical research reveals that German and U.S. respondents score higher in their attitudes of valuing romantic love in their dating relationships than do Japanese respondents (Simmons, Wehner, & Kay, 1989). Furthermore, some traditional collectivists (e.g., in India, Iran, and northern Nigeria, where arranged marriages are still the norm) often opt to get married first and then take their time to fall in love. In reviewing cultural perspectives on romantic love, intercultural love experts (Dion & Dion, 1996) conclude that the high divorce rate that characterizes U.S. society is due in good part to the culture's exaggerated sense of individualism. They observe that in the larger U.S. society, romantic partners who subscribe to "expressive individualism" often confront the emotional dilemma of trying to "reconcile personal freedom and individuality, on the one hand, with obligations and role requirements of marital partner and parent, on the other" (p. 286).

In the United States, while intimate partners desire to "lose" themselves in a romantic love-fused relationship, many also struggle with their desires for independence and personal freedom. Comparatively, for many traditional collectivists, the meaning of being "in love" takes long-term commitment and time to develop. Thus, they can continue to learn to fall in love after their marriages. Alternatively, as they learn to "grin and bear it" in dealing with intercultural-intimate conflict situations, they may also have a change of heart and learn to accept the flaws and virtues of their lifetime partners.

Different Expectations on Autonomy-Connection

In developing a relational culture between persons from two contrastive cultures, romantic partners often face choices about how to competently manage autonomy and connection issues. Here *autonomy* means the need for privacy and personal space in a relationship. *Connection*, on the other hand, means the need for relatedness and fluid merging of personal space. For intimate partners who are independent self-individualists, the autonomy-connection theme is often a delicate high-wire act, balancing "me–we" dialectical forces (Baxter & Montgomery, 1996). For interdependent self-collectivists, on the other hand, autonomy and connection are often viewed as a quadrangular contest, a "me–we–they–they" juggling act between the two partners and both family networks. For collectivists, the two partners are never truly free from the grip of their family obligations, duties, and extended family reactions.

In terms of relational commitment issues, independent self-individualists tend to expect voluntary personal commitment from their partners in approaching their intimate relationships. However, for interdependent self-collectivists, structural commitment may be more important (if not on an equal footing) than personal commitment in a long-term romantic relationship. Here *personal commitment* means the individual's desire or intent to continue the relationship based on his subjective emotional feelings and experiences; *structural commitment*, on the other hand, means the individuals take into consideration various external, social, and family reactions in deciding to either continue or terminate a relationship (Johnson, 1991). For collectivists, a long-term committed relationship involves the approval and consensus of immediate families, extended families, and their closest friends.

Communication Decoding Problems

Many interesting things can happen during the journey of intercultural-intimate relationship development. At a minimum, to reduce initial interaction anxiety, the two cultural strangers need to be proficient in a shared language and the use of everyday slang and idioms of a culture. Alternatively, it is critical for the native language speaker to develop cultural sensitivity for his romantic partner. Beyond cultural sensitivity, in-depth knowledge of the other's cultural values, changing identity issues, relational expectations, verbal and nonverbal interaction habits, and romantic connection rituals is essential for increasing interpersonal intimacy and satisfaction.

While individualists often use a low-context, direct verbal approach in initiating, maintaining, and ending a close relationship, collectivists often use a high-context, indirect approach in dealing with relationship formation and development issues (Hall, 1983; Ting-Toomey, 1999). Low-context communication means intentions and expectations concerning the relationship are spelled out clearly and directly. High-context communication, on the other hand, means meanings and intentions can be inferred through various subtle nonverbal channels or shared background contexts. Research shows that low-context individuals have been found to self-disclose more of their feelings and emotions directly and explicitly in intimate relationships, whereas high-context folks disclose their emotions indirectly and in a subtle, hinting manner (Ting-Toomey, 1991). Take for example the movie, *Crouching Tiger, Hidden Dragon* (Hsu, Kong, & Lee, 2000). The main male character is never explicit about his deep emotional feelings for the woman he loves for years—until the very end when he is dying. Actually, even to the very end, the emotional exchange between these two relational partners is so very subtle and nuanced. In the United States, we often scoff at such emotional understatement as shyness. In an individualistic low-context culture, it is generally expected that relational partners will engage in active verbal self-disclosure with explicit phrases such as "I love you" and "I miss you." In a collectivistic high-context culture, other-centric nonverbal caring gestures often speak louder than any explicit and direct verbal expressions. From the collectivistic cultural lens, if you love someone, you reveal it through your sincere caring actions. For traditional collectivists, love is in the details of paying careful attention to the other person's desires, wishes, and underlying needs. From the high-context communication mode, meanings—especially during an escalating conflict episode—should be expressed tactfully or in a circumspective manner so that everyone in the conflict situation can save face or preserve relational harmony. For high-context collectivists, not destroying *wa* or "relational harmony" is critical, so that both partners can still "save face" or maintain dignity with each other.

If partners both use high-context communication approaches, they will be able to understand each other's implicit nonverbal gestures. However, in an intercultural-intimate relationship, when relational partners use different communication approaches, they may carry very different relationship expectations and interpretations and, ultimately, experience major communication breakdowns. In fact, numerous conflict style research studies (Oetzel & Ting-Toomey, 2003; Oetzel et al., 2001) have uncovered dynamics that suggest even more complexity in intercultural-intimate relationship conflicts. While low-context cultural members tend to use confrontational, competing, dominating, defending, and assertive conflict styles, high-context cultural members tend to use accommodating/obliging, avoiding, defusing, compromising, forbearance, and passive-aggressive conflict styles. Confrontational or assertive conflict tactics are reflective of individualistic, "I-centric" cultural values. Comparatively, accommodating or avoidance conflict tactics are reflective of collectivistic, mutual face-saving cultural values (Ting-Toomey & Takai, 2006). However, in the high-context conflict system, repressed conflict emotions can also often turn into passive aggressive conflict expressions when emotions go unacknowledged or unresolved for a prolonged period. Additionally, since high-context folks tend to resort to the use of indirect, "smoothing" conflict styles, when they do "voice" via the passive aggressive mode, their emotional agitations can become more high pitched and carry strong resentment overtones.

To work with their differences, both partners need to learn to verbally code-switch skillfully and learn to decode and encode both low-context and high-context messages with cultural accuracy. Decoding means that the receiver tries to interpret the meaning and the intention of the message from the sender's viewpoint. In an intercultural-intimate relationship, the decoder or the interpreter of the message has to practice ethnorelative perspective-taking by taking into account his partner's cultural frame of reference that shapes the meaning of the message. On the other hand, *encoding* means that the sender constructs the meaning of the message in such a manner that the receiver can comprehend the message as accurately as possible. Thus, intercultural-intimate couples need to make a strong commitment to communicate in a culturally sensitive manner and to accurately decode the content (i.e., task or instrumental issues), relational (i.e., socioemotional and relational definition issues), and identity (i.e., multiple layers of cultural-ethnic, gender, and personal identity, etc.) meanings of the conflict interaction process.

Furthermore, intercultural conflict research (Ting-Toomey & Oetzel, 2001) indicates that while individualistic, low-context communicators tend to be more outcome- or content-oriented in their conflict outlook, collectivistic, high-context communicators tend to be more process or relational oriented in their conflict viewpoint. Low-context communicators like to " fix" or "repair" damages or hurts in their relationships, while high-context folks sometimes like to "gloss over" or use "forbearance" to wait for the conflict episode to simmer down. Additionally, while low-context individuals often prefer to go to an impartial or neutral third party for relationship counsel or guidance, high-context folks often prefer to seek out trusted relatives or wise elders for advice, especially when the conflict becomes highly intolerable. For high-context communicators, seeking help from individuals who already have some prior knowledge of their relationship history and context appears to be a reasonable request when dealing with a complex, multilayered conflict event. However, low-context partners might view this as an intrusion by close relatives or elders on relationship intimacy and privacy spheres. Alternatively, a third-party counselor will need to work extra hard to gain the trust of high-context individuals by building relationship rapport and spending time to really know the multilayered contexts of the conflict situation and the twist-and-turn processes of the evolving intimate relationship.

In sum, both relational partners need to pay mindful attention to the other's cultural worldviews, beliefs, values, expectations, and communication codes in framing their conflict approaches and styles (Ting-Toomey et al., 2000). Because intercultural couples often argue implicitly or explicitly about core cultural/ethnic identity issues, I will now turn to a discussion of how intimate partners can bring mindful awareness to the meanings and interpretations they make regarding cultural and ethnic identities.

Understanding Cultural/Ethnic Identity Issues: Extending Identity Support

According to identity negotiation theory (Ting-Toomey, 1993, 1999), satisfactory identity negotiation process includes the feeling of being understood, the feeling of being respected, and the feeling of being affirmatively valued. To the extent that intimate partners perceive that their desired identities have been mindfully understood, accorded with due respect, and affirmatively valued on a sustained basis, they will likely experience a high degree of identity and relational satisfaction. To the extent that one or both intimate partners perceive that their desired identities have been mindlessly bypassed, misunderstood, or disconfirmed on a continuous basis, the entangled partners will likely experience a high degree of identity and relational dissatisfaction.

Thus, on the identity level, the feeling of being understood is one of the most powerful means of being validated. The feeling of being understood connotes an echoing voice outside oneself that empathizes with one's thinking, feeling, and experiencing. To engage in an accurate and positive identity validation or confirmation process, it is helpful to understand something about theories of cultural and ethnic identity development. While cultural and ethnic identity development happens for all individuals, these aspects of identity may be especially salient for immigrant partners or racial minority partners.

Ethnic Identity Conceptualization and Identity Support

According to interethnic attraction research, the strength of individuals' ethnic identities is related to intergroup attraction and dating patterns (Chung & Ting-Toomey, 2001). Individuals with assimilated, bicultural, or marginal identities have a greater tendency to date and/or marry out of their own groups than those who view their ethnic identities and traditions as very important aspects of their self-concept (Gudykunst, 2004; Ting-Toomey, 2005; Ting-Toomey & Chung, 2005).

According to Berry (1994, 2004), immigrants who identify strongly with ethnic traditions and values and weakly with the values of the dominant culture subscribe to the traditional-based or ethnic-oriented identity option. These individuals emphasize the value of retaining their ethnic heritage culture and avoid interacting with the dominant group. As a result, there may be a higher degree of stress or interaction vulnerability when there is contact with the dominant group. They are also least likely to date or marry out of their own ethnic groups.

Those individuals who identify strongly with ethnic tradition maintenance, and at the same time incorporate values and practices of the larger society, have internalized the bicultural identity or integrative identity option. Bicultural individuals feel comfortable being a member of both cultural groups and also are likely to date and marry out of their own groups. Individuals who are dating or married to bicultural partners should be mindful that their partners have a sense of double belongings— at the same time that they value their ethnic traditions, they also want to be viewed as full-fledged "U.S. Americans."

Individuals who identify weakly with their ethnic traditions and identify strongly with the values and norms of the larger culture tend to practice the assimilated identity option. Individuals who are dating or married to assimilated partners should be sensitive to the assimilated "Americanized" identities of their relational partners. Having an assimilated U.S. identity can also mean that the value content of a partner's ethnic/cultural identity empha-sizes a strong individualistic "I-identity" value orientation. By understand-ing how our relational partners define themselves ethnically and culturally, we can communicate with them on a culturally empathetic level.

Finally, individuals who identify weakly with their ethnic traditions and also weakly with the larger cultural worldviews are in the marginal identity state. They basically have disconnected ties with both their ethnic group and the larger society and often experience feelings of ambiguity, frustra-tion, disconnection, and identity alienation. Those with marginal identi-ties might also look strongly to their relational partners for their identity support, as well as for emotional reassurance and relationship validation. Understanding others' self-conceptions requires mindful identity probing skills and sensitive identity dialogue work.

Sensitive identity dialogue work requires both introspective dialogue with self and empathetic dialogue with one's relational partner using the following types of questions. Who am I in this relationship? Who are you in this relationship? Who are we together in this relationship? How do my culture, family socialization, and past relational experiences shape who I am now? How do your culture, family socialization, and past rela-tional experiences shape who you are now? How do my cultural world-views and values shape my conflict outlook? How do your cultural worldviews and values shape your conflict outlook? What does it mean to my culture or your culture to "hurt" someone, to "betray" someone, to be "angry" with someone, or to "forgive" someone? What does "intimate fighting" or "intimate relationship healing" mean in my culture or your culture? What does "silence" mean in my culture or your culture? What reactive judgments or assumptions am I formulating about my conflict partner or the conflict situation? What conflict emotions and physical sensations am I experiencing and why? What conflict emotions and physi-cal sensations is my partner experiencing and how could I address such vulnerable emotions and strained physical sensations mindfully? What does "seeking third-party help" mean in my culture and in your culture? Furthermore, what relationship visions do we co-share now and for the future? What can we create together based on the best of who we are? How can we transform our relationship crisis to an uplifting relationship healing and rejuvenation process? Working with such questions, partners can learn to lend appropriate self-conception support via attentive obser-vation, mindful listening, emotional empathy, relational appreciation, and authentic inquiry and dialogue.

Conclusion

In this chapter, I focused on the obstacles to and challenges in developing an intercultural-intimate relationship. Despite the many pressure points in their relationship lives, many intimate couples often mention the following relationship rewards in their intercultural relationships (Romano, 2001; Rosenblatt, Karis, & Powell, 1995): (a) experiencing personal enrichment and growth due to the day-to-day opportunity to continuously clarify their own beliefs, values, and prejudices; (b) developing multiple cultural frames of reference due to the opportunity of integrating multiple value systems such as "doing" and "being," "controlling" and "yielding"; (c) experiencing greater diversities and emotional vitality in their lifestyles because of participating in different customs, ceremonies, languages, celebrations, foods, and cultural network circles; (d) developing a stronger and deeper relationship with their partners because they have weathered intercultural prejudice and racist opposition and arrived at a forgiving, healing place; and (e) raising open-minded, resourceful children who see the world from a multicultural lens and have the ability to be "at home" wherever they find themselves.

Finally, drawing from the main ideas in this chapter, the following guidelines may help intercultural-intimate couples to manage diverse conflict issues in their everyday living:

1. Pay close attention to culture-based obstacles and challenges in developing an intercultural-intimate relationship.
2. Be mindful that individualists and collectivists hold different expectations concerning relationship development issues such as love and commitment and autonomy and network connection.
3. Be flexible in learning the communication styles of your intimate partner and learn to code-switch from low-context/direct to high-context/indirect communication styles and vice versa.
4. Be unconditionally accepting of your intimate partner's complex layered identities—you must make your partner feel that you try hard to understand the ethnic-racial field experience or context from which he is situated.
5. Be sensitive to the reactions of your relational partner's family and close friends—learn to deal with racism and prejudice in a timely manner and display emotional empathy for your partner's feelings, pains, and hurts.
6. Be committed in developing a deep friendship with your intimate partner as a cushion to deal with both internal and external stressors down the road.

7. Do not neglect the everyday "emotional tasks" that face an intimate couple (Gottman & Silver, 1999)—learn to dialogue in a culture-sensitive manner about issues such as work stress, money, sex, household chores, and raising children and their peer pressure influence.
8. Be mindful of the evolving cultural-ethnic identity development issues in your bicultural and multicultural children and learn to respect their emotions and accept their identity choices during their growing up period.
9. Foster a secure sense of personal self-esteem and self-worth and tune into other important identity spheres (e.g., particular adolescent identity development stage) in your children—above and beyond racial and ethnic-cultural identity struggles.
10. Remember to engage in positive relationship memory reflections. Remember the common ground of universal human needs: to be understood, to be loved, and to experience emotional security in a nurturing home environment.

A mindful approach to intercultural-intimate conflict management means learning to listen deeply to your own inner voices and relational dilemmas and to the attending cultural issues that compound them. It means understanding your own cultural and personal value systems and conflict communication styles. It also means probing deeply how your underlying relationship desires and assumptions are connected to your cultural conditioning and personal life developmental and change processes. Concurrently, a mindful orientation from a relational system viewpoint also implies extending exquisite attunement and interpersonal sensitivity to your relational partner's cultural frame of reference. A mindful other orientation means taking the time to sit side-by-side with your intercultural partner with a nonjudgmental posture or with an "empty mindset." It means being comfortable with stillness or relational confusion and uncertainty. It means the ability to feel vulnerable and be able to share it with your intimate partner in his language code. It means the willingness to stretch and adapt to different conflict sensibilities and cultural rhythms. A mindful orientation to intercultural-intimate conflict really means having an intuitive grasp of the timing of when to approach an intimate conflict or when to "let go" of the aggrieved conflict emotions. A willingness to be consistently "in the moment" with your partner on a day-to-day basis, a willingness to genuinely forgive, and a willingness to engage in meditative conscious living may help you to hone an everyday mindful conflict practice.

Author Note

I thank Terri A. Karis and Kyle D. Killian for their thoughtful comments and suggestions on an earlier version of this chapter.

References

Baxter, L., & Montgomery, B. (1996). *Relating: Dialogues and dialectics.* New York: Guilford.

Berry, J. (1994). Acculturation and psychological adaptation. In A.-M. Bouvy, F. van de Vijver, P. Boski, & P. Schmitz (Eds.), *Journeys into cross-cultural psychology* (pp. 129–141). Lisse, The Netherlands: Swets & Zeitlinger.

Berry, J. (2004). Fundamental psychological processes in intercultural relations. In D. Landis, J. Bennett, & M. Bennett (Eds.), *Handbook of intercultural training* (3rd ed., pp. 166–184). Thousand Oaks, CA: Sage.

Chung, L. C., & Ting-Toomey, S. (2001). Ethnic identity and relational expectations among Asian Americans. *Communication Research Reports, 16,* 157–166.

Chogyam, T. (1976). *The foundations of mindfulness.* Berkeley, CA: Shambhala.

Cupach, W., & Canary, D. (Eds.). (1997). *Competence in interpersonal conflict.* New York: McGraw-Hill.

Dion, K. K., & Dion, K. L. (1996). Cultural perspectives on romantic love. *Personal Relationships, 3,* 5–17.

Gao, G. (1991). Stability in romantic relationships in China and the United States. In S. Ting-Toomey & F. Korzenny (Eds.), *Cross-cultural interpersonal communication* (pp. 99–115). Newbury Park, CA: Sage.

Gottman, J., & Silver, N. (1999). *The seven principles for making marriage work.* New York: Crown.

Gudykunst, W. (Ed.). (2003). *Cross-cultural and intercultural communication.* Thousand Oaks, CA: Sage.

Gudykunst, W. (2004). *Bridging differences: Effective intergroup communication* (4th ed.). Newbury Park, CA: Sage.

Gudykunst, W., & Ting-Toomey, S. (1988). *Culture and interpersonal communication.* Newbury Park, CA: Sage.

Hall, E. T. (1983). *The dance of life.* New York: Doubleday.

Hofstede, G. (1991). *Cultures and organizations: Software of the mind.* London: McGraw-Hill.

Hofstede, G. (2001). *Culture's consequences* (2nd ed.). Thousand Oaks, CA: Sage.

Hsu, L. K., Kong, B., & Lee, A. (Producers), & Lee, A. (Director). (2000). *Crouching tiger, hidden dragon* [Motion Picture]. Beijing: China Film Co-Production Corporation.

Johnson, M. (1991). Commitment to personal relationships. In W. Jones & D. Perlman (Eds.), *Advances in personal relationships* (Vol. 3, pp. 117–143). London: Kingsley.

Kabat-Zinn, J. (1994). *Wherever you go there you are: Mindfulness meditation in everyday life.* New York: Hyperion.

Langer, E. (1989). *Mindfulness.* Reading, MA: Addison-Wesley.

Langer, E. (1997). *The power of mindful learning.* Reading, MA: Addison-Wesley.

Markus, H., & Kitayama, S. (1991). Culture and the self: Implications for cognition, emotion, and motivation. *Psychological Review, 2,* 224–253.

Oetzel, J. G., & Ting-Toomey, S. (2003). Face concerns in interpersonal conflict: A cross-cultural empirical test of the face-negotiation theory. *Communication Research, 30*(6), 599–624.

Oetzel, J., Ting-Toomey, S., Masumoto, T., Yokochi, Y., Pan, X., Takai, J., et al. (2001). Face behaviors in interpersonal conflicts: A cross-cultural comparison of Germany, Japan, China, and the United States. *Communication Monographs, 68,* 235–258.

Robins, C., Schmidt, H., III, & Linehan, M. (2004). Dialectical behavior therapy: Synthesizing radical acceptance with skillful means. In S. Hayes, V. Follette, & M. Linehan (Eds.), *Mindfulness and acceptance: Expanding the cognitive-behavioral tradition* (pp. 30–44). New York: Guilford.

Romano, D. (2001). *Intercultural marriage: Promise and pitfalls* (2nd ed.). Yarmouth, ME: Intercultural Press.

Rosenblatt, P., Karis, T., & Powell, R. (1995). *Multiracial couples: Black and White voices.* Thousand Oaks, CA: Sage.

Simmons, C., Wehner, E., & Kay, K. (1989). Differences in attitudes toward romantic love of French and American college students. *International Journal of Social Psychology, 129,* 793–799.

Tannen, D. (1990). *You just don't understand: Women and men in conversation.* New York: William Morrow.

Tannen, D. (1994). *Talking 9 to 5.* New York: William Morrow.

Thich, N. H. (1975). *The miracle of mindfulness.* Boston: Beacon Press.

Thich, N. H. (1998). *Mindful living.* Berkeley, CA: Parallax Press.

Ting-Toomey, S. (1988). Intercultural conflict styles: A face-negotiation theory. In Y. Y. Kim & W. Gudykunst (Eds.), *Theories in intercultural communication* (pp. 213–235). Newbury Park, CA: Sage.

Ting-Toomey, S. (1991). Intimacy expressions in three cultures: France, Japan, and the United States. *International Journal of Intercultural Relations, 15,* 29–46.

Ting-Toomey, S. (1993). Communicative resourcefulness: An identity negotiation perspective. In R. Wiseman & J. Koester (Eds.), *Intercultural communication competence* (pp. 72–111). Newbury Park, CA: Sage.

Ting-Toomey, S. (1994). Managing conflict in intimate intercultural relationships. In D. Cahn (Ed.), *Intimate conflict in personal relationships* (pp. 47–77). Hillsdale, NJ: Lawrence Erlbaum.

Ting-Toomey, S. (1997). Intercultural conflict competence. In W. Cupach & D. Canary (Eds.), *Competence in interpersonal conflict* (pp. 120–147). New York: McGraw-Hill.

Ting-Toomey, S. (1999). *Communicating across cultures.* New York: Guilford.

Ting-Toomey, S. (2004). Translating conflict face-negotiation theory into practice. In D. Landis, J. Bennett, & M. Bennett (Eds.), *Handbook of intercultural training* (3rd ed., pp. 217–248). Thousand Oaks, CA: Sage.

Ting-Toomey, S. (2005). Identity negotiation perspective: A theoretical framework. In W. Gudykunst (Ed.), *Theorizing about intercultural communication* (pp. 211–233). Thousand Oaks, CA: Sage.

Ting-Toomey, S., & Chung, L. C. (2005). *Understanding intercultural communication.* Los Angeles: Roxbury.

Ting-Toomey, S., & Kurogi, A. (1998). Facework competence in intercultural conflict: An updated face-negotiation theory. *International Journal of Intercultural Relations, 22*, 187–225.

Ting-Toomey, S., & Oetzel, J. (2001). *Managing intercultural conflict effectively.* Thousand Oaks, CA: Sage.

Ting-Toomey, S., & Takai, J. (2006). Explaining intercultural conflict: Promising approaches and future directions. In J. Oetzel & S. Ting-Toomey (Eds.), *The Sage handbook of conflict communication: Integrating theory, research, and practice* (pp. 691–723). Thousand Oaks, CA: Sage.

Ting-Toomey, S., Yee-Jung, K., Shapiro, R., Garcia, W., Wright, T., & Oetzel, J. G. (2000). Cultural/ethnic identity salience and conflict styles in four U.S. ethnic groups. *International Journal of Intercultural Relations, 24*, 47–81.

Triandis, H. (1995). *Individualism and collectivism.* Boulder, CO: Westview Press.

Wood, J. (1997). *Gendered lives: Communication, gender, and culture* (2nd ed.). Belmont, CA: Wadsworth.

Section II

Examining Prevalent Assumptions about Intercultural Relationships

4

"I Always Wanted to Marry a Cowboy"
Bilingual Couples, Language, and Desire

Ingrid Piller

This chapter investigates various forms of desire that are intermeshed with the desire for another language, a phenomenon I described as "language desire" in Piller (2002a). In particular, I am concerned with two distinct forms of desire—romantic desire for a partner from a different language background than one's own native language and, once such a relationship has been established, a desire to raise one's children bilingually. Unrelated as these two forms of desire may seem at first glance, they are often inextricably linked in the lives of linguistic border crossers by marriage. I will draw on data from the semiprivate conversations of English- and German-speaking bilingual couples, as well as the representations of bilingual couples in the media. Such public discourses are often drawn upon in private discourses and help to structure desire.

The corpus of semiprivate conversations is described in detail in Piller (2002a). To summarize briefly: 36 bilingual couples, with one partner a native speaker of English and the other a native speaker of German, agreed to tape themselves in a conversation. The conversations are based on an open-ended questionnaire that partners administered to each other. Participants self-selected; i.e., they responded to recruitment advertisements. The German-speaking partners are natives of Germany and Austria; the English-speaking partners are natives of Australia, Ireland, South Africa, the U.K., and the United States. At the time of data collection (1997–1998) participating couples resided in Belgium, Germany, The Netherlands, the U.K., and the United States. The international distribution of the participants results from the fact that they responded to ads placed mainly on the Internet (but also in local and regional publications). The conversations range in length from a few minutes to 2 hours and constitute a corpus of just under 19 hours in total. I consider the conversations semiprivate because, although they are between partners without anyone else present, the tape recorder leads to a situation where an audience, often imagined as the researcher by the participants, is virtually present. However, as the researcher was not present in actual fact, I have not met most of the participants, and I had no chance to ask follow-up questions during the conversations. Therefore, some interesting points remain unexplored. My knowledge about the participants comes mostly from what they say about themselves in the conversations, a background questionnaire I asked them to fill out, and, in a few cases, further interactions I had with the participants (usually one partner only, rather than both). Those interactions included e-mail discussions and face-to-face interactions.

The chapter is structured as follows: I first outline the relationship between bilingualism and romantic desire, before I explore the concept of "language desire" in some more detail. I then describe how a bilingual relationship can serve as a way into a second-language community. Thus, desire for a partner who speaks another language may also be related to a desire for greater interactional opportunities in that language. In the next section, I then move on to discuss the desire for bilingualism in one's children. In the concluding section, I outline implications for couple therapy.

Bilingualism and Romantic Desire

Theories of language and desire have long been explored in the psychoanalytic tradition. However, as Cameron and Kulick (2003a) point out, "It is notable that theorists engaged in debating the nature of desire and its linguistic instantiation seldom refer to any empirical research that examines how desire is actually conveyed through language in social life" (p. 93). Consequently, these researchers argue that the study of language and desire needs to move beyond theories of "inner states" to investigations of the ways in which a variety of desires are discursively accomplished (see also Cameron & Kulick, 2003b). Unlike in psychoanalysis where desire is always seen from a developmental perspective and as an internal phenomenon that is not amenable to direct observation, discursive psychologists argue that desire is instantiated in language. Cameron and Kulick (2003a, 2003b) conceive of desire in a fashion similar to Foucault's understanding of power; i.e., as circulating in specific social spaces. Structures of desire are constitutive of the ways in which desire is enacted in the microdomain. Such an understanding of the relationship between language and desire is similar to the Bakhtinian concept of heteroglossia (e.g., Bakhtin, 1929/1981, 1952/1986). Bakhtin and his collaborators use the concept of heteroglossia to model the interrelationship between the macrolevel of ideologies and the microlevel of conversation. For them, language use in the microdomain cannot be understood without reference to larger discourses. In this view, individuals' desires and expressions thereof are structured by the discourses of desire and the values, beliefs, and practices circulating in a given social context.

As an example, take the comment "I always wanted to marry a cowboy," from which this chapter takes its title. It was made by Natalie,[1] a 35-year-old German woman married to an American man, as she was trying to explain her relationship to the German and American cultures. On one level this comment can be read as an individual expression of romantic desire. However, at the same time it is an instantiation of macro-discourses in which the United States is represented stereotypically as the "Wild West" and American men as cowboys. Based on the information I have about Steven (see the description of my data above), Natalie's U.S.-born partner of 11 years, he seems quite removed from the description "cowboy": he is college educated, holds a humanities degree, and works in a skilled trade in an arts-related business. Thus, describing him as a cowboy clearly draws on discourses outside of their relationship. Indeed, evidence for the stereotypical representation of the United States as the frontier society of the 19th century West abounds. The entertainment industry has produced its own genre of the "Western" where cowboys with their rugged masculinity, their self-reliance, and clear sense of right and wrong figure as heroes. The advertising industry's "Marlboro Man" and his countless clones are further instantiations of the same myth. The statement "I always wanted to marry a cowboy" is almost a literal translation of the title (and refrain) of a German pop song from the 1960s entitled "Ich will nen Cowboy zum Mann" (I want to marry a cowboy). The song was sung by a young female artist and it topped the charts in Germany in 1963 (Gitte, n.d., para. 4). Incidentally, 1963 is the year that Natalie was born. The song's refrain explains the attraction of a cowboy as follows: "Dabei kommt's mir gar nicht auf das Schießen an, denn ich weiß, das so ein Cowboy küssen kann" (I don't care about the shooting because I know that a cowboy knows how to kiss). By contrast, Natalie's attraction to a cowboy is associated with his relationship to English:

> Like, I just said this jokingly but even as a kid I always wanted to marry a cowboy. I always liked America, and the idea of America, and having married you was NOT AT ALL coincidental, like you just happened to be American. [...] I like English. . @ I studied English. I've always liked English. Everything that has to do with English. Old English, Middle English, American English, British English.[2]

One could almost substitute the pop song's explanation for a cowboy's desirability ("a cowboy knows how to kiss") with the explanation "a cowboy knows how to speak English." There are numerous participants who profess such a desire for a second language and explain that it was the pursuit of that desire, usually through studying abroad, that led them into contact with their current partner. For instance, Maren, another German-born participant, who now lives in the U.K., states "I came over because I liked England. I loved English. I love British culture. I wanted to live here." Steven, Natalie's husband, provides another example. Although Natalie and Steven met in the United States, prior to their first meeting he had spent extended periods in Germany, where they now live, in order to study the language:

> I used to love- I used to love German. I mean I studied it, but I don't know now since I really don't have much to do with the language other than using it daily as a tool just to communicate, and to- . yeah. just go about my business I guess erm, cause I'm not really all that interested any more. I'm not really particularly interested in German literature anymore. I think. I hardly ever read anything in German any more.

In yet another example, a clear link between desire for a second language and romantic desire is established. This example comes from a letter that a German woman married to a Briton wrote to me when she learned about my research interest:

> I have to say that I have been attracted to the English-speaking culture from my earliest childhood, and I listened to BFBS [British Forces Broadcasting Service - IP] all afternoon. I loved the chants of the soccer fans and the fact that "love" was such an easy word for these people. Later I chose English as a Leistungskurs [specialization for the high school diploma - IP] and after I graduated from high school I went over to England as an au pair for a year. I majored in English for my translating and interpreting degree at X-University, and during my studies I spent another year in England as an assistant teacher. I can't imagine a life without English and without the English culture. I would have moved to England after I graduated if I had not met my husband, who substitutes England for me here, so to speak. [...]

A range of desires are enmeshed in these examples. To begin with, there is the desire to master another language. Second, there is the desire to become a member of the community of speakers of that language. The road to such membership is envisaged via romantic involvement with a native-speaking partner in the cases under discussion. Third, there is a romantic desire for a type of masculinity (or femininity) that is stereotypically associated with another language. I will first discuss the latter, before I move on to a discussion of the desire for mastering a second language and its relationship to the desire for joining the community of its speakers through marriage.

Language Desire

The larger societal discourses that structure these desires must by necessity be language and culture specific, as discussed for the cowboy example above. Unsurprisingly, there are many more expressions of desire for English, English-speaking partners, and English-speaking communities found in my data than the other way round. This is not a German-specific phenomenon, as evidence from around the world testifies to the use of English in the media to connote desirability (see Piller, 2003, for an overview). In the face of the hegemonic status of English in ever-expanding areas of the globe, desire for languages other than English—be it from English- or non-English-speaking societies—is less likely to emerge. Steven, quoted above, is one of the few Americans in my data to express such a desire for a language other than English, namely German. Later in the conversation, he explains that his love of the German language stems partly from his heritage, as he is the son of German immigrants. Kate, another American participant, lives with her German-born husband in the United States. The couple speak German with each other, and in this quote Kate explains how good it feels to speak German to her partner:

> […] haben wir uns dann beide gefreut, dass wir Deutsch sprechen konnten, und unsere Beziehung fing eigentlich an aus Kaffeetrinken und Sprechen, und so war das- das Sprechen ganz wichtig fuer uns. und wenn wir ein ernstes Gespraech haben, dann muessen wir das eigentlich auf Deutsch haben, sonst laeuft es nicht richtig, und fuehlt sich nicht richtig an. ([…] we were both happy then that we could speak German, and our relationship started with drinking coffee and speaking, and so speaking was- was very important to us. and whenever we are having a serious conversation, it really needs to be in German. otherwise it doesn't go well, and it doesn't feel right. […])

While my research concentrated on English and German, the work of others suggests that the foreign language most likely to connote desirability in the United States is French. Evidence from advertising texts explicitly links "love" and "French," as in the slogan "Because you love French accents" (Lippi-Green, 1997). Similarly, Hollywood movies regularly feature love affairs set in France and/or involving a French partner. A recent example is the movie *French Kiss* (Kasdan & Brooks, 1995), a romantic comedy, in which an American woman transfers her love from her unfaithful American fiancé to a "a sexy, mysterious Frenchman" (*French Kiss*, n.d.). Discourses such as these sustain the desire to learn French and to study in France that Kinginger (2004) describes in her longitudinal work with Alice, a young disadvantaged American woman who overcomes much personal hardship to pursue a university education in French. This is how Alice describes the France of her dreams: "Before I went umm it's always been kinda like Oz, it was like the fairytale land like you know like Wonderland" (Kinginger, 2004, p. 227).

In the American context, languages other than French are relatively rarely linked to desirability. Indeed, as Lippi-Green (1997) points out, foreign languages and English accented by a foreign language background are, more often than not, likely to evoke negative reactions, particularly if it is "linked to skin that isn't white, or signals a third-world homeland" (p. 238). An exception to this pattern that links French to desirability—if a foreign language is linked to desirability at all—comes from the farcical comedy *A Fish Called Wanda* (Crichton & Cleese, 1988). The main female character, Wanda Gershwitz, an American in London, lusts after men who speak foreign languages. For her, hearing her lovers speak Italian or Russian—or rather "pretend Italian" and "pretend Russian"—leads to almost instantaneous sexual arousal.

A Bilingual Relationship as a "Way in"

Mastering a second language can be described as consisting of two components: learning the language in terms of its lexical and grammatical properties and getting access to social interactions in the language (Norton, 2000). Evidence from a diversity of contexts shows that the latter can be as difficult as the former (e.g., Kouritzin, 2000; Miller, 2003; Norton, 2000). Consequently, it does not come as a surprise that forming a romantic relationship is often seen as a convenient way in. As calculating as this statement may sound, in most cases it is unlikely that a range of desires—for mastering a language, for a way into the community of its speakers, attraction to a particular person, lust, etc.—can be clearly separated. A number of participants describe how their relationship has opened doors for them in terms of language learning and, particularly, access to using the language in interactions with native speakers. Claire, for instance, an American who lives with her German-born husband in California, describes how she has helped to improve his English:

> Actually you speak much better than you did erm seven or eight years ago. You still have some accent, but you actually have very good control over it. Getting on with some slang and stuff. And I don't have- like when we were first married, there were a lot of times you asked me like what does this mean and what does that mean. And I had to explain a lot of stuff. Now I don't have to do that ever anymore. It's pretty unusual for you to ask me about- but the other day you asked me something and I couldn't figure out what you mean. And I was out of practice, I was like, oh I can't do this anymore. I used to be able to be really—just like that I could come up with erm definitions. I used to practice all the time.

In another example, Corinna, a German-born woman, describes how her marriage provided her with instantaneous access to an extended American family and American friends when she moved to the United States:

> wir haben uns in Deutschland kennengelernt und am Anfang auschlie-auschliesslich Deutsch mitnander gesprochen. und nachdem wir dann geheiratet haben und in die USA gezogen sind, haben wir eigentlich mehr und mehr Englisch gesprochen, weil wir auch mit der englischsprachigen Familie dort zusammen waren. erm, unsere Freunde waren alle englischsprachig. (We met in Germany and in the beginning we only spoke German with each other. And then after we got married and moved to the USA, we really spoke more and more English, simply because we were with the English-speaking family there. All our friends were English-speaking too.)

For these participants, language learning, language use, and a bilingual marriage are one package. The same was found in other studies of linguistic intermarriage as well. In her interviews with migrant women to the United States, Espín (1999), for instance, found that many of her interviewees felt that learning English and becoming romantically involved with an American partner somehow belonged together. Again, it is important to explore how these individual experiences are structured by larger societal discourses.

A romantic relationship is not, however, a universally available avenue to success for aspiring second-language learners. Pavlenko (2001), for instance, cites a study that found that female Asian immigrants and international students in the United States had a much greater chance of forming relationships with American men than their male compatriots had of forming relationships with American women. Similarly, in an ongoing ethnographic research project with English as an Additional Language (ESL) users in Sydney, Australia, who consider themselves to be either successful or unsuccessful second-language learners, all those who considered themselves successful were romantically involved, or talked of their desire to be romantically involved, with an Australian partner (Piller, 2004). However, romantic relationships were avenues to linguistic success only for European participants, Asian women, and a Chinese gay man. By contrast, heterosexual Asian men and Muslim women (there is no male Muslim participant) did not report romantic relationships or desires, dovetailing with discourses in the host society, which sees itself as largely European. Relationships between Australians and Europeans are viewed as unremarkable while dominant cultural stereotypes cast Eastern European and Asian women as exotic and desirable. Others portray Asian men as undesirable sexual partners for Australian women and largely view Muslims as outside the pale of romantic interest. Indeed, while the relationship between globalization as a form of contemporary imperialism and sexual relationships remains to be explored, the evidence from comparable international relations of dominance such as colonialism and slavery suggests that sexual relationships are closely tied to political, social, economic, and military domination (Hyam, 1990; Nandy, 1983). In English studies, the concept of linguistic imperialism (Phillipson, 1992) has been much discussed in recent years. It refers to the global spread of English during the 20th century and the active roles institutions such as the British Council, British and American publishing houses, and missionaries have played in this spread. Those active roles tend to be hidden, and English as a global language is naturalized, viewed as neutral and beneficial (Pennycook, 2001). One is tempted to speculate that if sexual relationships are indeed part and parcel of all relationships of dominance (as argued by the above-mentioned authors in relation to colonialism and slavery), then it is likely that the linguistic dominance of English is producing its own concomitant sexual relationships: bilingual couples constituted of a native and nonnative speaker of English.

There is clear evidence that the desire for English as the global language, iconic of the West and modernity, is intermeshed with a desire for a romantic and sexual relationship with a speaker of that language (Takahaski, 2006). Drawing on promotional materials of private language schools in Japan, this researcher argues that many language schools promote English to Japanese women by playing on their *akogare* (desire) for Western men and suggesting that learning English might make romantic dreams come true (see Piller & Takahshi, 2006, for a detailed discussion). There is ample evidence in Takahashi's ethnographic work with Japanese women studying and living in Sydney, Australia, that the larger societal discourses of *akogare* for Western men, as a way into the community of English speakers, become an important part of the ways in which these women approach both romantic and sexual relationships on the one hand and learning English on the other. Likewise, a Japanese participant in my ethnographic project with ESL users in Sydney (see above), a young woman in her early 30s, describes in an interview how she began to be interested in studying English after she had graduated from high school:

> Top Gun, I- I when I first saw it I absolutely fell in love with Tom Cruise and I had a lot of articles about him and I- I you know you have this fantasy about you know […] I saw the movie during the high school years, but never really erm came to me as an incentive to do something you know oh er to- to study English but I had nothing to do so I was kind of working part-time and I just fooled around with a group of friends who were no good, you know, false society. And erm er I said to my parents that erm I wanted to study English erm because that's an important sort of tool to have. But really what I wanted to do was learn English so that I could write a letter to Tom Cruise? or- or go to America and- and do something to get to know- […] marry Tom Cruise or people who looked like Tom Cruise. And so he was- I mean it sounds ridiculous, but he was the biggest ins- in- ins- er in- inspiration for me to study English. I wanted to be like people who could talk to- to Tom Cruise or people who looked like Tom Cruise erm […]

Entering a couple relationship with a speaker of the world's most powerful language is attractive not only to Japanese women but also to German men, as is evidenced in the following extract. This one comes from Martin, a German man in his 30s, who is married to an American-born woman. They live in Germany, and Martin discusses the reactions of his coworkers, as well as family and friends, to the fact that he is married to an American:

> I can hear, I don't know how I see it, it's of like- with friends or co-workers, when they hear that you are American, or that I am married to an American, I can hear and see this like- this little like surprise and coolness about it. I don't know what's cool about it. […] I don't know, I just met you because you are you

and not because you are from the States. But for some people it's kind of that mystique thing, or cool having someone from the States. They think it's great, or whatever. @ you are laughing. It's like, I could even hear my dad sometimes, when he was saying, oh actually he's married to an American. I don't know. He definitely would see it different. I think if I would be married to a girl from Kenya or from Turkey or from you know what I mean? It's kind of like, I don't know what the States has but it never has any negative influence […]

A Desire to Raise Bilingual Children

Couplehood is often seen as a transitional stage on the way to starting a family (Fitzpatrick & Caughlin, 2002). In this section, I ask how language desire gets transformed once a bilingual relationship has been established. My data shows that language desire remains a powerful theme in the participants' lives. However, at the family stage, i.e., when the couple are raising (young) children or are planning to have children, language desire takes on a new form. It becomes a desire for their children to be bilingual, very often for them to be perfectly bilingual. Natalie and Steven, for instance, have this to say about their childrearing practices (they have two young children):

> *Steven:* […] to give them the advantage of- of having- . of being able to speak two languages, and erm and- well since they have both citizenships and might possibly choose to live either here or- or- or there erm. they sh- should be able to function in both places equally well. I [think-
> *Natalie:* [yeah and it's- it's pretty obvious also that erm-
> *Steven:* Yeah it's well [that's-
> *Natalie:* [living in Germany and having an English-speaking, one English-speaking parent. English as being a world language and erm stuff. The decision is very easy to say our kids should by all means have as much of that as possible.

All the participating couples expressed an unambiguous and strong commitment to the bilingual education of their children (see also Piller, 2001a, 2002a). This desire is rooted in a range of reasons. First, there is the functional argument that it is useful to be able to speak two languages and, particularly, for English to be one of these languages (as expressed by Natalie and Steven). However, given that at least one partner in all the couples interviewed, and in many cases both, are bilinguals themselves, there must be other reasons as well. Above, I argued that language desire as romantic desire can be seen as a desire to find a way into the second-language community, to become one of them. However, the strong emphasis on bilingual acquisition from birth for the children points to the fact that the parents do not see their project as complete. Even as highly advanced and proficient second-language users, they still grapple with their legitimacy as speakers of that language. Consequently, their dreams are for their children to be fully legitimate speakers of both. A pervasive ideology of native speakership engenders the belief that only speakers who learned a language from birth are legitimate speakers of that language (Davies, 2003; Kramsch, 1997). Despite the fact that applied linguists and second-language teachers have argued against the native speaker myth for years (e.g., Braine, 1999; Canagarajah, 1999; Cook, 1999; Liu, 1999; Piller, 2001b; Rampton, 1990), advanced second-language users oftentimes continue to feel like impostors, who are putting on a passing act (Piller, 2002b). Unsurprisingly, they desire for their children to be double "the real thing." The metaphor of giving them "the best of both worlds" comes up frequently. An American woman, who lives with her German husband and their 2-year-old daughter in Germany, for instance, says: "You know, hopefully Katja will get the best of both worlds from it." *It* refers to her bilingual relationship, and also their efforts to raise the child bilingually.

The hope to raise children who are native speakers twice over is rein-forced by the assumption that native speakers are better language teachers than nonnative speakers. This assumption leads to a fear in some par-ents that they might teach their children errors if they use a language other than their native one with them. As far as second-language learning is concerned, the applied linguists and educators cited above have made it abundantly clear that being a native speaker alone does not turn one into a good teacher of that language, and teaching skills, empathy, or bilingual ability may be of more use in the language classroom. As far as child-hood bilingualism is concerned, the argument for parents to use their native language with their children persists. Tokuhama-Espinosa (2003a), for instance, an educational counselor, exhorts parents as follows: "Mom, speak only your native language; Dad, do the same."

While raising children is a daunting process for anyone, fear of doing the wrong thing linguistically—teaching language errors to one's own children—and the desire to do the right thing linguistically—raising one's children bilingually—may make childrearing even more daunting for bilingual couples. Indeed, it emerges from my data that the parents of small children or couples who are as yet only planning to have children are full of the highest hopes for their children's bilingualism. By contrast, the parents of older children often exhibit a palpable sense of linguistic failure.

This sense of failure is most eloquently expressed in Fries (1998), the memoir of an American woman who followed her French husband to France and tried to raise her two children to become English-French bilinguals:

> As time passed I felt a deep sense of grief. I realized that throughout the years I had always considered my daughter's bilingualism as the most precious gift that I was giving her, and that an exceptional grade in English on the baccalauréat would be the official sanction of that endeavor. As it turned out, there was no recognition, no applause. [The daughter had scored 13/20 on her English test - IP]. [...] Ultimately, English became one more thing that was less important to my children than to me. (pp. 136–137, 140)

There is no doubt that the human language faculty is multilingual and that children can acquire two or more languages from birth and routinely do so in many different contexts around the world (Meisel, 2004). However, that does not mean that a bilingual is a monolingual twice over. Rather, multilinguals use their various languages in different contexts, with different people, for different purposes, and are usually good at doing some things in one of their languages and others in another. Very often, children who have been bilingual from birth develop a much wider repertoire in the language in which schooling takes place (e.g., Cummins, 2003; Mills, 2004). Or they may have a much stronger grip on their mother's language than on their father's language because—even if both use their first language with their children all the time—in most families, particularly those that follow a traditional "male breadwinner" model, children tend to spend much more time with their mothers. Unsurprisingly, the mother's language is often stronger than the father's language, particularly if the mother's language is also the community language (Boyd, 1998).

The widespread desire among bilingual couples to raise their children bilingually represents a most welcome change away from earlier beliefs that bilingualism might be harmful to a child's normal development (see Romaine, 1995, for an overview). This shift is supported by my own and others' data (Cunningham-Andersson & Andersson, 1999; Harding & Riley, 1986; Tokuhama-Espinosa, 2003b) and is reflected by the growth of publications, such as the *Bilingual Family Newsletter*, that seek to encourage and aid bilingual couples in their efforts. However, at the same time it is unsettling that the old beliefs have been supplanted by new ones that often seem to lead to unachievable desires. The "deep sense of grief" described by Fries above may also lead parents to recriminate each other for their perceived failure to raise perfect bilinguals. An example comes from the conversation of Gerda and Dennis, a German-British couple:

Dennis: As a bilingual couple which language do we usually speak together?
Gerda: That's a sad question.
Dennis: A sad question? no, I think it's a wonderful question. [@@
Gerda: [@@ It's from your point of view.
Dennis: and the answer is [of course-
Gerda: [@English.@
Dennis: English. But you know why this is?
Gerda: erm
Dennis: the reas- reason for that?
Gerda: Yes, but the reason doesn't apply anymore.
Dennis: Yeah the original reason is, that you would be at home all the time
        speaking German. With the children. So it's only fair that we should
        speak English together to balance it. However, @things turned out
        a bit differently from what we expected.@
Gerda: And if I remember rightly, we spoke English most of the time when we
        used to living in Germany, [or?
Dennis: [no.=
Gerda: =yes!=
Dennis: =das stimmt nicht. (that's not true.)
[…]
Dennis: […] Has your language use changed in the course of your relationship?
Gerda: Yes.
Dennis: Yes. It's become even more English.
Gerda: Yes, and that's just because you are too lazy to speak any German.
Dennis: And it's also because of Julian's school where English is the language.
Gerda: Which is not true because this boy de- decided not to speak any German
        anymore when he was three.
Dennis: Yê:s[3] that's true. But then why did that happen?
Gerda: Yeah. I don't know.
Dennis: We don't know the answer to that, do we?

Throughout the conversation, Gerda expresses her sense of disappointment at her family's language situation, particularly her children's choice of
English. She implicitly and explicitly blames her partner for that situation
and rebuffs various conciliatory moves on his part, as in the excerpt above.

Not only may parents turn against each other if their dreams of raising
bilingual children do not match the reality of their children's linguistic
repertoire, but there is also evidence of persistent self-recriminations and
a sense of failure. Okita (2002) notes that there is a widespread assumption
that raising children bilingually in bilingual families is easy and that the
advice literature for bilingual couples is often permeated by the assumption "that not raising children bilingually in mixed marriages is in a sense
a failure for parents" (p. 52). Using the life history method, this researcher
interviewed 28 bilingual families in the UK, with a Japanese-speaking
mother and a British father. Okita found that bilingual education was

hard work that was placed squarely on the shoulders of the mothers as the minority parent. It was work they had to undertake simultaneously with other pressing demands in their lives, including the multiple tasks of childrearing, establishing social networks in the UK, fitting in with their husbands and extended family, and coping with a sense of isolation as immigrant women. This hard work was—like other (emotional) work in the family—not perceived and valued as work by the research participants and significant others in their lives; hence, the title of Okita's book *Invisible Work*. Acknowledging this invisible work stands in stark contract to statements about the supposed ease of early childhood bilingual acquisition that permeate the advice literature, as in the following example: "Raising children bilingually in a monolingual community requires minimal effort but maximum commitment" (Bérubé, 1998, p. 3). Most disturbingly, Okita (2002) demonstrates that advice and recommendations to bilingual families that exhort them to raise their children bilingually without the recognition of the demands this places on the minority mother "lead to disempowerment, intensified pressure, guilt and personal trauma" (p. 230).

Conclusion

In this chapter, I have attempted to show that individuals who enter a bilingual relationship are oftentimes guided by multifaceted but interlinked desires. I have therefore termed these desires *language desire*: the desire to master another language; romantic and sexual desire for a partner who is a native speaker of a particular language; a desire for access to interactional partners in the target language; a desire for one's children to become fluent bilinguals; and a desire to be legitimate members of both language communities. These desires of individuals are structured by the discourses and ideologies available in a specific larger societal context: here I have focused on stereotypical representations of another country and its people; on the dominance of English as a global language; on persistent myths about native speaker status; on ideas about the frequency of perfect or balanced bilingualism; and finally on the supposed ease of raising perfectly bilingual children.

Counseling for bilingual couples has (hopefully) come a long way since psychoanalysts asserted that partners "can't love each other in their language," the title of a psychoanalytic case report, "I Can't Love You in Your Language" (Prado de Oliveira, 1988). In Piller (2002a) I argued that such a view of bilingual partners as essentially incapable of loving each other is symptomatic of a larger ideology that sees monolingual and monocultural couples as the norm and bilingual couples as inherently problematic. I hope to have shown that any problems such couples might have are not a result of their bilingualism per se. I believe that any helping professional working with bilingual couples should carefully consider whether the issues they are dealing with are in any way related to the fact that the partners were raised in different linguistic and national contexts. If there is a class of problems that is specific to bilingual couples, these may be issues rooted in beliefs and desires that the larger society makes available.

Notes

1. All the names of the participants are pseudonyms.
2. See transcription conventions at the end of the chapter.
3. Rising-falling intonation and lengthening on the vowel.

References

Bakhtin, M. M. (1981). *The dialogic imagination: Four essays* (C. Emerson & M. Holquist, Trans.). Austin: University of Texas Press. (Original work published 1929)

Bakhtin, M. M. (1986). *Speech genres and other late essays* (C. Emerson, M. Holquist, & V. W. McGee, Trans.). Austin: University of Texas Press. (Original work published 1952)

Bérubé, B. (1998). Two polyglots, three languages. *The Bilingual Family Newsletter, 15*(2), 3–5.

Boyd, S. (1998). North Americans in the Nordic region: Elite bilinguals. *International Journal of the Sociology of Language, 133*, 31–50.

Braine, G. (1999). *Non-native educators in English language teaching.* Mahwah, NJ: Lawrence Erlbaum.

Cameron, D., & Kulick, D. (2003a). Introduction: Language and desire in theory and practice. *Language and Communication, 23*, 93–105.

Cameron, D., & Kulick, D. (2003b). *Language and sexuality.* Cambridge: Cambridge University Press.

Canagarajah, A. S. (1999). Interrogating the "native speaker fallacy": Non-linguistic roots, non-pedagogical results. In G. Braine (Ed.), *Non-native educators in English language teaching* (pp. 77–92). Mahwah, NJ: Lawrence Erlbaum.

Cook, V. (1999). Going beyond the native speaker in language teaching. *TESOL Quarterly, 33*(2), 185–209.

Crichton, C. (Director/Writer) & Cleese, J. (Writer). (1988). *A fish called Wanda* [Motion picture]. United States: MGM.

Cummins, J. (2003). Bilingual education: Basic principles. In J. M. Dewaele, A. Housen, & L. Wei (Eds.), *Bilingualism: Beyond basic principles* (pp. 57–66). Clevedon, UK: Multilingual Matters.

Cunningham-Andersson, U., & Andersson, S. (1999). *Growing up with two languages: A practical guide*. London: Routledge.

Davies, A. (2003). *The native speaker: Myth and reality*. Clevedon, UK: Multilingual Matters.

Espín, O. M. (1999). *Women crossing boundaries: A psychology of immigration and transformations of sexuality*. New York: Routledge.

Fitzpatrick, M. A., & Caughlin, J. P. (2002). Interpersonal communication in family relationships. In M. L. Knapp & J. A. Daly (Eds.), *Handbook of interpersonal communication* (pp. 726–777). Thousand Oaks, CA: Sage.

French Kiss. (n.d.). Retrieved August 11, 2008, from http://www.movieweb.com/movies/film/65/1865/summary.php

Fries, S. (1998). Different phases: A personal case study in language adjustment and children's bilingualism. *International Journal of the Sociology of Language, 133*, 129–141.

Gitte. (n.d.). Retrieved August 11, 2008, from http://www.schulla.com/covergalerie/DATEN/G/GITTE/Gitte.htm

Harding, E., & Riley, P. (1986). *The bilingual family: A handbook for parents*. Cambridge, Ontario: Cambridge University Press.

Hyam, R. (1990). *Empire and sexuality: The British experience*. Manchester, UK: Manchester University Press.

Kasdan, L. (Director) & Brooks, A. (Writer). (1995). French kiss [Motion picture]. United States: Polygram Filmed Entertainment.

Kinginger, C. (2004). Alice doesn't live here anymore: Foreign language learning and identity reconstruction. In A. Pavlenko & A. Blackledge (Eds.), *Negotiation of identities in multilingual contexts* (pp. 219–242). Clevedon, UK: Multilingual Matters.

Kouritzin, S. G. (2000). Immigrant mothers redefine access to ESL classes: Contradiction and ambivalence. *Journal of Multilingual and Multicultural Development, 21*(1), 14–32.

Kramsch, C. (1997). The privilege of the nonnative speaker. *PMLA, 112*(3), 359–369.

Lippi-Green, R. (1997). *English with an accent: Language, ideology, and discrimination in the United States*. London: Routledge.

Liu, J. (1999). Nonnative-English-speaking professionals in TESOL. *TESOL Quarterly, 33*(1), 85–102.

Meisel, J. M. (2004). The bilingual child. In T. K. Bhatia & W. C. Ritchie (Eds.), *The handbook of bilingualism* (pp. 91–113). Oxford, UK: Blackwell.

Miller, J. (2003). *Audible difference: ESL and social identity in schools*. Clevedon, UK: Multilingual Matters.

Mills, J. (2004). Mothers and mother tongue: Perspectives on self-construction by mothers of Pakistani heritage. In A. Pavlenko & A. Blackledge (Eds.), *Negotiation of identities in multilingual contexts* (pp. 161–191). Clevedon, UK: Multilingual Matters.

Nandy, A. (1983). *The intimate enemy: Loss and recovery of self under colonialism.* Delhi, India: Oxford University Press.

Norton, B. P. (2000). *Identity and language learning: Gender, ethnicity, and educational change.* London: Longman.

Okita, T. (2002). *Invisible work: Bilingualism, language choice and childrearing in intermarried families.* Amsterdam: Benjamins.

Pavlenko, A. (2001). Bilingualism, gender, and ideology. *International Journal of Bilingualism, 5*(2), 117–151.

Pennycook, A. (2001). English in the world/the world in English. In A. Burns & C. Coffin (Eds.), *Analysing English in a global context: A reader* (pp. 78–89). London: Routledge.

Phillipson, R. (1992). *Linguistic imperialism.* Oxford, UK: Oxford University Press.

Piller, I. (2001a). Private language planning: The best of both worlds? *Estudios de Sociolingüística, 2*(1), 61–80.

Piller, I. (2001b). Who, if anyone, is a native speaker? *Anglistik: Mitteilungen des Verbandes Deutscher Anglisten, 12*(2), 109–121.

Piller, I. (2002a). *Bilingual couples talk: The discursive construction of hybridity.* Amsterdam: Benjamins.

Piller, I. (2002b). Passing for a native speaker: Identity and success in second language learning. *Journal of Sociolinguistics, 6*(2), 179–206.

Piller, I. (2003). Advertising as a site of language contact. *Annual Review of Applied Linguistics, 23*, 170–183.

Piller, I. (2004). *Success and failure in second language learning.* Unpublished manuscript, University of Sydney.

Piller, I., & Takahashi, K. (2006). A passion for English: Desire and the language market. In A. Pavlenko (Ed.), *Bilingual minds: Emotional experience, expression, and representation* (pp. 59–83). Clevedon, UK: Multilingual Matters.

Prado de Oliveira, L. E. (1988). "Je ne peux pas t'aimer dans ta langue." *Plurilinguismes, Suppl. 1*, 98–115.

Rampton, B. (1990). Displacing the "native speaker": Expertise, affiliation, and inheritance. *ELT Journal, 44*(2), 97–101.

Romaine, S. (1995). *Bilingualism* (2nd ed.). Oxford, UK: Blackwell.

Takahashi, K. (2006). *Language desire: A critical ethnography of Japanese women learning English in Australia.* Unpublished doctoral dissertation, University of Sydney, Australia.

Tokuhama-Espinosa, T. (2003a). First choice option: From birth. In T. Tokuhama-Espinosa (Ed.), *The multilingual mind: Issues discussed by, for, and about people living with many languages* (pp. 109–113). Westport, CT: Praeger.

Tokuhama-Espinosa, T. (Ed.). (2003b). *The multilingual mind: Issues discussed by, for, and about people living with many languages.* Westport, CT: Praeger.

Appendix: Transcription Conventions

Intonation and Tone Units

,	clause final intonation ("more to come")
.	clause final falling intonation (no space after the unit ends)
!	clause final high-fall
?	clause final rising intonation

Words and Pauses

.	short pause; i.e., less than half a second (preceded and followed by a space)
-	truncation; i.e., incomplete word or utterance
CAPS	emphatic stress (in keeping with standard orthography, I have capitalized "I" throughout, and the first letter of German nouns; these are not to be taken to indicate stress)

Paralanguage

@	laughter (one @ per syllable; e.g., @@@ = "hahaha")

Conversational Organization

[	beginning of overlap
=	one utterance latches on to another

Analytic Intervention

[...]	omission

Translation

italics	translations of speech that was originally in German are in italics

5

The Luckiest Girls in the World

Jessie Grearson and Lauren Smith

We were almost on Oprah. We had just finished a book on intercultural romance, and *The Oprah Winfrey Show* called, looking for a backup for their Valentine's Day program. In the end they didn't need us, and the show went on as originally scheduled, but as American women who chose spouses from other countries, we watched the broadcast first with interest and then with disappointment.

The lead story had obvious appeal: a young woman, a princess from Bahrain, escapes from her aristocratic family to marry an American Marine; but it was the same old flag-waving it's-so-great-to-be-an-American cant that we have struggled against since our own first sparks of international love. The program, its two young guests apparently shy and a bit star-struck, emphasized the tragedy of being female and growing up "Over There." "We're the luckiest girls in the world to be born in this country," Oprah shouted, revving up her already enthusiastic audience, welcoming the young princess into the land of the free (*Bahraini Princess Fights to Stay in America*, 2001).

Then came the second part of the show, designed to emphasize how the other half lives by depicting the kind of life the lucky princess had escaped. Oprah talked with two Indian women who had been pressured into arranged marriages. These women's stories did not have happy endings, though interestingly enough, both women remained loyal to their Indian culture, even trying to defend the tradition of arranged marriage, to explain the cultural values that had prompted their parents to find mates they thought well-suited to their daughters. But it hadn't worked out. And Oprah wasn't in a mood to listen.

It became clear that these Indian women, whose own arranged marriages had failed, were there to make a point: We are so lucky to be in America and not "Over There", which could be almost anywhere in the

71

developing world. Our own spouses and our families-in-law are from India and West Africa, and watching Oprah's show helped us articulate one of the unexpected challenges that has resulted from our intercultural marriages: we have come to realize that Americans typically view non-Western marriage practices such as arranged marriage (India) and polygamy (West Africa) as hopelessly backwards. As women who are committed to men from the developing world, then, we have had not only to negotiate cultural difference itself, but also to grapple with U.S. citizens' simplistic, sometimes complacent, view of other cultures and their traditions.

Although we do not defend the practices of arranged marriage and polygamy in this essay, we do argue for a less simplistic reaction to them, a more thoughtful understanding of why such practices might make sense within a cultural framework other than our own. We also suggest how our own development of less reactive and more nuanced understanding of the marriage practices of other cultures has changed us. We are less fully invested in the love stories our own culture tells and have a more flexible understanding of what relationships might be like, what they offer, and why and how we might cherish them.

We begin by considering the overly simplistic way in which Americans see the marriage practices of other cultures. Americans tend to have a black-and-white perspective on marriage, contrasting oppressive Third-World practices with liberating American practices. In the next part of the essay, we retrieve arranged marriage and polygamy from this good/bad dichotomy by reflecting on the literary responses of Indian and West African women writers to these institutions, which, in their complexity, resist a monolithic Western perspective. Finally, we draw upon our own family histories in order to argue for a more multifaceted and less judgmental attitude toward the cultural practices of the developing world and for the enhanced relational possibilities that become available when we open ourselves to the complicated realities of other people.

Arranged Marriage

> Around the world, women's lives are restricted by cultural traditions. Arranged marriages, in which parents choose mates for their children, are still common practice in many cultures. Today, two women shared their stories of marriage without a choice.—(*Bahraini Princess Fights to Stay in America*, 2007)

Oprah serves as a voice of popular culture, for she has a powerful influence in shaping public opinion, and the overwhelming popularity of her show indicates its reflection of the American mainstream. Her emphasis on the words *choice* and *choose* in the above description suggests that American reactions to arranged marriage, as opposed to "love marriage," are more protective of the ideas of freedom and choice than of romance. The concept of arranged marriage interferes with Americans' dearly held sense of independence, their right to decide for themselves and to live their own lives. Although more than half of their marriages end in divorce, Americans cannot imagine anyone choosing a partner for them, and they have a hard time imagining this fate for anyone they know. Another aspect of Oprah's objection to arranged marriage, which again we find echoed among our acquaintances, rests partly on feminist principles that would fight the oppression of women whose lives are "restricted by cultural traditions" that are "still common practice in many cultures." Oprah assumes that women in arranged marriages inevitably experience their situation as oppressive, without actually considering the opinions of the women themselves.

The writing of Indian women raises questions about Western feminism's wholesale dismissal of arranged marriage practices. Professor Monisha Pasupathi (2002), in an essay on arranged marriage, challenges the assumption that the practice necessarily results in "denying women choice and power and treating them as commodities … a feminist nightmare" (p. 214). While not suggesting that all arranged marriages are wonderful or ever doubting the "real horror stories" (p. 212) of uneducated child brides, stories worthy of an Oprah hour, Pasupathi does depict a more complex reality, including a view of contemporary arranged marriage as more than "monolithic rituals with no loopholes that provide the possibility … of resistance" (p. 215).

Although historically women may have had less say in the arrangements than their potential mates, Pasupathi (2002) points out compelling evidence (both from research and her own experience) that this is no longer the norm, a change that has occurred not only in India but also in the many other countries that practice arranged marriages. In contemporary arranged marriage, both partners typically retain the ability to meet and accept or reject a potential match, always mindful of their families' reactions. She argues that a modern perspective of the practice might be better characterized as "treating both sons and daughters as parts in a collective whole—that of the family. As parts of a family, sons and daughters should not select their spouses independently of the concerns of the family as a unit" (p. 231). This union between two people is "collectively chosen and collectively maintained" (p. 231). She also notes that increased levels of education do not necessarily lead to people abandoning the practice of arranged marriage, indicating that well-educated, privileged persons do subscribe to this cultural practice.

Considering whether arranged marriages produce power inequities in marriage partnerships, Pasupathi (2002) wonders whether these inequities are greater in Indian marriages than in their Western counterparts, pointing to research showing that the burden of marriage rests more heavily on women in either culture, as women "do more housework, make greater career sacrifices, and ultimately have less negotiating power in the marital relationship" (p. 229). Increasing freedom to choose a spouse, she notes, is not necessarily accompanied by improved status overall, and it might be that it is "less important to take a stand against arranged marriage, and more important to take a stand against inequitable educational and career opportunities" (p. 231).

Contemporary Indian writers such as Jhumpa Lahiri and Chitra Bannerjee Divakaruni offer examples of this updated view of arranged marriage, and both writers are loath to simply condemn the practice. In fact, Jhumpa Lahiri (2003) describes as seductive the pleasures inherent in Pasupathi's updated arranged marriage practice in her novel *The Namesake*. Lahiri describes the comfort two central characters feel as they come together with the approval of their families, "fulfilling a collective, deep seated desire" (p. 224). Although Moushumi, like her fiancé Gogul, has had the freedom to choose other romantic attractions, "[a]fter years of clandestine relationships, it felt refreshing to court in a fishbowl, to have the support of her parents from the very start, the inevitability of an unquestioned future, of marriage, drawing them along" (Lahiri, 2003, p. 250). While Lahiri resists simplified endings (this couple marries but they do not live happily ever after) she pinpoints the fault line of tension on which "Americanized" Indian offspring stand—raised as part of a collectivist culture but operating within the individualist culture of America.

Divakaruni (1995) also explores the tension that her characters experience in this collision of cultures, either submitting to family expectations or departing from them. Though her collection of short stories is entitled *Arranged Marriage*, the subject is never treated directly; rather, she uses the practice to set characters in motion, challenging them and letting the pull of tradition send them off into different outcomes. In "The Word Love," a young Indian woman who has moved in with her American lover despite her family's disapproval cannot explain or escape from the unhappiness she feels (Divakaruni, 1995). In "Clothes," a young woman who ambivalently accepts an arranged marriage finds happiness following her husband to America. (Divakaruni, 1995). As she later grieves the loss of this partner and considers whether to follow tradition and return to India, donning the white sari of the widow, she instead chooses to wear the Western clothes he purchased for her and to pursue the education he urged her to have. Both writers perceive arranged marriage as a complicated, interesting practice with roots deeply tangled in cultural ways of being, never as something merely to be dismissed at the border of a more "enlightened" way of life.

Jessie's Story

Exactly how Indian is he? Someone once asked me about my husband, and I remember replying, "Oh, he's very Indian." I offered as proof the fact that he would have had an arranged marriage had it not been for me. I was just going for shock value, but I realize now that I did in fact name something essential about my husband: Viren, my kind mate and the father of our children, would have been perfectly content to have had his parents help him find a bride, to begin his married life with their devoted assistance. I have come to understand this truth over time, through knowing my husband and his Indian family. It was much harder to grasp when we were first dating, and back then I pursued the subject of arranged marriage with him relentlessly, wanting to know more details, despite his reluctance. He didn't think I would understand, and at first, I could not. How could he believe—even when he was in love with me—that an arranged marriage would also have worked for him?

Over time he explained the process to me. His parents would have "put out the word" in their community that their son was ready "to begin his life." They would have begun with basic preferences about the girl's religion, level of education, and horoscope and more general preferences about a pleasing personality and appearance. They would have learned about potential families, and their son would have met with a carefully selected pool of candidates, screened by their concerns and desires for him. Parents of eligible daughters would have been told of his educational accomplishments and his pleasant nature. Their horoscopes would have been compared. Personal anecdotes and details—stories of his fondness for freshly made roti, for example—would have made it into the final rounds, where the prospective partners would have met for a date to see if they liked each other.

Now I see that by attempting to understand arranged marriage, I was also coming to grips with the central role of Viren's family in his life, how his happiness and their happiness were joint accounts, not separate. This idea of a collective happiness felt new to me. I was in love with a man who would not always put his personal interests first, someone who would not see his happiness as easily distinguishable from that of his extended family. I was glimpsing a future where I would sometimes struggle with my own desires in the context of this larger happiness—understanding that going after what I wanted would from now on be more complicated, requiring discussion and consensus. I would need to think about the feelings and reactions of a much wider group of others than I had been used to considering.

It wasn't just Viren I would be marrying, I realized, but his whole family, a fact that he made sure I understood once we were serious. He was expected to take care of them; I should understand that they would come and stay with us, not just for short visits. When he wrote to tell his parents more about me, his respectful letter catalogued what he knew of my family, documenting their jobs and educational achievements, and introducing us as a "good family."

I don't recall how it was exactly that we moved from dating to engagement, though to me in my American time frame, it seemed we moved quickly. Viren had only a student visa; we needed to make up our minds in a matter of months. I do remember traveling to Devon Avenue in Chicago, which we jokingly referred to as "Little India." There Viren's other life surrounded me with its bold smells, bustling crowds, but most of all its potential brides: beautiful brown-skinned women with thick black braids, dressed in colorful silks, gold jewelry. Out of respect for tradition, he gently refused to hold my hand on Devon, and I felt our lack of connection keenly, as though we were weakly bonded atoms held temporarily together by whim. I envisioned him moving off to join another family, carrying someone's groceries, stopping in Patel Brothers for fresh samosas with them, and I felt stung by the thought. I didn't want him to marry an Indian woman, I realized, but it was still hard for me to commit to marriage, a hesitation that is still a matter of some interest to my extended family. What took you so long to decide?

Looking back, I think it was my knowledge that Indian marriages were different, without the understood "return policy" of divorce that silently accompanies American marriages. Despite my own parents' long marriage, I had absorbed our culture's idea of divorce as part of a learning curve, but I could tell that marrying into an Indian family would be different. When we did let his parents know, I recall their first words: "If you make up your mind, stick to it," they advised us. To me they said, "Jaysi ho, achchhi ho," a lovely play on my name that roughly translates, "As you are, you are ours."

I realized not long after we made our decision how lucky I was that Viren's family was so accepting, "broadminded." We had a friend, the eldest son of a conservative Indian family, whose family broke off all contact with him when he married an American woman. But Viren's family wanted him to be happy, and they trusted his judgment. Viren's great-grandfather may have prepared the way by traveling abroad to educate himself at Oxford. And although my husband's own grandmother was married extremely young and had children by the time she was a teenager, her own daughters appeared to live anything but traditional lives: one of Viren's aunt's married a Muslim man, and three other daughters remained unmarried, devoting themselves to India's struggle for independence, travel, social work, and art. In fact, of the five, Viren's mother was the only daughter to have a traditional arranged match, and she told me recently that there was "no pressure, no hurry" for her to make up her mind. She describes her marriage as an adventure she willingly embarked upon, as her own choice.

Sometimes I think of Viren's other bride, though I no longer view her as competition, but as a part of some alternative, equally acceptable reality. The woman I imagine (she is modern, and wears a sari only on special occasions though she knows the complex folds required to don one) is a cook, companion, mother, someone who would not have nagged Viren to stop smoking, someone who would have been more deferential to him, who would not have needed his constant translations in Hindu temples. She would have known rules I know nothing of, would have understood how to care for his parents. They would all be living in the heat of India, not in Maine, and their grandchildren would not be singing "Jesus Loves Me" some Sundays or hunting for Easter eggs in the spring time. Sometimes I feel sad that I disrupted what I imagine would have been a simpler happiness for all of them, but it's a sadness of my own making: I feel cherished by my Indian family.

I am grateful for the ways in which my Indian family's definition of collective happiness has enhanced my own life. When each of my two children was born, Viren's parents came to live with us for months, caring for my infant daughters with a devotion and pleasure that gave me peace of mind while I continued to work at a job I enjoyed. They never made this gift feel like a favor for which I should be grateful or indebted, although each time my father-in-law left his job for months and both cheerfully left behind their own busy lives in Bombay. I have, in turn, tried to be a good daughter-in-law to them, learning to cook my husband's favorite dishes from his mother, learning the family stories, and respectfully receiving the wisdom of my elders.

They tell me that their advice to me is the same that they would have given to that other daughter-in-law: Happiness in marriage is about adapting, having realistic expectations, patience, and a sense of humor. At a recent get-together with them, I told my Indian relatives about a book I'd just heard of—Rachel Greenwald's (2003) *Find a Husband After 35 Using What I Learned at Harvard Business School.* Greenwald suggests that her clients envision themselves as a product and that they advertise their personal brand in order to market themselves to potential husbands. She encourages women to call on everyone they know and directly ask these acquaintances to fix them up with someone. Women should further broadcast their intention to marry by sending out cards and photographs to any acquaintances who could introduce them to more single men. My Indian family gave a collective shudder at Greenwald's ideas, extending their compassionate sympathy to any woman who had to suffer through such a public embarrassment, asking for this kind of help from strangers. This reaction stopped me in my tracks. Before I could bring up similarities between Greenwald's methods of finding a mate and their own practice of arranged marriage, my Indian family had already parsed the extreme differences: the blatantly public and commercial versus the familial, private, and loving nature of the transaction. They decried the embarrassing and objectifying treatment of women, who saw themselves as products competing on a shelf instead of individual people with feelings.

Their sympathy for these American women struck me as ironic. These were Oprah's "lucky girls," the luckiest—American middle-class women, exercising choice over every element of their lives. I imagined my sister-in-law hosting a talk show that turns the tables. "Do you see what they go through?" she would say to her audience, "objectified and humiliated, turning themselves into products for the market. We are so lucky," she says to her Indian audience, "the luckiest girls in the world."

Polygamy

Our understanding of American mainstream views of African polygamy is mostly anecdotal, based on the comments of friends and family members. ("Your brother-in-law isn't polygamous, is he?" Or "How do you know your husband doesn't have other wives in Africa?") Like most things African, sub-Saharan marital relationships are all but invisible in American popular culture, except perhaps in images of African male virility—like the brief bed scene in *The Scorpion King* (Russell, 2002) involving an African tribal lord and two of his female subjects. When Americans talk about American polygamy in the context of popular culture, the conversation focuses on the most sensational cases and provokes the most unequivocal reactions. "Thousands of young girls, trapped in secret sects ruled by religion, sex and incest," reads the Web site description of an Oprah show on polygamy (*Porn Star Gone Straight*, 2003). The video that follows this summary calls for increased women's rights. While we agree that women should have more choices and more power in the United States and all around the world, the Web site puts forced marriage, pornography, incest, and polygamy in the same bag and implies that a feminist perspective requires an absolute rejection of them all.

It is exactly this all-in-one-bag perspective that some African women scholars object to in the American feminist view of Africa. According to Stonybrook professor Oyèrónké Oyewùmí (2003), American women tend to "recreat[e] all women in the image of the Western woman" (p. 27) by looking for sexism and gender oppression in Africa that mirrors Western women's experiences. Instead of listening to the range of different African women's voices on gender issues in Africa, Oyewùmí argues that American women interpret African institutions based on Western perspectives, flattening African women's experiences and understanding them as Western (acceptable, understandable) or the opposite (ignorant, unacceptable). Such thinkers ignore or distort what does not fit into their interpretive framework. When they constantly portray African men as backwards and brutal, and African women as victims, Oyewùmí argues, Western feminists perpetuate harmful stereotypes by confirming the basic, primitive otherness of Africans: "[I]n relation to 'his' women, the African male could not be portrayed as anything but a bestial savage. In this regard, polygamy was singled out and represented as a special evil, symbolizing the degradation of African women and hence the low state of Africans" (Oyewùmí, 2003, p. 31). Oyewùmí and like-minded African thinkers want their cultures and cultural practices to be viewed in all their variety and specificity and for African women to be left to define their own experiences. The absolute rejection by Western women of practices labeled "uncivilized," "brutal," and misogynistic also serves to construct African women as spectacles of victimization, focusing their attention and calls for social transformation and emancipation "Over There", eclipsing the problems with patriarchy that persist "Right Here."

Of course, it is not just Western feminists who express disapproval of the institution of polygamy. Some African women writers are quite critical of polygamy, too, though their critiques are more ambivalent, shaped by cultural context and by the particular stories the writers are telling. Ama Ata Aidoo's (1993) understanding of African polygamy, for example, as expressed in her novel *Changes*, captures these mixed feelings. Aidoo tells the story of a hard-working and successful, middle-class Ghanaian woman Esi who becomes the second wife of the wealthy and attractive Ali. Esi's polygamous marriage has its rewards, including the freedom from the constant demands of domesticity: "[T]here was no doubt at all that she enjoyed the fact that she was free to attend all the conferences, workshops, seminars, and symposia on her schedule" (Aidoo, 1993, p. 148). Certainly, this second marriage is no worse than Esi's first marriage, which was monogamous and, for Esi, stultifying.

However, her marriage with Ali is ultimately ungratifying because her new husband is too busy with his other family—and later with his secretary—to spend much time with Esi. The problem is partly with Ali's sexual restlessness and partly with the institution of polygamy itself. "Well, just remember that if a man can have two wives ... Then he can have three wives ... four wives, ..." Esi's best friend had warned her (Aidoo, 1993, p. 156). The viewpoint suggested by the novel is complicated because neither polygamy nor monogamy works out for Esi. But Esi's own developing understanding locates the problem with her first marriage in the relationship between Esi and her first husband and the problem with her second marriage in the institution of polygamy itself. While Aidoo's perspective on polygamy is much different than Oyewùmí's, it is also far away from Oprah's brand of American feminism, at least as that feminism is expressed in unreflective or dismissive shows addressing polygamy and arranged marriage.

Less ambivalent about polygamy is the writer Mariama Bâ (1979/1989). In her famous epistolary novel *So Long a Letter*, Bâ follows the lives of two women, both of whom begin as happy young brides but who eventually face the unhappy prospect of a second wife. One of the women, Aissatou, promptly packs her bags and moves on to a lucrative job and a life of independence in the United States. The second character, the letter writer and narrator, Ramatoulaye, chooses to remain married to a husband, Modou, who increasingly shuts her out of his life—lavishing affection instead on his new and demanding child bride. The comparison of Aissatou, who goes on to live a happy and successful life as a single woman, and Ramatoulaye, who experiences nothing but betrayal and humiliation, makes the author's perspective clear. Ramatoulaye has made an understandable choice in accepting her polygamous marriage, but Aissatou has made a better choice in rejecting it.

Bâ's critique of polygamy takes place on two levels. First and foremost is the emotional level. The marriages of both Aissatou and Ramatoulaye arise out of the love and shared values of the partners, happy choices for all involved. In contrast, both second marriages have less credible origins—a controlling mother-in-law in Aissatou's case and a mid-life crisis in Ramatoulaye's. In taking second wives, both husbands have betrayed not just their first wives but their own emotional integrity. There is an economic aspect of Bâ's critique, but this is muted. Ramatoulaye suffers financially when she is left to fend for herself and again when she loses the house at her husband's death, but she does successfully provide for her family.

While this novel voices disapproval of polygamy, it is simultaneously ambivalent in its treatment of polygamous men. Bâ shows that her main character suffers because of polygamy, and her critique of the practice is pointed, but she does not participate in the vilification of African male characters that Oyewùmí targets. The character Daouda provides a good case in point. Daouda is an accomplished man, a doctor with enough resources to support two families—and he is portrayed as intelligent and kind-hearted, an ideal husband in every way but one: He is already married. In a letter to Daouda, Ramatoulaye writes, "Abandoned yesterday because of a woman, I cannot lightly bring myself between you and your family" (Bâ, 1979/1989, p. 68). Ramatoulaye does not reject Daouda so much as she rejects the institution of polygamy.

Like Aidoo, then, Bâ critiques the institution of polygamy, but both maintain a complicated perspective on the institution, and neither offer Western-style monogamy as an ideal alternative. None of the female characters discussed has a satisfying polygamous relationship, nor do they have satisfying monogamous relationships. Most importantly, neither falls prey to the vision Oyewùmí finds so offensive: of African men as brutes and African woman as victims. Both African male and female characters are complicated, and both are able to make choices within their cultural contexts.

Lauren's Story

On a recent trip to the country of Burkina Faso, West Africa—my husband's country—I discovered that I had acquired three extra husbands. Before long, I found that these husbands were not "extra" at all, but essential to my life and work while I was in Africa. I was there doing research on AIDS, and I was, for an extended period of time, by myself—without my home, my routines, my car, and especially my daughter and my husband, Hassimi. My newly acquired spouses, all family members and friends of my legal husband, rallied around. Together, they provided me with a place to stay, a car and driver, valuable contacts, advice, and company. They took time out from their work and family lives, shared their food and resources with me, and took my problems on as their own, searching thoughtfully for solutions to each major or minor dilemma as it arose. My brother-in-law Alassane became the most indispensable. My "compagnon de tous les jours" (companion of all the days), he drove my car, listened to endless stories about my daughter, and served as a kind of public relations manager—smoothing the way for me in countless situations. If I remarked on his generosity, my listeners responded in the affirmative, adding, "But of course he must take care of you. He is your husband."

As a feminist by profession, as well as personal commitment, I thought it wonderfully ironic to find myself so implicated in the ideology, if not the practice, of polygamy. I love a joke, and this one provided endless opportunities for mock fights, divorces, and remarriages. My "cowives" played along joyfully, making elaborate pretenses of jealousy or arranging to swap spouses. "You can have all these guys; I'll take Hassimi." "Do you miss Hassimi?" friends would ask, and I made a ritual pleasantry out of denying it. "Oh, that guy?" I would respond, "No, no, no. He is the least important of all my husbands." Likewise, whenever one friend had done something especially kind, the others would pay a joking tribute to him. "Oh no, now he is the most important husband, and our case is very weak."

My adventures in polygamy were mostly funny and entirely metaphorical. However, like most successful metaphors, these figurative adventures hinted at certain truths. Among other things, they suggested an important difference between the way Americans see marital relationships and the way Burkinabé people see them. In the United States, the story of husbands and wives is the story of romance and sexuality first, and family commitments a distant second. In West Africa, Burkinabé family commitments are embodied in a series of obligations, like the rearing of children for women and the provision of financial support for men. In other words, marriage is more about providing care for family members than about sexuality. In this sense, my Burkinabé spouses were real husbands because they fulfilled their most important family obligations toward me, providing for my safety and well-being.

Once I appreciated the family-centered nature of polygamous unions, I could move toward understanding why so many Burkinabé women choose to participate in them. At first, I assumed these women didn't have a choice, but this is not true. In Burkina Faso, partners make a legal agreement when they marry that commits them either to a polygamous or monogamous marriage, so if the woman does not agree, there can be no second legal wife. So why would a woman choose to share her husband? The first reason that made sense to me was based in a rural subsistence economy. Bigger families provide more people to work the land and are more prosperous. In the United States, *prosperous* might mean a fancy entertainment center and not having to shop the sales, but in the context of rural Burkina Faso, it means that your children can eat and go to school. Big families also provide better "social security" in the form of young people to care for the aging. Even now, my husband provides financial assistance for his mother's cowife when he can. Finally, the more able-bodied women there are in a family, the lighter the workload on any one woman—and women's work in a rural context can include childcare, housework, cooking, and gathering wood, as well as work in the fields.

"In the village, it is the women who ask for second wives," I was told over and over again by proponents, mostly men, of polygamy. I felt skeptical, but the assertion was confirmed by a surprising source. My friend Angélique, a retired teacher and community activist in Ouagadougou, does not necessarily talk the feminist talk, but she definitely walks the feminist walk, participating in numerous committees and civic groups addressing the problems of women in West African cultures. She herself is monogamous, but when the subject came up, she spoke with enthusiastic nostalgia about the large, polygamous families that were part of the village life of her girlhood. "Oh yes, the women were the ones who would ask their husbands for a second wife, and often they would choose the woman. Your girlfriend might want you, for example," she said, laughing at my surprise. "The women would choose, and they would bring you gifts, flatter you, court you on behalf of their husbands." It is easy to imagine the joy—the company and friendship—of sharing family life with another woman, the pleasure of working side by side with her, if family well-being and not sexual competition is placed at the center of consideration.

The lives of urban women, especially if they are middle class, do not involve the same kinds of labor or the same hardships as do the lives of village women, so the benefits of polygamy are limited for them. Of those urban, middle-class women who choose polygamy anyway, many have simply succumbed to pressure from their families, and others are afraid that they will not find a husband if they won't share him. "What difference does it make?" said one woman, whose cynical response reflected the feelings of other women I met. "If we sign up for monogamy, he can still have a mistress." But there are important differences between a monogamous man who takes a mistress and a polygamous man who takes a second wife, and those differences make monogamy look bad to some women.

In a Western-style monogamous relationship, the husband would be justified in abandoning the first relationship in order to be with the mistress, no matter what kinds of hardship that might mean for the first wife. "It just didn't work out," people might say, "he doesn't love her anymore." In a traditional polygamous relationship, on the other hand, the husband is obliged to maintain support for and connection with both women. The first wife keeps not just her husband but also all the support his extended family can provide. The harsh realities of our own monogamous culture are masked by our romantic mythology of exclusive relationships. For example, we don't always acknowledge the frequency of infidelity and divorce, or the poverty of fatherless families, the deep imperfections of our own marriage practices. If I were a wise Burkinabé woman, I might well choose a responsible polygamist over a Western-style serial monogamist.

Or I'd choose a life of celibacy—which is what I always told my "extra" Burkinabé husbands when we talked about the issue. "It's not worth it, I just wouldn't get married," I would say. We had such talks about gender issues, and polygamy in particular, fairly often. I remember the night of our most heated conversation vividly, partly because it turned out to be so engaging. My friends and I, in this case all male, drank tall bottles of Flag beer, ate greasy chicken, and talked under the stars for more than 4 hours.

The discussion centered on whether or not a sexual double standard that allows multiple partners only to men could be justified by cultural difference. I said it could not. Women should have the same freedom as men; polygamy (multiple marriage) should allow for polyandry (multiple husbands) as well as polygyny (multiple wives) or it was unfair. The argument became anthropological, theological—and very intense. The men listened to all my arguments with tolerant attention, and nothing I said that night or later pushed me outside the circle of their friendship. They conceded this or that point in principle, very little in practice. There was more beer, more animated conversation. I was named head of the women's union. No matter what I said, however, they could not dismiss or abandon me. I was family.

I can make jokes and engage in all-night discussions about polygamy in the abstract, but the real-life complexities of Burkinabé marriages render me mute. We are close to a man I'll call Hamidou. As a young person, he married and had two children. At some point, still early in his marriage, he had the opportunity to receive training abroad and so left his family behind for a year. As a result, he was offered a good job in the north of the country, which he accepted, finding himself again far away from his children and his wife, who had a good job in the capital. Hamidou could not have chosen differently, since to do so might have meant menial labor or unemployment. However, the distance—and maybe other issues as well—caused problems in the marriage. At some point, there was another woman and a child.

I am in the car talking with Hamidou. We are bouncing through potholes and narrowly missing bicycles and mopeds. "What should I have done?" he asks me. "Leave the baby without a father?" In the United States, Hamidou would probably have left his first family, but in Burkina Faso, divorce would have pinched the resources of Hamidou's first family even more than it would in the United States. That family would no longer be able to live in Hamidou's house, and his wife would lose the respectable title "Madame" (Mrs.). In fact, Hamidou's relationship with his first wife has deteriorated, and he would prefer a divorce. "What do you think I should do?" he asks me, less rhetorically this time. Before spending time in Burkina Faso, I would have answered easily in favor of divorce, but life is more complicated than I once imagined, and now I don't have an easy answer. I do know that Hamidou is my friend, part of my family's community, and none of the decisions he might make will weaken that connection.

Conclusion

People's reactions to arranged marriage and polygamy differ. As one friend put it: "People hear about arranged marriage and think 'that's sad,' but when they hear about polygamy they think 'that's bad.'" Yet these reactions have in common a blindness to the cultural values that shape our American perceptions. A "love" marriage is understood as the good in a good/bad dichotomy partly because personal choice, personal freedom, and personal happiness are such important values for us, within our independent, individualist culture. If maintaining family cohesion and prioritizing family happiness were prime values, as they are in other cultures, then we might see things differently. Likewise, if the cohesion and well-being of our extended family members were more important than our ideas about romantic love, polygamy might seem a less heinous option. In other words, our individualist culture values independence over interdependence, and this affects our choices and vision of the world.

These days, when we consider the issues of arranged marriage and polygamy, we are not just thinking about ourselves, whether or not we are "lucky girls." We think of our husbands, too. Are they lucky? Having lived with these men for so long, we can see their other lives. The Indian wife, who would have learned to cook Viren's favorite meals from his mother, made roti without complaint, and cared for his parents with a better understanding. The African family weaving Hassimi into its huge and loving net—maybe more wives, more children, more in-laws, all an important and immediate part of everyday life.

We consider our children: three girls. Are they lucky? We think they are, not because they are American, but because they have two cultures to draw from, a growing knowledge of and commitment to a wider world. Emma and Eleanor understand that they are connected to distant cousins who live on the other side of the globe in a country they long to visit. For now, this world visits them when their grandparents do, when they listen to stories about the elephant god Ganesh or learn to make chapatti, the soft, fresh flatbread that their father loves. They are experts at yogurt rice and ask for a pinch of heeng to put into the "sizzle" without a hint of self-consciousness. Words from their father's language are an extension of their vocabulary; we like to think they come easily because they were first absorbed when the girls listened to them as infants in their grandparents' care.

Myriama has chased chickens and goats in a dusty savannah village in West Africa. She loves the story of Safagamamourou, the playful monkey, enjoys African stews with couscous, and is learning to greet Burkinabé visitors in French, taking the time to shake hands with each one in turn. Adult friends she calls "tantie" or "ton-ton" (aunt or uncle) as a reflection of the sense of community we want to cultivate. We nurture the loyal heart that is natural to her and hope she will develop an African sense of commitment to match it, not just to her nuclear family but also to her extended family. It was to this end that we took her on the arduous journey to Africa, not easy for a small child or her parents, but one that has left her with memories and photographs that make her African friends and family real for her. All three of our daughters have a broader sense of family than we did at their age, an understanding that extends past the nuclear family and cousins-at-Christmas to include more distant blood relations and close friends of the family—and larger intercultural communities as well. If, many years from now, our girls want to marry, we hope that they will make their decisions knowing the depth of their choices, seeing them in the fuller light an international family can provide. If they can weather the complications, if they can see marriage as a compelling and beautiful fable that varies from culture to culture, then maybe they will be able to write their own stories. Then maybe they really will be the luckiest girls in the world.

References

Aidoo, A. A. (1993). *Changes*. New York: The Feminist Press at CUNY.

Bâ, M. (1989). *So long a letter* (M. Bode-Thomas, Trans.). Portsmouth, NH: Heinemann. (Original work published 1979)

Bahraini Princess Fights to Stay in America. (2001). Retrieved April 13, 2007, from http://www.oprah.com/tows/pastshows/tows_past_20010215_b.jhtml

Divakruni, C. B. (1995). *Arranged marriage*. New York: Anchor Press.

Greenwald, R. (2003). *Find a husband after 35 using what I learned at Harvard Business School*. New York: Ballantine.

Lahiri, J. (2003). *The namesake*. New York: Houghton Mifflin.

Oyewùmí, O. (2003). *African women and feminism: Reflecting on the politics of sisterhood*. Trenton, NJ: Africa World Press.

Pasupathi, M. (2002). Arranged marriage: What's love got to do with it? In M. Yalom & L. Carstensen (Eds.), *Inside the American couple* (pp. 211–235). Berkeley, CA: University of California Press.

Porn Star Gone Straight: The Tracy Lords Story. (2003). Retrieved April 13, 2007, from http://www.oprah.com/tows/pastshows/200310/tows_past_20031009.jhtml

Russell, C. (Director). (2002). *The Scorpion King* [Motion Picture]. United States: Universal Pictures.

6

"We're Just a Couple of People"
An Exploration of Why Some Black–White Couples Reject the Terms *Cross-Cultural* and *Interracial*

Terri A. Karis

> I just look at this relationship as she is my wife and I am her husband.... Everyone else is looking at it as a black and white couple, which I think is really stupid because we are just a married couple. We are no different than a Chinese couple that were married or a white couple that were married or a black couple that were married. We're just a couple of people who decided we wanted to be with one another. [African American man in a black–white relationship.] (Rosenblatt, Karis, & Powell, 1995, p. 25)

> The fact that I'm in an interracial relationship is, it's not a label that I apply to my relationship.... That's an external label [used by] ... people outside [who] have a need to categorize. [African American man in a black–white relationship.] (Rosenblatt, Karis, & Powell, 1995, p. 19)

The growing literature on Black–White couples suggests that a significant subset of these couples take issue with the labels *cross-cultural* and/or *interracial* (Karis, 2003; Killian, 2002). Although these terms often are used interchangeably, from a metaphoric perspective they are not synonymous. Using theories of metaphor and categorization, I will consider what is highlighted and what is obscured by each label when it is applied to Black–White heterosexual couples. After reflecting on differences and similarities between these labels, I offer preliminary thoughts on the discursive work done when couples use or reject a label. I argue that learning more about couples' interpretive repertoires—how and when they use these terms and what is accomplished socially and politically by their usage—is a potentially fruitful path for deepening understanding of Black–White couples and how they make sense of race in their daily lives.

A Theory of Metaphor

Metaphor is often regarded as just "a figure of speech in which a word or phrase that ordinarily applies to one kind of object or idea is applied to another, thus suggesting a likeness or analogy between them" (Rosenblatt, 1994, p. 12). The theory of metaphor put forth by Lakoff and Johnson (1980) suggests, instead, that metaphor is basic to how humans conceptualize. In this view, all language is saturated with metaphor that shapes how we perceive and think about the world. A metaphor is a mapping from one conceptual domain to another. We use our experiences with entities or aspects of one domain to make correspondences to entities or aspects of another. While these mappings are always partial, they are not arbitrary. Drawing on our everyday embodied experiences, we make connections between concrete physical patterns of experience and the corresponding elements of more abstract conceptual domains.

Some metaphorical mappings seem to be universal, based on our human experience in bodies (Lakoff & Johnson, 1980). Our primary physical experience includes spatial orientations such as in–out, front–back, and up–down, and we draw on these to organize our understanding of whole systems of concepts. Thinking that the future is in front of us, rather than behind, is an example of how concrete experiences in one domain (the physical body) are mapped onto another domain (the abstract relationship to time). Human experiences of space lead to numerous sensory and spatial metaphors that are fundamental to how we understand more abstract concepts. Similarly, we use experiences with substances and physical objects, especially our bodies, as the basis for a wide range of ontological metaphors (Lakoff & Johnson, 1980). More abstract aspects of experience, such as thoughts, feelings, states, or ways of viewing events, are conceptualized as entities or objects. For example, talking about "my hope for the relationship" makes the abstract experience of hope into an entity that can be present or absent, have aspects, or be quantified. Metaphors grounded in orientation and ontology are so pervasive that they generally are taken for granted as self-evident descriptions and are not thought of as metaphorical.

Our embodied experience as physically separated from the rest of the world by the surface of our skin is the foundation for a variety of "container" metaphors (Lakoff & Johnson, 1980). Because we experience ourselves as bounded entities with an inside and an outside, we project these qualities onto other physical objects, as well as onto more abstract concepts. Buildings are obvious containers, but the essential qualities of boundedness and in–out orientation are evident when we talk about categories such as interracial and cross-cultural. "Being in an interracial relationship" or "visiting another culture" reference interracial relationship and culture as things that can be entered into or left, with specific qualities, and with beginning and ending points in time and space. As these examples illustrate, we impose boundedness even when there are no physical boundaries. Events and actions, activities, and various kinds of states all might be conceptualized as containers.

Categories as Containers

The ways that people understand and act upon the world are shaped by how they categorize, and the processes of categorization involve metaphor rooted in bodily experiences (Lakoff & Johnson, 1980). This experiential approach moves beyond the classic Aristotelian idea of "categories as sets of equivalent members, upon which logical operations can be performed" (Edwards, 1991, Introduction, ¶ 3) to consider how the generation and application of categories is shaped by human embodiment. The pervasiveness of container metaphors used in the process of categorization stems from our human experience of being in "separate skinbags" (Dogen, trans 2007). This containment is then mapped onto other experiences. Sorting or grouping people, for example, involves selectively attending to particulars and drawing distinctions between those who belong within the container or category and those who fall outside of it. Our distinctions create the limits of the category; a focus on different characteristics would result in different categories. The abstract nature of a category becomes concrete when we project the properties of a container onto it. Thus, it is common practice to talk about the category of interracial couples and to assume that a couple either belongs inside the category or outside of it. The border between inside and outside creates a boundary, and within this system of categorization it doesn't make sense to talk about a couple sometimes being an interracial couple and sometimes not; a couple is either included in the category or not, but being both inside and outside, or neither inside or outside, are not options within a system of categorization.

Interracial and Cross-Cultural as Metaphors

Although the terms *cross-cultural couple* and *interracial couple* often are used interchangeably, from a metaphoric perspective they are not necessarily equivalent. Dictionary definitions provide a starting place for exploring their similarities and differences. According to the *American Heritage Dictionary* (2000), *cross-cultural* is defined as "comparing or dealing with two different cultures" and *interracial* is defined as "relating to, involving, or representing different races." Both definitions elicit the container metaphor, implying distinct categories marked by boundaries or borders between different entities, and movement between them. In one case the groups are separate and distinct cultures, whereas in the other the groups are different races. The commonality between cross-cultural and interracial is the fundamental assumption of separate categories—an assumption that highlights difference—marked by the boundary of being in or out of the group, whether that group is named as cultural or racial.

As an essential aspect of the container metaphor, the boundary delineates an inside from an outside. Boundary is defined as "something that indicates a border or limit" (*American Heritage Dictionary*, 2000). It implies marking one territory from another, in this case cultural groups or racial groups. Highlighting the difference or boundary between groups invites thinking of racial and cultural groups as homogenous, unified, monolithic, fixed categories that one is either in or not in. By extension, it invites thinking of racial and cultural identities or selves as fixed, rather than as fluid or multiple. Categorization requires that which is ambiguous, uncertain, contradictory, or paradoxical to fit within the defining border or boundary of the container.

While the modifiers of *inter* and *cross* claim the possibility of relationship, connection, or movement between the different categories, they presume distinct boundaries between one group and another, between one self and another. This emphasis on the border or boundary obscures whatever doesn't fit neatly within its limits, including processes such as the relationships within racial or cultural groups, the contexts within which groups are embedded, the difference between crossing the boundary in one direction versus crossing it going the other way, and what one crosses into or over when moving out of the bounded container of race or culture.

The terms *cross-cultural* and *interracial* are similar in that each is based on the assumption of a relationship between two separate categories, but looking through a metaphoric lens requires drawing distinctions between race and culture, both of which are complex concepts with multiple, sometimes contradictory, definitions. One way to look at the differences between race and culture is to explore the entailments, or automatic associations or connections, elicited by each concept. Metaphors are systematically structured by entailments that highlight or focus on certain aspects of experience while obscuring or hiding others (Lakoff & Johnson, 1980). For example, "Feeling at home in a relationship" is related to particular associations (e.g., "I feel nurtured," "I can relax") that are different from the associations linked with "Feeling imprisoned in a relationship" (e.g., "I feel trapped," "I've got to keep my guard up").

With any complex concept, such as relationship, experience is structured not just in terms of one metaphor or another but based on two or more overlapping, sometimes conflicting, metaphors. "Feeling at home" might name a part of my experience in a significant relationship but not get at how I also sometimes "feel burdened" by it or experience the relationship as an "uphill battle." Although all these metaphors are container metaphors, each has related entailments that highlight different aspects of relationship: as a place, as a heavy object, as a difficult journey.

Investigating what is highlighted and obscured by the metaphoric entailments of the terms *interracial* and *cross-cultural* will lay a foundation for understanding Black–White couples' practices of using and rejecting these labels. Edwards (1991) recommends thinking about categorization discursively by looking at the specific contextual deployment of terms and the social functions served by their use. He argues that "[c]ategorization is something we do, in talk, in order to accomplish social actions (persuasion, blamings, denials, refutations, accusations, etc.)" (Introduction, ¶ 5). Edwards acknowledges the link between bodily experience and human categories but maintains that a category item is always a specific situated thing, event, or group of things that performs "moral work." He therefore recommends exploring the social nature of terms and how they function in achieving social outcomes. In the next sections I apply Lakoff and Johnson's (1980) approach to metaphor to explore what is highlighted and obscured by the terms *cross-cultural* and *interracial*. After that, I follow Edwards' (1991) suggestion and consider what social actions are accomplished when Black–White couples use or critique the use of labels that are applied to them in their everyday lives.

What Is Highlighted by *Cross-Cultural*?

Culture as a Physical Location

In the literature on cross-cultural couples, culture often is portrayed as a place or location. Concrete physical aspects of a specific place or location are used to represent the many intangible and abstract aspects of culture.

A place or location is a variation of a container metaphor, and like all metaphors, it shapes thinking in particular ways as it draws awareness to some aspects of an experience more than to others. Conceivably, culture could be represented by alternative metaphors such as an information processing system, an organism, or a psychic prison, but these are not the metaphors used in the writings on cross-cultural couples.

Perel's (2000) chapter on cross-cultural couples, entitled "A Tourist's View of Marriage," provides one example of using place to represent culture. Perel writes that:

> [C]ross-cultural partners are like immigrants or tourists.... Plunged into an unfamiliar world, each "tourist"-partner wonders, "How can I feel comfortable here?" The "tourist" notices all kinds of things the indigenous local misses or takes for granted—"Why is this building here? What does that sign mean?"—often reawakening the local's own curiosity about his or her own surroundings, and his or her place in those surroundings, affording a fresh look at customs or landmarks or traditions that the local formerly hadn't noticed for years—if at all. In one type of cultural adjustment the newcomer slowly takes hold of this new world by imitating, identifying, and internalizing its key aspects and familiarizing himself or herself with its landmarks. (p. 180)

In this example, the "new world" and "its landmarks," including the concrete objects of a building and sign, are used to characterize culture as a place or location, and being "immigrants or tourists" implies vivid, yet markedly different relationships to that place.

The most significant aspect of a place or location metaphor, as with all container metaphors, is that it implicitly references a boundary or border. A boundary, by definition, marks entities as separate and distinguishes an interior from an exterior. It draws attention to the distinction between "in" and "out." Boundaries not only highlight difference but, more accurately, they create difference, drawing attention to the border, edge, or margin (Rosenblatt, 1994). As sociocultural constructions, boundaries are established and maintained by rules about who or what belongs or is included and who or what is excluded. Those who are "in" are assumed to be bonded by something in common that differentiates them from those who are "out." Boundaries function as a barrier between inside and outside and regulate movement across the line that separates the two.

One implication of referring to culture as a place or location is that it invites thinking of partners' cultures as relatively stable and unchanging. This assumption is shaped by our actual day-to-day experience of physical and geopolitical locations. Even though landmarks and buildings change over time, our everyday experience of them is that they are more or less permanent. Think of Paris, and images of landmarks such as Notre Dame and the Eiffel Tower come to mind. Similarly, we commonly experience the boundaries of places as set. This may be especially true for those of us in the United States, as state lines and borders between neighboring countries have remained unchanged for so long that their existence is taken for granted. Within this metaphor it is a common-sense assumption that places are pretty much fixed or permanent. By extension, we are invited to think of the more abstract aspects of culture, and of cultural identities, as established and unchanging. What is obscured by these metaphoric entailments is awareness that cultures and identities are fluid and diverse and that change and uncertainty are a constant reality.

A second implication of thinking about culture as a location is that it invites thinking about culture and cultural selves as natural rather than as socially constructed. We tend to experience our current physical surroundings as a given, decontextualized from the past and the evolving political and social choices that have shaped them. For example, even though I know that the interstate highway I regularly drive was not always there, I usually take its existence for granted. I may not think about or even have conscious awareness of these facts: the highway was built right through the center of a once-thriving Black neighborhood; its creation not only disrupted the community and led to a decrease in property values but also was linked with the relocation of White families to the suburbs. I may not think about how these changes were supported by tax dollars and government subsidies or how declining property values are linked to racial disparities in wealth accumulation. I may not think about how any of this has shaped my sense of self or the selves of those who live in the neighborhoods through which I drive. The highway is simply an established, and unexamined, part of my taken-for-granted daily routine. Accepting one's experience as a natural given results in a dehistoricized and depoliticized perspective, obscuring the social processes that have contributed to things as they are (Brown, 2007).

A third implication of using the location metaphor to represent culture is that concrete aspects associated with a place are highlighted. When we think of a specific cultural location it includes cultural artifacts, typical foods, dress, and music. Even though culture includes values, beliefs, goals, attitudes, and a multitude of customs and relational practices, thinking of culture as a physical place makes tangible cultural objects especially salient and obscures the ways that each culture is complex, diverse, and ever-changing.

Relationships within the Cultural Location

As a variation of the container metaphor, a place or location metaphor is defined by its emphasis on a boundary between inside and outside. When culture is represented as a place, the boundary defines cultures as separate and distinct, raising questions about the relationships that cross-cultural partners might have to that boundary. In Perel's (2000) example, partners are "like immigrants or tourists." The metaphor of tourist highlights having the freedom and resources to enter a culture for the purpose of pleasure, adventure, and exploration. Visits are usually quite short; tourists see the sights and meet the locals but generally do not stay long enough to develop deep or meaningful relationships. Being a tourist is often considered a break from one's usual life, not an ongoing journey or lifestyle. Applying the tourist metaphor to cross-cultural couples highlights the excitement of learning about different cultural practices, such as music, food, and holiday traditions, and the adventure of being an "outsider within" (Collins, 1990), such as when a White woman is included on a visit to a Black barber shop. The cultural "native" might experience the familiar through new eyes and enjoy sharing special places and practices or grow weary of being the "tour guide" or the "navigator."

Regardless of how the tourist experience goes, the metaphor of immigrant conveys significantly different associations. While tourists may be able to move freely into cultural landscapes that appeal to them, immigrants are subject to laws regulating their movements across borders and often are not welcome. As an example, Otto Santa Ana studied the language used in the *Los Angeles Times* coverage of California state propositions related to Latino immigrants (UCLA News, 2002). Over a 6-year period (May 1992–July 1998), 98% of the quotes characterized the United States as a body or a home (container metaphors), and immigrants or immigration were most commonly represented as disease, weeds, animals, and a threat to the national health or hearth. Even if tourists are experienced as annoying, they generally are welcomed in; immigrants are more likely to experience a tightening of boundaries to restrict their entry and to be viewed in ways that preclude being treated as full citizens with the same rights and privileges as those who "truly belong." Even when they are allowed in, immigrants often experience the alienation and isolation of not really being included.

Perel's (2000) use of the tourist and immigrant metaphors highlighted different particular ways of relating to a new cultural location, but it is possible to imagine numerous other metaphorical roles that a person could take. Cross-cultural partners might, for example, be thought of as reformers, revolutionaries, clowns, storytellers, outcasts, bridges, or pilgrims, just to name a few possibilities. Each metaphor has an associated set of entailments that leads to a particular way of thinking about one's relationship to the cultural location and its inhabitants, including one's partner. In all likelihood, one's role might change in different situations and in different relationships. For example, a White partner might function as a bridge, helping White family members connect to Black culture, feel like "one of the family" with Black in-laws, and yet feel like an outcast at a Black family reunion.

Even though the metaphor of cross-cultural may get at some aspects of Black–White couples' experiences, there may be other ways that this term does not fit, especially when its metaphorical entailments are considered. Because every metaphor highlights some things and obscures others, no one metaphor is sufficient to name the complex realities of any relationship. Exploring what is obscured by the term *cross-cultural* when it is applied specifically to Black–White couples may support a deeper understanding of these couples and why some reject the labels *cross-cultural* and *interracial*.

What Is Obscured by *Cross-Cultural*?

Shared American Culture

Defining Black–White couples as cross-cultural obscures their shared American cultural background. Cross-cultural assumes two separate and distinct cultural entities with movement between them. The term implicitly assumes that one partner comes from a homogeneous, essentialized "Black culture" and the other from a homogeneous, essentialized "White culture." When both are from the United States, however, they share the experience of the American cultural landscape that is dominated by what Myrdal called "the American creed" (Kouri, 2003, p. 365). This set of ideals includes a value system based on equality, freedom, and justice. Even though there has been a huge discrepancy between these ideals and our country's ability to put them into practice, it could be argued that the influence of the American creed is so powerful that Black and White partners have a shared common ground rather than separate and distinct cultural landscapes.

Life in the United States is characterized by underlying belief systems about many dimensions of culture, such as individualism, time, the nature of the universe and attitudes toward life, family structure, thinking and feeling, and power and gender roles (Perel, 2000). While partners may have differing interests or practices associated with their own racial group (for example, preferences in food or music), when it comes to values like self-reliance, independence, pragmatism, privacy, task focus, acquisition of goods, and controlling one's destiny, interracial couples may have many common values that reflect the individualism characterizing American culture.

One example of how this common ground shapes the experience of interracial couples is the pervasive belief in the right to choose a partner based on romantic attraction and individual preference. Partners in a Black–White relationship often emphasize that they are with "a person" they love, rather than with someone who is "Black" or "White" (Kouri, 2003). In the following example, a Black man, "Lorenzo," draws on the cultural values of individualism and romanticism to explain his choice of a partner.

> Both of my parents give some due to sort of the Afro-centric worldview and neither of them really, in their heart of hearts, thinks that that's particularly important.... As I was growing up, things relating to Africa, that side of my heritage, was always very important to me and so I asked myself some questions ... what is it going to mean for me personally, like on a level somewhere between the social and spiritual, 10 years from now, 20 years from now, to be married to this white woman? ... I ... wrestled with that stuff, but decided at the time that it probably wasn't really all that important and that the love and my hopes for the relationship were really the more important thing. I can't think, honestly, of any moments when I've had to ... seriously wrestle with it as an issue. (Rosenblatt, Karis, & Powell, 1995, pp. 184–185)

This example illustrates that, despite the importance of his African American heritage, this man framed his selection of a relationship partner in terms of the American cultural values of personal choice and individual love and self-fulfillment.

Asymmetrical Racial Categories

Viewing Black–White couples as cross-cultural obscures not only their shared American cultural background but also hides the reality that racial categories are not symmetrical. The idea that partners come from different cultures is based on thinking of racial categories as being equivalent to cultures, with one partner coming from Black culture and the other from White culture. The notion that partners are positioned to cross boundaries into each other's racial territory rests on the assumption that Black and White are simply two parallel cultures with interesting and unique cultural differences, without acknowledging their hierarchical ranking in terms of power.

Using the term *culture* to reference Black and White racial categories draws attention away from the power relations inherent in a racially stratified country, such as the United States. In everyday language the word *culture* is used in numerous ways (Mio, Barker-Hackett, & Tumambing, 2006). It can refer to countries, history, normative standards, traditions, food, clothing, and activities such as music, dance, and art. One distinction, regularly drawn, is that race has to do with politics and power, whereas culture does not. As an example, McGoldrick, Giordano, and Garcia-Preto (2005) write that "Race, unlike culture, is not an internal issue, but rather a political issue, operating to privilege certain people at the expense of others" (p. 20). Although this understanding reflects common usage of these terms, it neglects the psychological and interpersonal implications of racial identities and racial group membership and obscures the ways culture is shaped by power dynamics and political processes. It implies that cultural "values, beliefs, knowledge, and customs ... exist in a timeless and unchangeable vacuum outside of ... racism" (Razack, 1998, p. 58) and that it is possible to be an innocent, dehistoricized, and depoliticized subject, standing outside of power relations. The label of *cross-cultural* not only draws attention away from asymmetrical racial categories but also takes attention away from the dominance of Whiteness.

The Dominance of Whiteness

The term *cross-cultural* obscures the fact that the very existence of a boundary or border between White and Black reflects a history of dominance and exclusion and the systematic obstruction of movement across or between groups. Historically, Whiteness has been created by excluding those viewed as non-White (Haney Lopez, 1996). The shared experience of those within the White category has been access to privilege, including the privileges of citizenship and property ownership, leading some to suggest that White culture is empty—that there is nothing to White culture other than its power and privilege (Roediger, 1991). As the defining universal standard, Whiteness is not just one racial identity among many but is the taken-for-granted yardstick used to measure all non-Whites (Mahoney, 1995). Only Whites have been perceived as raceless, as American, as simply individuals, while non-White Others have been viewed through the lens of their racial group membership and thus have not been regarded as fully American (Haney Lopez, 1996). Viewing Whites as racially neutral, as just individuals, not only hides White racial dominance but leads to the mistaken belief that it is only non-Whites who have culture and that Black culture is more "genuine" and "natural" than White culture (Hartigan, 2005).

Asymmetrical Racial and Ethnic Identities

Use of the term *cross-cultural* masks the asymmetrical salience of racial and ethnic identities for Black and White partners. Because of the taken-for-granted dominance of Whiteness, many Whites have underdeveloped racial awareness. Prior to their interracial relationships, or until they've attempted to talk with their children about their White racial heritage, White partners might not even have thought of themselves as having a racial identity. In contrast, for Black partners, whose survival is dependent on a high degree of racial consciousness, race is likely to be a significant aspect of personal identity.

Black and White partners also may have major differences in how they relate to their own ethnic identities. The term *ethnicity*, like race and culture, is used in numerous ways. Here, I am using it to mean the belief that one shares membership in a socially defined group, based on common ancestry. The racial history of the United States has contributed to the fact that race and ethnicity are not important aspects of self-identity for many White people (Roediger, 1991; Waters, 1990). European immigrants were encouraged to downplay or let go of their ethnic identities in order to become White Americans (Roediger, 1991). Although there are enduring communities of White ethnics, Americans of European heritage often have chosen what role, if any, ethnicity would play in their lives and increasingly have identified as just "American" (Alba, 1990). Perry (2002) writes that "cultural identity formation involves, above all, a process of investment in and identification with the meanings attached to one's social location" (p. 73). As members of the dominant racial group, Whites have been socialized to think of themselves as individuals and to distance, rather than identify, with their racial positioning. In contrast, ethnicity has been especially important for non-White racial groups who haven't had the option to identify as simply American. Blackness frequently is personally meaningful, as both an ethnic and a racial identity and as a source of belonging in relation to others who share this identity. What this means in terms of Black–White couples is that partners are not equally positioned in terms of racial and ethnic identities. White partners are likely to have much less identification, not only with their racial identities but with their ethnic identities as well, leading to lack of awareness of "the dimensions of their lives that both exceed and inform their individuality" (Hartigan, 2005, p. 28).

This lack of symmetry between White and Black cultures and identities often gets highlighted for Black–White couples when they grapple with how to transmit each parent's cultural heritage to their children. Blackness more often is associated with concrete cultural practices, such as specific foods or hairstyles, and with historical events that symbolize solidarity and pride in one's heritage. Black parents can share particular foods and types of music with their children, for example, but White partners typically do not identify their cultural practices with Whiteness and sometimes have little knowledge of their own ethnic heritage. A further complication is that White parents may find themselves at a loss regarding what to convey to their children about Whiteness; while the history of Blackness elicits pride in a struggle against great odds, the history of Whiteness can evoke guilt and shame associated with colonization and being the oppressor. Imagining the creation of a White cultural center highlights how Whiteness and Blackness are not parallel or comparable cultural or ethnic categories. It is relatively straightforward to name specific cultural artifacts that would be appropriate for a Black cultural center, but it is not so simple with a White cultural center. This exercise makes explicit the significant overlap between American and Whiteness and the asymmetrical relationship between Black and White cultures.

Border Patrolling: The Difficulty of Crossing Racial Boundaries

Cross-cultural, with its emphasis on movement across cultural lines, draws attention away from the fact that despite an increase in interracial marriages, the borders between racial groups are still patrolled from both sides (Dalmage, 2001). Although partners can and do choose to be with the person they love, there are social consequences for crossing racial boundaries. Lorenzo, in the earlier example, can marry a White woman, but he cannot travel freely, as a tourist might, into the White racial landscape. Nor is it an option to immigrate into Whiteness. At the same time, he may be viewed suspiciously within the landscape of the Black community, his loyalty, and his Black identity, suspect because of his White partner. In the following example, a Black woman describes her experience of this dynamic.

> ... But you always feel people will discount because you are with someone white. It's like, "Well, we know where you stand!" ... People will assume a lot about your political beliefs, about how you grew up.... When people start robbing my identity from me ... or discount me because I'm with someone white, that I have no concern about the black community, I'm not black identified ... that's been the hardest thing to deal with for me (Gloria). (Rosenblatt, Karis, & Powell, 1995, p. 180).

White partners, too, may face opposition and judgment from White friends and colleagues and even be disowned by their families, but it does not necessarily mean that they will be welcomed into the Black community. Thus, thinking about Black–White couples through the cross-cultural lens may obscure or oversimplify the complicated relationships that partners have with their own and each other's racial communities as they and those around them attempt to sort out issues of belonging and difference.

Why Some Black–White Couples Reject *Cross-Cultural* and *Interracial*

In previous sections I have considered *cross-cultural* and *interracial* as metaphors and have examined some of what is highlighted and hidden by their entailments. In this section I offer preliminary thoughts on how these terms might function socially and discursively for Black–White couples in their day-to-day lives. As couples use or critique these labels, what is the argument or challenge being made? Is something being denied or avoided? Rejection of these terms might be viewed through the lens of the moral work that is accomplished—what are the moral judgments, values, and desired outcomes reflected by the use or rejections of these labels?

Rejecting or Challenging Categorization

Some Black–White couples may reject the terms *cross-cultural* and *inter-racial* because they experience any imposed label as objectifying. The process of categorization necessarily oversimplifies; as it attempts to fit complex relationships into a predetermined container, it obscures individual uniqueness and what is special about this particular relationship. Being categorized as either *cross-cultural* or *interracial* highlights divergence from the unmarked normative standard of White middle-class heterosexual couples and subjects couples to the stereotypes associated with these categories. Because partners emphasize that they are with the person they love, and not with a representative of a category, the containers of race and culture may be particularly irksome.

As container metaphors, *cross-cultural* and *interracial* both emphasize the boundary or difference between groups. When a Black–White couple rejects these labels it might be because they object to this emphasis on difference over similarity. In addition to shared American culture, couples may have numerous similarities, including educational and class backgrounds, religious or spiritual values, political beliefs, family values, and shared interests or hobbies. Some couples emphasize the life they have built together (Killian, 2001) in a single, shared container. In the following example a White man describes the similarities he and his partner share.

> If you're really looking at who out of all the people I ever dated is most like me in terms of values and what we want to do with life, Patricia is more like me than anybody I've ever known.... It felt to me as if the first time in my dating relationship I'd ever been with someone that I could frankly, openly talk about ideals and things that I believed in, and that there was a kind of a connection, an ambition of things we wanted to do ... (Gary). (Rosenblatt, Karis, & Powell, 1995, pp. 58–59)

Categorization, by definition, sorts objects based on assumptions of difference and similarity. Another reason that some Black–White couples may reject categorization is that their experience with other such couples has led to the belief that they do not have much in common.

> I remember going to one of the interracial support group meetings and leaving thinking, "This is not enough." The fact that—the only thing we have in common is that we are in interracial relationships. Our values are different. Our belief systems are different, religion, where we came from. This fact that we are just married—white people married to black people, black people married to white people, is not enough common ground (Lynette, a white woman). (Karis, 2000)

A final challenge to categorization based on race or culture is the claim, made by some heterosexual Black–White couples, that it is gender categories, rather than racial ones, that are significant in their relationships. The following two examples, the first by a White woman, the second by a Black man, illustrate this point.

> I definitely felt there were man/woman issues between the two of us. Racial issues between the two of us ... I don't know ... problems ... or what I want different, I don't really attribute those to him being black and me being white. It's been things I've experienced with other men, period, you know. He's surprising[ly], or not surprisingly, he's very much like the men in my family. Better in some ways, but he's not so different than me (Rose). (Karis, 2000)

> ... really and truly there is a bigger empathetic, a bigger more fundamental, more cosmic empathetic gap between men and women than there is between any people of any two wildly disparate cultures that you care to put together in a room. And I think people shouldn't lose sight of that fact. (Rosenblatt, Karis, & Powell, 1995, p. 295)

Rejecting an Emphasis on Power Relations

Black–White couples who prefer the term *cross-cultural* but reject *interracial* might make this choice precisely because cross-cultural obscures the hierarchical stratification of couples' differing racial groups and the resulting asymmetrical racial and ethnic identities. Specific cultural practices, such as music and food, and locations (e.g., a Kwanza gathering) may be viewed as apolitical, untainted by power relations. They offer comfort when compared to the uncertainty of how to address the influences of racial stratification that show up, even in the privacy and intimacy of one's home and one's self. One White woman described the eye-opening experience she had when she attended a work training and learned about White privilege.

> ... the notion of race in our country and how it's really about economics and politics. And it's really not about, it's not about people, like it doesn't identify, it doesn't—I don't know, I just didn't like white. And I don't. Because I didn't feel like it talked about who I am either. Gosh, and then I think too with my kids ... they're more than the labels ... these labels were developed out of political and economic terms. I don't want to put that on my kid because they're human beings. They're children. And they have a rich background. And I want to stay away from those kinds of terms (Claire). (Karis, 2000)

In the above example Claire associates race with "economics and politics" and grapples with how to make sense of Whiteness and racial categorization in relation to herself and her children. Although Claire still displays a considerable amount of "not knowing" regarding race, she is actively engaged with trying to make sense of racial dynamics. In contrast, some White partners seem oblivious to the power dynamics of race.

> I told him someone yelled, "nigger." I was on the corner down there; I was with the baby, just driving by. And his first reaction is, "Well, what did you do to

provoke that?" (laughs). And I thought, "That's the difference between being black and white. Why would I have to do anything to provoke it?" (Gloria). [a Black woman talking about her White husband] (Rosenblatt, Karis, & Powell, 1995. p. 240)

The drawback of not attending to power dynamics is that lack of awareness does not make them go away. White partners sometimes comment on the enrichment they experience by being exposed to the social landscapes of their Black partners. There generally is not a parallel process for Black partners who may express weariness at being the minority in predominantly White settings (Rosenblatt, Karis, & Powell, 1995) or remain silent when White partners interpret racial awareness as "hypersensitivity" (Killian, 2002).

Rejecting Interracial Because It Doesn't Fit Their Experiences

Some Black–White couples may reject the term *interracial* because race, as they understand it, does not fit with their actual experience of racial realities as fluid and shifting. Just as racial categories can be considered as a type of container, a person also can be thought of as a container that holds substances or characteristics, such as a racial identity. The container metaphor supports thinking of places—in this case, racial categories—as fixed, bounded, and natural, rather than as constructed.

Focusing on the cultural landscapes of Black–White couples implies one of two things: either racial difference is located in the place—the landmarks or features of their landscapes are different—or racial difference is located in persons (i.e., race is a personal characteristic that belongs to individual partners). The widely accepted view on race—that it is based on physical characteristics such as skin color and other physical features—aligns with the idea that racial difference is located within persons. When difference is assumed to be located in a specific person, what is missed is how race is socially constructed and reflects social relationships between individuals and groups who have been defined as different.

Thinking of difference in terms of social relations rather than simply in terms of individuals presents a way to understand how those in Black–White relationships make sense of race in their lives. The term *interracial*, which emphasizes crossing over a boundary between distinct entities—fixed racial groups—hides the fluid and changing nature of racial categories and racial identities. Just because they have crossed this boundary does not mean that Black–White couples have moved beyond the commonly understood definition of race. At the same time, though, those in Black–White relationships routinely experience how race matters differently in different situations and relationships and how it does not necessarily replicate racial dynamics at the larger social level.

It may be that some Black–White couples reject the term *interracial* because of the discrepancy between the term *race*, as they understand it, and their actual experience of racial situations and identities. Perhaps because race is commonly understood as a fixed categorical characteristic, these experiences often seem difficult to articulate. There are, however, numerous accounts by Black–White couples illustrating how racial meanings shift in different situations and different relationships as partners get included in the "Other" group or excluded from their own group in ways that move outside of normative racial standards. In the following example, a Black man describes the shifting significance of race in relation to his White wife and in-laws.

> Race just really hasn't made a lot of difference; it hasn't intruded very much. Early on, it's still early on, I would kind of look over and realize there was this white woman (he laughs) with my name (still laughing). How did that happen? Or sometimes I'd forget; ... and when I see her relatives, "Oh, that's right, these are my in-laws (laughing). How odd." But most of the time, I don't think about it. She's Laura. (Rosenblatt, Karis, & Powell, 1995, p. 27)

As this quote illustrates, racial interpretations are sometimes in the foreground, but at other times race is not the central concern or primary interpretive lens used by Black–White couples. When the term *interracial* is rejected, it might be in opposition to cultural stereotypes that assume Black–White relationships are only, or primarily, about race. In the following example, a black woman challenges this assumption.

> We talk about money; we talk about the other things that couples [talk about]. ... People assume that when you have arguments or discussions it has to be about race and race is so central all the time to what's going on. I'm not saying race isn't there, but it's not like we spend more time talking about, or arguing about, things related to race. ... And so I think to normalize these relationships ... I just think interracial couples go the gamut the same way as same-race couples in terms of issues. (Rosenblatt, Karis, & Powell, 1995, p. 247)

Rejecting an Emphasis on Homogeneity

When Black–White couples reject the label *interracial* it might be a challenge to the way that within-group variability and difference are obscured by the process of categorizing, which highlights difference across groups. The following example illustrates how abstract conceptualizations of Whiteness as dominance and privilege are complicated by social class, leading this White woman to feel more connected to communities of color that share her class background than to "White culture."

> I identify more with people who struggle with day-to-day living and making ends meet. So that it's hard for me to really feel like I identify with white culture … my family has always been pretty down-to-earth; we don't put on very many airs. What you see is what you get, and we'll tell you what—say what we mean and mean what we say. And that, I think, is not the norm in white culture. And so, that has made us feel less part of white culture, and that is part of what has made us fit more with communities of color (Rose). (Karis, 2000)

As the above example demonstrates, ideas about separate and distinct Black and White cultures may not fit the complex realities of partners' lives. The following quote, from a Black woman raised in a predominantly White neighborhood, shows how life experiences shape a sense of belonging that doesn't necessarily follow racial lines.

> All the kids I played with were white so I always felt very comfortable around Caucasians. And I went to school and I majored in psych and in a lot of my classes I was the only Afro-American person in there and it was fine with me. (Kouri, 2003, p. 361)

Rejecting Uncomfortable Racial Realities

When Black–White couples challenge use of the term *interracial* it might be because they are under the influence of the dominant American discourses of colorblindness (Karis, 2003), of not talking about race, and of minimizing the significance or racial and cultural histories (Killian, 2002). While these strategies may serve important functions as couples navigate their intimate relationships and their daily lives, these approaches also may constrain couples' abilities to engage with the complexities of living in a racially stratified culture.

Conclusion

This chapter might be viewed as an extended metaphor, highlighting some things and obscuring others, trapped in the containers of societal discourses about couples, culture, and race (P. C. Rosenblatt, personal communication, February 12, 2007). As Black–White couples make sense of the differences and similarities that matter in their lives, they draw on interpretive repertoires that both reflect and challenge the hierarchical stratification of racial categories. Within the place-specific dynamics of their social locations they reject dominant discourses and they replicate facets of dominance and subordination. Hartigan (1997) draws attention to the family as the location "that generates a great degree of variation in how racial categories gain and lose their significance" (p. 184), and the family life of Black–White couples is a rich terrain for investigating multiple, overlapping, and shifting identities.

The concept of culture has sometimes been pointed to "as a key means of refashioning racializing notions of difference into more palatable, seemingly innocent public forms" (Hartigan, 2005, p. 258). This chapter is a beginning attempt to consider how the terms *culture* and *race*, and *cross-cultural* and *interracial*, are used by Black–White couples. Although racism can be found throughout American culture, this fact does not explain everything about when and how race matters in their day-to-day lives. Attending to what is accomplished socially and politically as these couples make sense of their lives offers a path for understanding, not only Black–White couples, but more about how we as human beings establish and draw boundaries around forms of difference.

References

Alba, R. D. (1990). *Ethnic identity: The transformation of White America*. New Haven: Yale University Press.

American heritage dictionary of the English language (10th ed.). (2000). Boston: Houghton Mifflin.

Brown, C. (2007). Dethroning the suppressed voice: Unpacking experience as story. In C. Brown & T. Augusta-Scott (Eds.), *Narrative therapy: Making meaning, making lives* (pp. 177–195). Thousand Oaks, CA: Sage.

Collins, P. H. (1990). *Black feminist thought: Knowledge, consciousness, and the politics of empowerment*. Boston: Unwin Hyman.

Dalmage, H. M. (2001). *Tripping on the color line: Black–White multiracial families in a racially divided world*. New Brunswick, NJ: Rutgers University Press.

Dogen, E. (2007). Shobogenzo: The treasure house of the eye of the true teaching (H. Nearman, Trans.). Mount Shasta, CA: Shasta Abbey Press.

Edwards, D. (1991). Categories are for talking: On the cognitive and discursive bases of categorization. *Theory & Psychology, 1*, 515–542. Retrieved February 25, 2007, from http://www.psych.ucalgary.ca/thpsyc/VOLUMES. SI/1991/1.4.Edwards.SI.html

Haney Lopez, I. (1996). *White by law: The legal construction of race.* New York: New York University Press.

Hartigan, J. (1997). Locating White Detroit. In R. Frankenberg (Ed.), *Displacing Whiteness: Essays in social and cultural criticism* (pp. 180–213). Durham, NC: Duke University Press.

Hartigan, J. (2005). *Odd tribes: Toward a cultural analysis of White people.* Durham, NC: Duke University Press.

Karis, T. (2000). [Racial identity constructions of White women in heterosexual Black–White interracial relationships]. Unpublished raw data.

Karis, T. A. (2003). How race matters and does not matter for White women in relationships with Black men. In V. Thomas, T. Karis, & J. Wetchler (Eds.), *Clinical issues with interracial couples: Theories and research* (pp. 23–40). New York: Haworth Press.

Killian, K. D. (2001). Reconstituting racial histories and identities. *Journal of Marital & Family Therapy, 27,* 27–42.

Killian, K. D. (2002). Dominant and marginalized discourses in interracial couples' narratives: Implications for family therapists. *Family Process, 41,* 603–618.

Kouri, K. M. (2003). Black/White interracial couples and the beliefs that help them to bridge the racial divide. In L. I. Winters & H. DeBose (Eds.), *New faces in a changing America: Multiracial identity in the 21st century* (pp. 355–370). Newbury Park, CA: Sage.

Lakoff, G., & Johnson, M. (1980). *Metaphors we live by.* Chicago: University of Chicago Press.

Mahoney, M. (1995). Segregation, Whiteness and transformation. *University of Pennsylvania Law Review, 143,* 1659–1684.

McGoldrick, M., Giordano, J., & Garcia-Preto, N. (2005). Overview: Ethnicity and family therapy. In M. McGoldrick, J. Giordano, & N. Garcia-Preto (Eds.), *Ethnicity and family therapy* (3rd ed., pp. 1–40). New York: Guilford.

Mio, J. S., Barker-Hackett, L., & Tumambing, J. (2006). *Multicultural psychology: Understanding our diverse communities.* Boston: McGraw-Hill.

Perel, E. (2000). A tourist's view of marriage: Cross-cultural couples—Challenges, choices and implications for therapy. In P. Papp (Ed.), *Couples on the fault line: New directions for therapists* (pp. 178–204). New York: Guilford.

Perry, P. (2002). *Shades of White: White kids and racial identities in high school.* Durham, NC: Duke University Press.

Razack, S. H. (1998). *Looking White people in the eye: Gender, race and culture in courtrooms and classrooms.* Toronto: University of Toronto Press.

Roediger, D. (1991). *The wages of Whiteness: Race and the making of the American working class.* London: Verso.

Rosenblatt, P. C. (1994). *Metaphors of family systems theory: Toward new constructions*. New York: Guilford.

Rosenblatt, P. C., Karis, T. A., & Powell, R. D. (1995). *Multiracial couples: Black and White voices*. Thousand Oaks, CA: Sage.

Waters, M. (1990). *Ethnic options: Choosing identities in America*. Berkeley: University of California Press.

UCLA News. (2002). Negative stereotypes perpetuated in '90s coverage of key anti-Latino propositions, UCLA linguist finds. Retrieved July 14, 2005, from UCLA News Web site: http://www.newsroom.ucla.edu/page.asp?menu=mediaserv&id=3369

7

Electronic Attachments
Desire, the Other, and the Internet Marital Trade in the 21st Century

Anna M. Agathangelou and Kyle D. Killian

Back in 1967, *Guess Who's Coming to Dinner* hit the big screens in the United States, helping to chip away at long-standing taboos via its depiction of a now famous cinematic border crossing: a Black man and a White woman falling in love and scandalizing their parents. Since then, Hollywood has portrayed romances between White men and Black, usually light-complexioned women (e.g., *Monsters' Ball, Guess Who*), probably betting that good old boys watching Billy Bob Thornton cavorting with Halle Berry are filled not with disgust but with voyeuristic envy and desire. In recent times, there has been a proliferation of movies depicting characters from separate social structures, forbidden to become involved in interracial and/or intercultural romances but doing so anyway (e.g., *Broken English, Mississippi Masala, Snow Falling on Cedars*). In this chapter, we explore how the use of media technology shapes the expression of this desire for "Others." The Internet, combined with a neoliberalist paradigm (Foucault, 1997) that encourages individuals to explore their desires and choose from people and products available "Out There," is creating a virtual marriage market, a major transnational, simulated zone facilitating connections between partners of different nationalities, races, ethnicities, sexualities, and classes.

First, we examine the medium of the Internet, which allows individuals to virtually connect, and the economies of seduction and desire (see Agathangelou, 2002, 2004). Second, we discuss electronic couple attachments; that is, attachments that are initiated through the Internet, a technology that seems to "transcend" racial, ethnic, national, and state borders, the crossing of which was once quite transgressive. We discuss the now commonplace occurrence of such border openings and the titillation and seduction associated with a simple Internet chat that could develop into something big. Third, we argue that the sundering of borders does not evade the sexualizing and racializing of bodies but can reinscribe people within racial and sexual architectures and matrices of violence and recolonization. In the crossing of borders to seek sexual intimacies, people do not pass just any borders and do not choose just any people. We argue that in a context of rapid technological development, electronic "love connections" highlight significant pressures of the contradictory registers of domestic and national, national and international, and, within these spaces, racialized, gendered, and sexualized relations. Our intervention articulates the shifts and disruptions that become possible through the crossing of these borders.

Cyberspatial (Re)Presentations and Seductions: The Internet as Contested Border of Social Relations and Governance

Picture if you will: the pressure from the press is mounting, and the authors feel the need to finish this manuscript, and then quickly and electronically send the copy to the editors. I (the first author) touch the keyboard, checking my notes on this project about electronic intimacies. Then I conduct yet another search on the Internet, surfing for any Web sites about international–intercultural intimacies. The authors work to identify in an a priori manner what they think they need for this chapter, the object of search, the object that would enable the production of the chapter. Similarly, we desire a finished product with a beginning, middle, and end, electronically generated within the private space of our office. This is the production of a narrative that has embedded within it a disciplinary epistemology, one that spatializes writing before it occurs, reducing the obscure, the poetic, and the unorthodox, as it embraces a strategic map upon which all details are accountable to and readily understood by the reader. In order to finish this chapter, some questions may not be asked: about the histories of subjectivities, their production and reproduction, which borders are crossed, and which need to be defined, the bodies of knowledge and bodies of practice that need to be examined. Why such a chapter? What intervention do we intend to make? What kinds of negotiations do the authors engage in to make it possible, and what spaces do both writers and readers of this text cross? All these questions could raise for "us" (the authors and the readers) questions about relations and intimacies in layered ways and yet a dominant linear approach to time and space demands that those issues be held in abeyance so that the chapter can be finished. Otherwise, the "seductive" process of answering these questions could demand too much time, and it is urgent to get this piece completed.

The Internet: Borderless Site of the Neoliberal "Free Market"?

In order to examine the medium of the Internet and economies of seduction and desire it is necessary to understand Foucault's idea of biopower. Foucault's major contribution, albeit fragmentary, was the idea of biopower, referring to the ways man's biological existence becomes the target of control and intervention by political power. This category of biopower was further distinguished as two distinct manifestations, anatomo-politics and biopolitics. *Anatomo politics* comprises a series of political strategies collectively targeting "man-as-species" (Foucault, 1976, p. 242) and *biopolitics* is "the attempt to regulate aggregrate biological occurrences at the population level" (Foucault, as cited in Elbe, 2004, p. 5). Population, according to Foucault, is not a "numerical aggregate of individuals" (Elbe, 2004, p. 6) but rather a "living being penetrated, compelled, ruled by processes, by biological laws. A population has a birth rate, a death rate, an age curve, an age pyramid, a degree of morbidity, a state of health, a population may perish or may, on the contrary, expand" (Elbe, 2004, p. 6, citing Foucault as cited by Curtis, 2003). Thus, biopolitics is the "endeavor, begun in eighteenth-century Europe, to rationalize the problems presented to governmental practice by the characteristic of a group of living human beings constituted as the population" (Foucault, 1976, p. 73). This biopolitical dimension of power, we think, is significant in shedding light on electronic technologies as political strategies and on their deployment to target, control, manage, and discipline in border crossings toward the formation of a different life.

The rapid proliferation of Internet technologies, as well as the growing digitization of a broad array of economic and political activities, has contributed to the formation of new cross-border flows operating partly outside the formal interstate system. Sassen (2002) argues that:

> these types of flows can be seen as having the potential for weakening sovereign state authority as it has come to be constituted historically, particularly over the last century. Insofar as sovereign state authority is the key building block of the interstate system, changes in the former conceivably will have an impact on the latter ... these developments have also altered key features of

cross-border relations such that there are consequences for states and for the place of the interstate system. (p. 1)

With online dating as an example of a "border flow," we are witness to a burgeoning million dollar industry (Alapack, Blichfeldt, & Elden, 2005). Many times, these businesses do not have to abide by interstate rules. On the contrary, many of these industries embody a major principle of globalism, the strategy of neoliberalism: "open and free markets" as the most effective social organization for generating profits. This openness enables the generation of many industries, including the trading of bodies on the Net; it reorganizes state borders long enough to generate profits without control and protectionist policies and yet simultaneously draws on asymmetries of power to recolonize and reracialize spaces and bodies. Indeed, it seems that these strategies intensify "Internet intimacies," eroticizing toward the fantastical both the subjects of the purchaser ("seek and you will receive") and the person to be purchased ("Bring me a ring for I am longing to be the envy of all I can see," "Find me a find, catch me a catch," and "I Want to be in America ..."; Chittenden, V., n.d., http://www.american.edu/TED/bride.htm).

Within the movements and exchanges of the global economy, the Internet acts as a site that mediates relations between "individuals" expected to follow different national rules and values. Constituted through a set of discourses (i.e., freedom, the ability to traverse spaces anytime, anywhere), the Internet becomes a geographical technology/space representing the "objective" desires of "humans" through Web pages and images that advertise possible partners. Zooming into the specificities of these borderless sites (i.e., the Internet and Web pages such as Helene International Marriage Agency, Latin Wives, etc.; see http://www.heleneinternational.com/ and http://www.latinwives.com/) we come to recognize the revenue-making border circuits where women's bodies are a key value (Szeman, 2002). Yet, these sites do become significant doors for many women in the Global South who are seeking "better" lives. New technologies facilitate and increase migration opportunities for those who seek these "better" lives. As Biemann (2000) described when discussing her video *Writing Desire*, the virtual bride market's expansion has been mediated extensively by the use of the Internet, which contributes to the raising of profits for many agencies and yet seems to accord possibilities to many women in the Global South:

> Women no longer have to travel to the West in the hope of finding a husband within the three months of their tourist visa. Migration is made easier with the use of email, enabling them to build up a relationship that will lead to an

engagement and consequent invitation to the West. In her writing, discourses
of romantic desire intertwine with a desire for survival. It is not surprising that
the Internet capitalizes on this vulnerable set of motivations. This is the topic
of *Writing Desire*, in short, an attempt to combine the various writing positions
without wanting to highlight a binary contrast between those female subjects
in the advanced societies who practice a self reflexive, postmodern discourse
of desire and sexuality out of fun, and those who struggle for survival and
offer their emotional, sexual and care-giving services to get out of the slums.
(Szeman, 2002, p. 6)

Biemann complicates the global economy's dominant discourse, which
argues that the world is becoming borderless, and the Internet a medium
for borderless embodiment. She complicates this very dichotomous fundamental logic of capital and argues that women use these opportunities,
however limited, to seek a fulfillment of their desires as well as to shape their
subjectivities in ways that do not "fit" some of the nationalist/patriarchal/
class expectations of their particular geographical sites/sights.

In reading Web pages that offer opportunities for cross-cultural dating, we wonder about the "banal everyday use" (Holloway & Valentine,
2001, p. 129) of the Internet in the search of what many are seeking
(i.e., "intimacy"), even if it has become a centrally important part of the
marital market or trade. It is a complex phenomenon. Many perceive
the Internet as a virtual site of equal exchanges, a technology that enables
exchange and communication of ideas, capital, and people. Others see it
as a border that is contested by social relations that disrupt dominant logics of racial and geographical asymmetries. Web pages epistemologically
relegate "dating" to a personal, individual register: the nuanced epistemes
and relations of power employed and deployed in dating are obscured
as the culmination of an individual exchange. What is concealed is that
the Internet and all Web pages are not simply neutral spatialities used
by generic individuals. In this globalized postcolonial age, they must be
understood in light of the very formation of Western capital, its motion,
and the formation and production of North American subjectivity. This
requires a geopolitical and genealogical rethinking, one that considers the
formation of North American subjectivity in relation to other subject formations within the capitalist business-oriented context.

In their intensive studies of cyber behavior, social science researchers
have detected some interesting aspects of online interaction. Sayer (2002)
writes, "Cyberspace represents a dimension where one can transcend the
laws of place and physicality and reach a realm of dreams with one touch"
(p. 60). The Internet as a medium offers a cyberspace of virtual connection,

promising liberation from stereotypes (e.g., Kruger, 2000), and sources of prejudice, such as ableism, sexism, classism, and racism, that beleaguer one's everyday, face-to-face interactions in the real world.

In support of the notion that one can transcend the physical and psychological constraints of one's everyday social existence, studies (e.g., Yurchisin, Watchravesringkan, & McCabe, 2005) have found that users, or consumers, of Internet dating services do indeed re-create their identities through their posted dating profiles and that online and offline validation of the identities presented in such profiles strongly influences individuals' beliefs about themselves and their actual behaviors in online versus offline environments. In other words, not only does what we type impact who other people think we are, but who *we* think we are, with considerable variation across the medium of social interaction. Cyberspace affords a unique flexibility, allowing us to exercise a great deal of poetic license in the process of identity creation and re-creation. If we are no longer hampered by peoples' "hang-ups" about our skin color, body type, accent, and numerous markers of "otherness," perhaps we should all go online and celebrate this electronic emancipation. With the availability of a medium in late modernity that creates such liberating new rules of engagement and permits the formation of "pure relationships" (Hardey, 2004), it would seem that electronic attachments are just around the corner. It is these intimate relationship shifts that we look at in order to make visible possible disruptions of dominant capital and moral/fundamentalist narratives of social relations (i.e., you can access anything anytime you want; "you will be sold like a doll," "sweet young lotus blossoms," "they are human beings too"), and to articulate alternative possible social relations (interviews with sex workers in Greece by Agathangelou, 2001, in Athens).

In looking at the Internet as a technology of governmentability (i.e., how the society controls and influences), some have argued that it challenges national borders and territorial limits. Yet, others are beginning to expose the paradox that lies within these arguments. "Emails conquer distance, emails maintain distance, emails mark exchanges" (Biemann, 2000). E-mails conquer the distance that has been generated because of racialized power relations (e.g., the Global South and the Global North)[1] and enable exchanges between people and, simultaneously, ironically, these same e-mails maintain and constitute a distance that is itself nationally, racially, sexually, and class produced. Who sends the e-mails, for what purposes, and under what conditions? What kinds of changes do these e-mails foretell? Does the Internet and the exchanges it makes possible open borders toward freedom, as capital claims, or does it "open"

borders and bodies to the kinds of contestations and paradoxes generated by the way a "society of control" functions, or governs? (see Deleuze,
1998). We are arguing that this society does not function based only on
the production of "identities" (e.g., the other, the marginalized, the abject)
whose logic still depends on individuation and subjectifying of individuals as "types" who can be "inclusively rehabilitated." This newer society of
control also depends on (a) dissecting and fragmenting the individual into
its smallest components and at the same time; and (b) creating/determin-
ing multiple subjectifications (Deleuze, 1990), which opens itself to other
kinds of contestations and paradoxes.

Before we all go online and post our profiles with an online dating
service, let us consider the findings from some other studies. Analyzing
701 archived discussions, Sussman and Tyson (2000) explored whether
sex differences in communication style would be eliminated or reduced
in the use of cyber-talk. It was hypothesized that gendered power differential in communication style would remain salient in this new medium
and that male communicators would display power behaviors via longer
and more frequent postings and more opinionated discourse as compared
to female communicators. Results found that while women communicated more frequently than men, men's entries consisted of a greater number of words and men tended to write more opinionated communications
in two of three sex-typed categories (i.e., masculine and gender neutral).
Their results suggest that cyberspace, "despite being a context where the
gender of communicators is not salient, remains a male dominated atmosphere, where gender differentiation and power displays in communication persist, similar to other communication models (Sussman & Tyson,
2000, p. 381). Even though many of us aspire to transcend our physical,
psychological, and cultural codes, or our social locations on ecosystemic
axes of power, the purportedly liberatory medium of the Internet does not
allow an escape from our locations as raced, gendered, classed, national,
and geographical selves or the accompanying social relations:

> There is a strong tendency in the literature to conceptualize the matter of use—
> to be distinguished from access—as an unmediated event, as unproblematized
> activity ... [but] electronic space is inflected by the values, cultures, power sys-
> tems, and institutional orders within which it is embedded. For instance, if we
> were to explore these issues in terms of gendering, or specifically the condi-
> tion of the female subject, we would then posit that insofar as these various
> realms are marked by gendering, this embeddedness of electronic space is also
> gendered at least in some of its components, and, further, that so is electronic
> space itself.... One way of conceptualizing these conditions is to posit that the

articulations between digital technologies and individuals—whether as social, political, or economic actors and organizations—are constituted in terms of mediating cultures. (Sassen, 2002, pp. 6–7; also see http://programs.ssrc.org/itic/publications/volumes/intro3.pdf)

According to Sassen (2002), electronic space is a social relation of power whose production cannot be understood outside the concrete aspects of expressions of power. The discourses and narratives that articulate it (e.g., what it is, how we come to know it) are themselves affected by the existence and mediation of historical legacies of colonization, genderization, racialization, sexualization, spatial, temporal, and class relations. In addition, the Internet as a technology of biopower "circulates ... rather as something which only functions in the form of a chain ... exercised through a net-like organization" (Foucault, 1976, p. 98). A plethora of actors, ranging from states to multinational corporations, business agencies, nonprofit organizations, and individuals of the civil society, work through the Internet to enable "electronic attachments." These attachments become possible through a series of political strategies and draw extensively on epistemologies of colonization, open borders and open bodies, racism, and historical legacies of power (e.g., Russian women as the new image of an old [territorial] enemy), which are informed by and inform larger environments such as capital relations and principles of the market and its desire to be "virile."

Disruptions of Worlds and Intimacies: Technologies of Social Relations

Briefly, how did this come to be so? After World War II (1945), the world was divided into three major regions among the victors (i.e., the United States, Britain, Russia, etc.): the First, Second, and Third Worlds.[2] These divisions drew extensively on the historical legacies of colonization, imperialism, and affective economies of revolutions (e.g., the affects mobilized in the struggles for change and transformation of the status quo, the racial, class, gender, and sexual structures of violence),[3] to divide sovereignties and regions. The First World came to embody the virile, the masculine, the White "norm" or meter stick against which other regions were to compare themselves to decide whether they were developed enough economically or socially. Whether these regions were equally developed internally was of no concern, especially to the elite and upper classes whose interest was ensuring their power, based on the accumulation of property. Within these divisions (i.e., within each region or across regions, or both, and within sovereign spaces) the crossing of people as laborers, the capturing of people as enemies or violent subjects/terrorists, the sale and purchase of people, is always regionally, nationally, geographically, racially,[4] and sexually coded. These divisions, indeed, mark the asymmetries of power: who has access to resources (e.g., land, bodies, labor, and money) and under what conditions? (Agathangelou, 2006).

Orientalist (Said, 1979) epistemologies presume particular bodies (White, Western, and male) as ontologically superior to "others," who could be used as mere objects to fulfill racialized, sexual, national, and geographical fantasies, which are part and parcel of economies of sex tourism, trafficking, and migration. For instance, if a woman is Black, and from the Caribbean, her body becomes synonymous with carnality, uncontrolled lust and desire, and animality. Similarly, if a woman is from Thailand, her body is synonymous with a lotus or bondage (i.e., "a sweet young lotus blossom or as objects of bondage"); see Agathangelou (2001) transcripts of interviews with sex workers in Athens, Greece. Indeed, many times these epistemologies are used as alibis in making invisible shifts of production relations (i.e., who produces and reproduces what and under what conditions?). In the contemporary moment, the division of the world into the Global North and Global South is shaped by axes of power, gender, race, sex, and class (Agathangelou, 2004; Grewal, 1998; Razack, 2004), which organize and restructure economies and social relations.

Since the 1970s, many women have sought "migration" as the solution to the dramatic economic and political restructurings of their debt-ridden countries. As international organizations like the World Bank and the International Monetary Fund threaten to shift multinational corporations to other sites, and countries move to privatize most of their social resources, many peoples, and a majority of women, have been disenfranchised or lost their basic access to employment. As the state's focus has been redirected to ensure the interests of a small elite at the expense of the welfare, and even the survivability, of a poor majority, many peoples have found themselves seeking options for a better life. New technologies are facilitating and increasing migration, leading some to characterize these migrating women as "noncitizens, phantasmatic, and exchangeable parts of a flexible market" (Maleno & Munoz, 2003, p. 3). With the growth of the international bride market, many women draw on the technology of e-mail, "enabling them to build up a relationship that will lead to an engagement and consequent invitation to the West" (Biemann, 2000).

Granted, the sale and purchase of bodies is nothing new. However, with the restructurings of the world economy, many countries in Eastern Europe, the former Soviet Union, Africa, Asia, and South America are directing subjects—women—into resources for exchange in the desire industries (Agathangelou, 2002, 2004; Agathangelou & Ling, 2003). Women's bodies are being sold to generate remittances for nation-states whose economies are in shambles and profits for corporations who see the promise of such a business. These neoliberal restructurings and exchanges, including those in cyberspace, cannot be abstracted from the historical, social, and material conditions within which they are embedded. As Gonzalez and Rodriguez (2006) argue, the Internet is still the domain of the first world:

> The basic technological infrastructure that enables the creation of search engines and the enormous databases they must support are owned and located mainly in the United States and a very few European nations.... Even now, with the rest of the world supposedly becoming wired, the United States and Europe still control how information is delivered on a simple search like "Filipina." Meaning making is not a democratic process. (p. 377)

Most of us daily draw on this technology of the Internet to accomplish many tasks, including finding and maintaining professional and intimate relations. This is the subject that this chapter addresses: How do people of different backgrounds (including race, gender, class, sexualities, or different geographical sites) come to form and develop intimate relations with each other? What kinds of borders are crossed, and what processes are engaged in to accomplish what they set out to do?

All e-mails are symptoms of larger social relations and the way they are organized. These e-mails conceal even as they reveal. These electronic exchanges may be about connection, or negotiation, or they may be about the purchase of whole lands and bodies for the generation of profits. They may be about expressions of desire for others' lives and others' bodies. Or they may be about traumas and anxieties about one's role/power in the world. Or they may be expressions of love. E-mail exchanges may reveal a certain identity, but they also conceal other identities.

Meanwhile, we are e-mailing back and forth to the press and editors, letting them know that the chapter is not yet complete. The arrival of these e-mails discloses much about these different processes including the environment within which they unfold: our own identities as professionals whose major measure of success depends on communications about publications, as well as other kinds of activities related to professionalization (e.g., intensified competition as well as a constant negotiation of "signs" to ensure the generation of money). In the authors' case, the finished product depends on our coming to intimately know how electronic attachments come to be initiated, developed, formed, and shaped. The whole environment of production (including of writing) depends on different kinds of seductions (e.g., the more you publish the more successful/famous you could become; the more you write the more pleasure you will receive, the more cutting-edge research you engage in the more you will forget your pain, trauma, and other kinds of violence you experience in your life; the more you can access your own resilience, the better you will be able to adjust to the environmental crises you face, etc.). There is a particular seduction in writing this chapter. It may generate a sense of fun and pleasure. Similarly, those who use the Internet to seek others for "intimacies" may find themselves ecstatic when they "find that special someone." However, as Biemann (2003) argues, the Internet does not take away power relations. Electronic communication has quickly been discovered as a tool to build romantic and erotic relations, but what is experienced by many in the Western world as a playful and fun seductive activity is, for many women in locations of weaker economies, a chance to address a White man as a way of getting out of poverty. Discourses of romantic desire intertwine with a desire for survival (Biemann, 2003).

What becomes apparent when we search the Net is that the many Web pages of agencies working to ensure productions of intimacies could be extremely appealing to people whose focus is survival: those seeking a different, better life because of alienation, conditions of violence, oppression and other traumas, restructurings of family relations, disenfranchisement, and exploitations that prevent people from continuing to live in the spaces where they were born. The moves by many agencies to respond to this desire for social reproduction have been very telling. The sundering and shifts of borders is disjunctive. Below, we gesture to some of the contradictions/disjunctures and shifts, as well as articulate other epistemologies that move us ontologically beyond the social relation of profit and superexploitation.

Crossings and Intimacies: International Dating and Electronic Exchanges

International dating is one of the many electronic intimacies that we are promised daily in the heterovirile market. (Others have also argued about the homovirile market; see Alexander, 2006; Ingram et al., 1997; Ingram,

2001.) International dating embodies itself through different technologies: ordering one's future partner through the mail or visiting the site/sights in search of that intimacy that could fulfill one's yearning. But, can any (body) date just any (body) by crossing electronic, spatial (i.e., national) territories? What does it require legally? How do brides who can be ordered through the mail turn into the objects of desire of others? Why? What kinds of scarcities mobilize some people's participation (albeit with their own "consent") in such processes? What kinds of resources are required in order to participate in international dating?

The mediation that enables these exchanges in the production of electronic attachments, and the resources necessary to constitute those who come to be interested in "diverse" dating, are many times made invisible when we exclusively focus on the object of intimacy. The production of intimacy as a marketable good closely follows the rules of the neoliberal market. A cursory surf of available Web sites and services reminds us that, as with traditional "personals" printed in newspapers, Internet intimacy does not escape commodification and exploitation. This is true even though the intimacies that are promised daily through the push of a button are promised in one's private space (i.e., one's household, one's office, one's jet). Anxieties about finding partners (and, especially, ideal ones) and anxieties around choice and selection range seem to be supplanting awareness of oppression and anxieties about immigration, labor, and biotechnology. Indeed, these moments and these particular formulations of the intimate prop up structures and institutions of dominant power relations. This next section explores several agencies (i.e., available sites on the Internet) through which the international marital trade becomes instantiated. The different processes that enable electronic attachment include seduction, violence, mystification, and other processes working simultaneously to ensure dominant and hegemonic gendered, raced, heterosexual, and class power relations.

Seductions and Simulations: Borders, Bodies, and Other Sites of Contestation?

Just as corporate structures of capitalism issue promises on a daily basis, the numerous Web sites on finding "intimacy" communicate promises of freedom and happiness. As most of us usually do not pay much attention to the conditions underlying the production of such messages or to how such visual and textual material may be received by other groups of people, we are not able to situate the interplay between medium and message within the larger context of global circuits of power such as the political economy of electronic mediums. Thus, we will look at a few sites out of the multitude available as part of the burgeoning multibillion dollar "desire industry" (Agathangelou, 2004).

A Web site called Russian Brides (http://www.russianbrides.com/), brought to you by a company called Anastasia Tours, features women from the former Soviet Union and Eastern Europe. Not all the women featured on the site are from Russia—some are from the Ukraine and other countries—but Anastasia is a tag that carries certain associations toward the production of a specific subject and body (i.e., what comes to be articulated as the "Western" male). The production of the Western subject depends on the commodification of the object of his desire: Anastasia. This page presents or codes itself as a "woman." It also trumpets an unbeatable success rate: "Anastasia is the Industry Leader in Matchmaking Tours!" (http://www.russianbrides.com/tours.asp). While this page at first glance appears quite generic and open to all men, a closer look reveals that this company's target audience is what the page terms the "Western" man:

> WE GUARANTEE that during our tour you will be exposed to HUNDREDS of beautiful ladies who are extremely interested in establishing relationships with Western men of all ages. This is not a "sex tour"! The women you will meet have high moral values and are from middle and upper class family environments. (http://www.russianbrides.com/tours.asp)

The message is that these women are not just available for sex but are women of high moral fiber, appropriate for serious men looking for long-lasting marital connections. The discourse of this company's advertisements is revealing: These women are waiting, in "feminized national spaces," for the penetration of Western capital and the virtual and eventual physical penetration by the Western man (Biemann, 2000). Biemann argues that these companies, which capitalize on the desire and affective economies of "capturing" transnational others, are arriving on the scene at a specific historical moment when "humanist" culture is in crisis. The modernist notion that a man, through his rationality, can understand everything, and that "the whole world can become material for his intellectual or practical activity and that he has no absolute point of reference" outside himself is being challenged theoretically and politically (e.g., Heidegger, Derrida, Foucault, Irrigaray). The search for bodies as a way to fulfill the "desires" of those Western males, through the resignification of "Russian" women's bodies as sexy and desirable,[5] emerges powerfully as a symptom of this crisis, occurring simultaneously in the context of globalization and socioeconomic restructuring the world over.

Before and during the Cold War, these female bodies were not on the radar. Socialist economies ensured employment, education, and the welfare of peoples, and, thus, those women and their bodies were not open terrains for the contestation of capitalist corporations. The collapse of the Soviet Union ushered in an intense economic crisis and struggle to survive. It is within this context that the Web page/corporation "Anastasia" becomes a site for the purchase and sale of "intimacies." Web pages such as Russian Brides resignify women's and men's desires toward the neoliberal and heterosexual fantasies of freedom, control, and management of one's life. Such Web pages constitute themselves through a series of catalogues that advertise potential Russian brides (e.g., Elena, Viktoria, etc.) accompanied by live videos with "personal" data: age, height, and weight. Such communications are highly subject to fantasy, as the semantic descriptions and visual depictions and the act of consuming these words and bodies become inextricably interwoven. Without real-time interactions in physical proximity, such data are consumed in a manner that promotes ultimate projection of ideals and fantasies, from both sides. Via cyberspace, the bodies of "featured ladies" appear on the left-hand side of the screen of one's desktop computer.

> Troubled by nothing
> Bodies moving through various spheres
> Through transnational spaces
> Shopping for another body
> That represents desire
> That represents pleasure
> The bodies turn to images
> The bodies turn to words
> The bodies turn to codes
> Culturally coded
> Always
> A simple electronic device has allowed the order [of] bodies
> Passing borders passing officials passing through transnational wires
> To some proper place. (Biemann, 2000)

Epistemologically speaking, the production of these bodies as objects of desire is hidden. The crossings of bodies in search of pleasure and desire, in search of those bodies that may come to fulfill those fantasies, go on daily without awareness that the presentation of these men and women has been "objectively" structured by this electronic device, the Internet. We take this presentation as a given, not asking who ordered these women and why, or why women seek these kinds of relations, daily entering their "passport numbers," surrendering their identifications to the invisible hand of the neoliberal market. To echo Edward Said, why are "Western" subjects seeking these kinds of relations? Why are non-Western subjects interested in this kind of ordering of their own subjectivities and bodies? Reflecting on these Web pages/corporations, we have an opportunity to ponder the structure and production of particular narratives as epistemes and to gain insight into why this phenomenon, and why now?

The Internet as a technology advances and reinforces conceptions of an advanced West and of the advanced "Western" male, referred to in "Anastasia," "Foreign Bride," and "Volga Girl." These technologies are, of course, part and parcel of our everyday social relations. Even those of us who have no access to the Internet know persons who do and thereby come to know the effects of particular practices, such as visiting international dating pages (e.g., CyberDating.net, n.d.). Through the mediation of "Anastasia," a "Western" man on a tour to Russia or the Ukraine is promised (and hopefully finds) a "loving wife," whom he rescues and brings back "home." Though these exchanges occur daily, they do not take place on a neutral ground. These exchanges take place within particular liminal zones (Reed, 1996) that occupy a place in what one might call imperial power.

The Internet might be thought of as a liminal space, a transitory "time out of time" in which one is "betwixt and between" social roles (Turner, 1967, p. 99). In the liminal zone of cyberspace, subjects come to engage in specific everyday practices, such as fabrications, acts that over time come to affect how subjects develop and organize their lives in relations to others (Thrift & Dewsbury, 2000). This liminality operates through the Internet in the way that women, men, transgender persons, and others are most likely to be brought into private homes of Western men who buy "foreign women" in such a way that does not disturb the public. As long as these crossings happen in private spaces, they take place unseen without perturbing or disturbing the public.

In a sense, these liminal zones turn Ukrainian, Russian, Bulgarian, and Filipina women, us (the authors and readers of this chapter), and our bodies and their integrity into borders delineating West and East. Western males are articulated into subjects who can afford to purchase access to these women and men as commodities and spectables of endless desires. Borders, Balibar (2002) argues, historically have been "lines or zones, strips of land, which are places of separation and contact or confrontation, areas of blockage or passage ... [f]ixed or shifting zones, continuous or broken lines" (p. 77). Thus, in the Internet marital trade, female bodies serve a polysemic function, in that bodies become borders, which have the ability to differentiate between individuals (Balibar, 2002). The "loving wives" or, rather, the fantasies of "loving wives," function as the border that is "an extraordinarily viscous spatiotemporal zone, almost a home" (Balibar, 2002). These women encounter and are regulated by the borders that capital sets up for them. These women's bodies become the borders and their very existence is "neither this nor that" (p. 83). Their bodies become tools and strategies of power especially when national borders fix their bodies as borders. Balibar suggests that borders have become heterogeneous and ubiquitous. Women's bodies become the borders that enable the asymmetrical power of the Western man once he is able to access those bodies that have crossed state borders to become "good wives." Moreover, the Western man may become the site of power that make possible the space for the fulfillment of the fantasies and desires of the women of the "South" (Agathangelou, 2004, 2006).

Electronic seduction and the contestation of territorial, organizational, state, market, and corporeal borders do not begin with the Internet. They begin within the communities in which each of us finds ourselves. We are reminded who we are and how we are supposed to live our everyday lives by the constant bombardment of spectacle from television advertisement and programming that "dramatizes state power" and manages images that articulate for us how to think, act, and organize our lives (i.e., you turn beautiful if you use Dove soap; you turn into a successful subject if you gain a college degree; Best & Kellner, 2005; Aretxaga, 2001). Sites also play a role in the reproduction of social relations. These narratives shape the questions we ask ourselves and inform us whether or not we are doing all right. Are you happy? Are you happily married? Are you successful? These spectacles are modes of seduction and also become modes of contestation. They seem to inform us of one major thing: if you do not buy this product, do not expect to become that which this ad defines. Seductions, as embodied through the logic of these Web pages, define the terrains of the struggles themselves. Following Maleno and Muñoz (2003), crossing borders becomes a way of negotiating identity formations and space formations that enable specific intimacies. It is within these environments that we can understand electronic attachments. Seduced into the struggles of intimacy and love, the political economy of electronic attachments is narrowly punctuated and articulated as being about freedom and the choice of finding the right, moral, and good partner.

Dating Web sites embody the principles of property relations and subject formations. Banners stating that the "above sites are open to all

nationalities, locations, genders, and sexual orientations" (http://www.
yourtangowiredating.com/html/your-interracial-dating-site.html) "normalize" the search for a partner. Does the Internet, in its liminality,
normalize the crossing? What is highlighted and what is made invisible?
Is the highlighting done in order to efface something and if so, what?

Perhaps any kind of cyber crossing is being done in the now, just for the
time being, for the sake of finding those bodies and those connections (and
perhaps, information) that comply with one's intimate desires (Gonzalez
& Rodriguez, 2006). Search engines change the Russian or Filipina woman
into "cyberscript, change and conflate[e] her body" (Biemann, 2000) into
an object of desire. The specific visualizations render Russian, Filipina,
and other women "the most immediately conjurable' embodiment" or
guise (Gonzalez & Rodriguez, 2006, p. 378) of "single women seeking
men." What is visible are the Internet and the body as a site/border of
seduction.

And when borders are crossed, both men and women may find themselves in situations that they did not fantasize about, or even if they did,
they may never have thought they would become a reality. Those realities not part and parcel of conversations about "free" access and choice
come to be recognized after prolonged intimate contact. In dealing with
the everyday, couples that began as an electronic attachment are often
confronted with the materialities and contexts that were suspended long
enough to make their connection possible.

> The irony of artificial practices: the peculiar ability of the painted woman or
> prostitute to exaggerate her features, to turn them into more than a sign, ... to
> incarnate the peaks of sexuality while simultaneously being absorbed in their
> simulation. The irony proper to the constitution of woman as idol or sex object:
> in her closed perfection, she puts an end to sex play and refers man, the lord
> and master of sexual reality, to his transparency as an imaginary subject. The
> ironic power of the object, then, which she loses when promoted to the status of
> a subject. (Baudrillard, 1979/1990, p. 15)

Baudrillard (1979/1990) argues that we "produce the other and what is
produced is the effigy of a 'masculine hysteria'. In this hysteria, the femininity of men is projected onto the production of women who are then
made to resemble man's utopian fantasy...." (p. 15). Baudrillard suggests
that such sexuality is a radical break with the past because erotic attraction once came as a result of the fascinating encounter with the "Other,"
but now erotic attraction has shifted from otherness to sameness and likeness. "The body has become a fetish, a project to avoid destiny, self, and

identity ... in toning, in makeup, in the performance of masculine desire, destiny is exorcised" (Vannini, n.d., para. 3). The women of "Anastasia," "Foreign Affair," and other Web pages are dressed to seduce. But seduction for whom, and for what purpose?

> Seduction does not consist of a simple appearance, or a pure absence, but the eclipse of a presence. Its sole strategy is to be there/not there, and thereby produce a sort of flickering, a hypnotic mechanism that crystallizes attention outside all concern with meaning. Absence here seduces presence. The sovereign power of the seductress stems from her ability to "eclipse" any will or context. She cannot allow other relations to be established—even the most intimate, affectionate, amorous or sexual (particularly not the latter)—without breaking them, or repaying them with a strange fascination.... Here lies her secret: in the flickering of a presence [...] Seduction supposes, Virilio would say, "aesthetics of disappearance." (Baudrillard, 1979/1990, p. 85)

And there is plenty of seduction to go around. The seductive subjects themselves are seduced by the fantasy of what crossing the borders of the Western man may offer them. Baudrillard does not talk of what seduction entails beyond the "aesthetics of disappearance." Others do. For example, Hartman (1996) argues that seduction is a process that enables the formation of pleasure through violence. These forms of power in the global political economic context emerge out of the production of body images that attempt to satiate. Female bodies in pages like "International Athena" and "Anastasia" become a complex production onto which male ideals and resources are invested, constituting a quintessentially contemporary Western project of finding oneself the "loving wife." In this situation, their female bodies function as borders.

But this process of contestation and struggle over the production of borders does not become part of the conversation; seduction as a process redirects the focus from the historical and material specificities of particular women, to bodies that are "exported and circulated as specular signifiers of broader socioeconomic formations such as 'the global assembly line,' 'export processing zone,' 'military prostitution,' and/or 'sex/tourism'" (Gonzalez & Rodriguez, 2006, p. 378) and subjects who buy "things." What is obscured, for instance, is who is able to cross what borders and under what conditions? Who becomes a border, and under what conditions? This production of borders (international, national, corporate, and corporeal) becomes constituted in banners such as: "Goodwife.com: The Foreign Bride Guide," a Web page providing pointers for the successful procurement of a foreign "good wife."

Crossing national, international, and corporate spatialities in search of a foreign goodwife is a code for racialized, sexual, national, and corporeal power contestations. These Web pages promise to open the doors leading to the exchange of flesh; Western subjects are promised entrance to the "mail order bride warehouse," where they can transcend their particular corporeality and access a body that could turn itself into a "good wife." The site "Mail Order Bride Warehouse" gestures once more to an episteme of "things" and "objects." After all, what are warehouses? On the one hand, these subjects are made hypervisible, indeed, bodies dressed mostly in swimsuits and big smiles. On the other hand, these women become the sites/borders that can define the Western man in relation to the "bride," in relation to other internal borders such as Western women, and other men, both domestically and internationally. This crossing of borders at these different levels is justified this way:

> Russian women want something better. A large number of Russian women prefer American men. "Our [Russian] men treat women like objects.... They drink, they smoke, they have bad hygiene and care only about themselves. These Americans don't smoke or drink. They really seem to want to settle down and take care of their family." (http://www.american.edu/TED/bride.htm)

These pages not only construct women but men as well. Who are these "dream men"?

> These men are tired of "career-obsessed" women and see Russian women as less materialistic and more appreciative of men. Many men are just frustrated by the American dating scene. One potential groom describes his searches through bars, clubs, coffeehouses, Laundrymats and grocery stores with no success. Russian women are seen as ideal over other nationalities as they "have a European face but the patience of an Asian." Russian women are seen as more feminine and more traditional.... Is it any wonder then that American men are attracted to the idea of finding an educated, good-looking wife who will appreciate the simpler things in life? (http://www.american.edu/TED/bride.htm)

The Western man frequenting these sites likely longs for times gone by, a nostalgic world where a traditional woman's whole purpose in life was serving (and servicing) her husband. As Biemann (2000) states, "The body is entangled in words that recount not a historical body, but a nostalgic body, in any case, a narrated body, imbued in electronic desire, imbued in electronic pleasure." It is no coincidence that sites advertising women from Asia, Eastern Europe, and the former Soviet Union sympathize with the "plight" of Western men—that they cannot find suitable women due to the "blight" of feminism (Cunneen & Stubbs, 2000). Western men who browse these sites are most likely having difficulty negotiating between their fantasy of ideal relationships (i.e., the assumption that the perfect partner will be an embodiment of their desire, both submissive and ecstatically sexual) and how real women operate as subjects with their own needs, wants, and desires. Western men who have a real encounter with an Asian woman who has a voice, preferences, and her own ideas about the relationship may find their power challenged, especially since their search has been for an object to control. Thus, it is "easier" to reassert one's hegemonic status (i.e., First World, Global North) by exerting power and control over a commodity (i.e., Third World, Global South) that one has purchased. Explicit and lethal violence is one strategy, among many, to try to conquer and assert dominance over the female "Other," and as the homicide rate of Filipino women in Australia shows, some men will kill for control.

Men are constituted as the seekers of foreign wives. Crossing borders to find a "foreign bride" becomes an ontological priority: "in seeking I find." Indeed, "I seek, I pay, I deserve, it is my right to possess you, to make your body mine," irrespective of trespasses, irrespective of the bride's body becoming a fluctuating space that serves to punctuate one's own identity. For instance, many Western men beat their "new brides" and their children if they do not obey their orders (Investigative Reports, 1999).

The Western man becomes an ultimate site of simulation, indeed, the simulacra of ultra-capitalist relations. This "man of money" is the alpha and the omega of social relations. He is the one that can overcome all to reproduce him/itself. International dating agencies draw extensively on this principle and generate their business out of such fantasies:

- Round-trip airfare
- Transportation to and from the airport
- 13 night stay at a 4 star hotel
- One 4 hour guided tour of the city
- One Intimate Social
- 3 Large Socials
- 24 hour hospitality service
- On-going introductions
- Full buffet brunch daily
- Free 3 month platinum membership and EZ-DO-IT Fiancee Visa Kit
- "New Applicants Interview" sessions. (A Foreign Affair, http://www.loveme. com)

As described in Trade and Environment Data Base (TED) Projects, "the Love Boat soon will be making another run. The Love Boat promises something for everyone. Set a course for adventure, your mind on a new romance" (http://www.american.edu/TED/bride.htm#31). The "Western" man just needs to set sail, his mind on an adventure of discovery (and colonization). This new narrative of recolonization echoes *Fiddler on the Roof*: "Did you think you'd get a prince? Well I do the best I can. With no money no dowry no family background, be glad you got a man!" (cited in http://www.american.edu/TED/bride.htm).

While this freedom and choice does not come without payment, the Web pages address the issue of the cost of the exchange as yet another aspect of seduction:

> We are not the least expensive, but when using agencies, you get what you pay for.... Athena follows in the fine Angelika NetWork tradition of service by putting the needs of the Ladies and Gentlemen using the service first. Because of our location, our backgrounds, our professional staff and our dedication to service we are able to offer you several exclusive services that nobody else can match. If you compare the costs and value of our Personal Tours, Email forwarding with Russian women, Translations and other services you will see that we offer very high quality services for a very reasonable price. (Ukrainian & Russian Women Marriage Agency, n.d., para. 5)

The International Athena Agency's episteme is that access to "loving wives" is costly but worth every penny. The agency has the expertise to ensure that one can access the best. In parallel fashion, the authors of this piece are producing themselves as the dedicated experts that can bring readers "several exclusive services (e.g., knowledge and insights about electronic attachments) that nobody else can match." The suggestion that the major goal is to meet the needs of "Ladies" and "Gentlemen" who use the service obscures the primary motive of profit. This approach is another kind of seduction for those whose fantasies are ridden with desire to find the loving "Lady" and for those "Ladies" in search of the "Gentleman" who can bring them to North America. These ladies represent borders that enable the Western man's possibility, and through the Internet, the Western man is seduced in search of his own freedom. Seduction represents women's symbolic power over men (Baudrillard, 1990). Similarly, "International Athena," "Anastasia," and so many other purveyors of the "ideal" wife for the "right" amount of money, represent the seduction of capitalism. Thus, women's bodies, or the symbolic power of their bodies, become the border, the border of simulation.

Read, for example, how "white mythologies"[6] (Derrida, 1982) are used in the international trade of mail-order Eastern European and Chinese brides toward the exchange of money for their bodies. These examples make Global North and Global South racialized relations invisible, but they reveal that this particular dating relation requires particular bodies, and that this romantic venture is necessarily a business relation, replete with tensions and contradictions (Filipina, http://www.filipina.com/). "Moldova Cupid is an introduction agency that brings together Western men and Moldova's beautiful women." "Chinese Dating Site. Say goodbye to the torture of blind dates. Say hello to your future. Professional Asian matchmaking featuring personalized one on one selection. This is the real way to get what you want."

These relations are organized in a way that enables "getting rid" of those real-life moments that can generate fear and loathing. The embedded episteme promises freedom from the many pressures and experiences people have (struggles, fear, anxiety, loss, loathing, "love at first sight") when they first meet someone. It is organized to simultaneously allow one to get rid of unwanted insecurities and to manage circumstances through the fantasy of control and empowerment (i.e., it is easy to find love; it does not require work to connect with somebody; the connection just happens naturally). This epistemology embodies colonization, racialization, and, of course, romance of social relations; it is always about the self and the alleviation of its own anxieties, irrespective of who is being bought and on what basis, irrespective of who purchases and on what terms. Moreover, do not worry because this "professional Asian matchmaking featur[es] one to one selection" and will accord you what "you want," and, indeed, what you desire. Seductively, these pages demonstrate that this exchange is about affirming a particular identity, that of the subject who purchases the services. The exchange and its direction seem to be "one-way" and, perhaps, about conquest. It presents the "women" described in the pages "as the objects of the action, not as an agent" (Spanos, 1998, p. 8). These women are the objects that can fulfill the desire of those who are already subjects of power and desire to continue to be so by disciplining, containing, and controlling those who are seen as "objects of those fulfillments." These pages embody the "oculacentric problematic" (Spanos, 1998, p. 4). The action in this case is "dating" (international dating, mail-order brides, etc.) but it is not a "free," borderless action even though it is presented as such.

Let's look at another case. Investigating constructions of masculinity and femininity in the context of the new global market for sex and marital trade via the Internet, Cunneen and Stubbs (2000) examined the representation of Filipino women on international sites that advertised them as partners for sex or marriage. Interest in the question of representation emerged from a striking statistic in the researchers' country of Australia:

the homicide rate for Filipino women in Australia was 5.6 times that of all women there, and nearly all the murders were committed by an intimate. From the available data, the majority of the couples involved met in the Philippines, and in about half of the cases, an introduction agency or some other mechanism for promoting international connections with Filipino women was involved.

Australian immigration regulations are quite strict in regard to Filipino immigrant women, and so their main means of entry is marriage to Australian resident men not from the Philippines. It is helpful to place choices to marry and migrate within a larger socioeconomic and international context. Not merely exercises of free will made by individual women, such choices often represent explicit governmental policies of human export in developing countries like the Philippines, in response to factors such as high unemployment and poor economies (Agathangelou, 2004). Migration as economic strategy signifies the stark inequality that persists between "North" and "South," and structural adjustment policies in the service of neoliberal export-led development have had especially deleterious effects on women (Harrison, 2006).

But why are Filipino, and migrant Asian women in general, targeted so frequently and disproportionately for intimate homicide in Australia? The answer may lie in masculine fantasies projected onto Asian women and the frustration and anger that explode when one's fantastical notions of how a partner is, or should be, unravel in the face of everyday relations. Pervasive myths about the submissive, compliant Asian beauty (with a dubious past) actually circulated in the discourse of Australian media reports about murdered "mail-order" brides in Australia (Cunneen & Stubbs, 2000). Following the outlawing of introduction agencies in the Philippines, Internet sites emerged to meet the demand for Filipino women. Sites provide detailed catalogs of "exotic" women from which to choose. These kinds of electronically facilitated couple attachments are grounded in words exchanged in a cyber environment that facilitates flights of fantasy. Internet connections with "Others" allow space for introductions written in words supersaturated with anticipated ideals, pleasures, and wish fulfillment.

Cunneen and Stubbs (2000) quote from an Internet site called "Asian Eyes": "The Asian female possesses an inner beauty not tarnished by western traditions ... generally men find Asian ladies to be loyal, honest, fun to be with ... Asian ladies are the essence of femininity, and you will see why [they] are known to be ideal marriage partners" (pp. 16–17). Such sites loudly trumpet the virtuous qualities of Asian women and simultaneously drum a sexual vibe, embedded, sometime subtly and sometimes obviously, in colonial discourses. Even at "legitimate" marital introduction sites, sexual fantasy and titillation are always near, with links to sites offering sex tours and erotica, in effect promising the availability of "bad girls" to supplement or complement the "good girls" to be found out there. One can see how patriarchal and racialized demands for a perfectly docile and accommodating partner could mold and shape one's expectations of an "Other" who has been, in a sense, advertised, idealized, bought and paid for on the Internet. The narrative structure of most of these corporations' Web pages (written for consumption by the Western male customer) is essentially Western, in the sense that the appropriating, distributing, and producing of these desires/fantasies is directed by "White" peoples of Europe and the United States. Moreover, it is Western in the sense that it assumes a directional movement toward a preconceived and productive end (i.e., find a wife who obeys, indeed, find a wife who enables one's reproduction of power as a White, masculine, heterosexual subject).[7] Marriages are commodified and conveniently packaged such that all one needs is a few dollars (a credit card) and a dream (a masculine and colonial fantasy of an ideal female partner; see http://www. filipina.com/eflp_nosoj.php?pid=61470&D=244221&C=193955&domain =filipina.com&V=10143&K=filipina&K2= to see how women are coded on the Internet as "exclusively mail-order brides, sex workers and maids"; Gonzalez & Rodriguez, 2006, p. 375).

Many pages that men use to find their future wives are filled with racial stereotypes that could fuel frustration and hostility when women are not as "controllable" as imagined. For example, see what several agencies ("A Foreign Affair," "A Volga Girl") tell the men who are seeking bodies for pleasure and wives for marriage: "Do Not Be a Victim of the 'Russian Woman' or 'Foreign Woman' Scam!" "A Volga Girl has standard practice that guarantees your initial investment" (http://www.volgagirl.com). These pages basically state that the "Russian woman" or "foreign woman" is often a devious gold digger. These racialized and gendered stereotypes (e.g., the Russian or the foreign woman as perverse deceiver) become part and parcel of the "free" market's epistemology that makes implicit or invisible a discussion of the conditions under which such exploitation and violence take place (e.g., under relations of intensified capitalism that superexploits labor and bodies). The absence of "the structures and social relations within which these exchanges take place constructs the authoritative and objective rescuer, always outside of history" (Grewal, 1998, p. 502).

Marital trade agencies invoke Western male power by stating: "Don't forget that a man is a maker of his own fortune"; "Remember there are millions of attractive, sweet young women in the former USSR ... who are seeking a better life with loving men in the West" (http://www.dating-world.net/index.htm). Protecting the Western male's privileged status, these agencies hire their own lawyers, banks, and "scam counselors" to ensure that their clients do not fall into the clutches of the "Russian mafia" (see http://www.loveme.com/information/scam_info.html) or other scams. The following supposedly "true" story actively participates in constituting the Russian woman as "just one of many people" who would do anything to deceive the Western man by extracting his resources:

> *Caller:* I have been corresponding with a woman from Lugansk for some time now. I met her from company other than yours, and she now wants to come here to visit me. I did not think that it would be easy for her to get a visa, especially from Lugansk, which seems to be the scam capital, but she assured me that she could do it.
>
> *Counselor:* How did she say she could do it?
>
> *Caller:* She had me call a travel agent and the travel agent told me that, yes, she could get the visa and the passport and the tickets all for $1,000.00. They would send her on a packaged religious tour, which is how they could obtain the US visa. That price would get her right to my city.
>
> *Counselor:* That is a classic scam. If you send the money, you will never see the money or the woman again. The woman may not even exist; there is a good chance that you may be speaking with just one of many people working out of a boiler room operation. The "Travel Agency" is probably just another person taking the call answering the phone as a travel agency but probably does not exist at all and is only there to trick you into sending $1,000.00.
>
> *Caller:* Yes, I had a feeling it was not right. I offered to go there to see her and she did not want me to come, kept saying it was a bad idea, and that she should come to see me.
>
> *Counselor:* That makes sense; she wouldn't want you to come there to see her, especially if she did not really exist. You are much better off going over to meet the women and even then you are much better off going with a group tour, if not ours than take another reputable company, but whatever you do—do not send the money!
>
> *Caller:* Ok thank you very much, I think a group tour may be the way to go as well.

This "story" confirms once more the dangers in seeking a "foreign woman" and offers a way of preventing such catastrophes through the use of the Internet agencies. Such narratives reinforce the notion that their clientele are moral, Western males seeking the "truth" regarding their searches for a bride, customers who need guidance and protection from evildoers who threaten them on their journey. But an Internet vision quest is ridden with fantasy, and cyberspace facilitates the emergence of fantastic desire. As Biemann (2000) states:

> In the isolation of the private space of writing, released from the experience of physical proximity, personal fantasies reach a heightened intensity, the sensation of pure desire, the perfect one, the one emanating from no image, no aura, no voice, no body, no physical experience whatsoever, one that emerges completely from one's imagination, culturally coded, of course, always. Suspended realities that simulate a permanent state of being in love, a fantasy forever unfulfilled in its enactments, a sense of always approaching, but never reaching.

This commodity status of bodies (i.e., both the purchaser and the bought), and all in the name of fulfilling intimacy, is constantly disrupted with statements by the children left behind by some of the women who are purchased or with statements by the women themselves who crossed the borders to become the wives of a "rich" man in the United States or Western Europe ("I am the one who keeps tightly your household."). More so, these fantasies are disrupted by the fact that imperialism is not an abstract set of social, economic, and political concepts and principles but a set of social relations that enables predation on the bodies of women from the Global South all in the name of freedom and smooth exchange.

International Coupling and International Border Crossings as Contradictions

In the context of particular women being deemed as exotic and as good wives to the Western man, how do we make sense of the Internet as a liminal zone? How do the bodies of Russian and Ukrainian women serve as borders, and how are these borders sites of contestation and tension?

We check our e-mail accounts again. Pressing a key will enable us to send this chapter to the press and perhaps, within this action, we experience a promise, or, rather, the fantasy of a publication promised, and with it, a fantasized contribution toward our professional development. Yet, many times these border crossings make invisible the stakes in these exchanges, in these social relations. Many times what seems to be a simple, short sentence, a single phrase, or the choice of a word actually translates into codes of power that can be read and critiqued, if only we felt we had the time to do so. Many times this writing happens at the expense of marginalizing other significant social relations: our partners, our children, our friends, our communities, and their struggles.

Regarding the subject of gender and "real" women, our participation in the production of knowledge itself is gendered, raced, sexualized, and class informed. In reading the personal stories of women who found themselves in the tentacles of the marital trade, we see stories of gender violence. Yet, success stories are also available for consumption. For example, Elena relates her story to us:

> John met me here. He paid my ticket to NYC and we have been living together since 2001. He brought me into this beautiful big house and he also paid for my daughter's ticket to come and live with us. Here we have cable TV. He is also paying for my six-year-old daughter to attend a private school. Here we have a full fridge and we go to restaurants quite frequently. I feel that I made it. (Biemann, 2000)

Many such stories circulate, intimating that dreams do come true, including the desire to "move up" through the helping, invisible hand of Internet technology. A ticket to come to the United States, a full fridge, private education in the Big Apple, visits to nice restaurants, and a nice house complete with cable are all symbols of Elena's increased social and economic mobility. Her story is one that subverts the socioeconomic and national relations of power between herself and John long enough to show us that Internet cross-cultural exchanges lead to happy cross-cultural social relations. Thus, bodies become borders of contestation as well as bodies of possibility. Such exchanges are themselves paradoxes—paradoxes that contest, negotiate, and reproduce asymmetries of power as desire—and fantasies that become mediated through technologies so ubiquitous that they are like water to a fish. The daily crossing of electronic borders can also subvert or challenge neoimperial seductions that try to maintain territorial frontiers, to reduce subjects to objects of purchasable flesh, and to turn bodies to borders.

Conclusion

The process of "trying out" different versions of cyberintimacy produces new subjectivities or identities, but subjects do not elude their "residual attachments" to embodied experiences, practices, or social relations as they are mediated through power. "The liminal zone of cyberspace is clearly not only virtual [a particular materiality]; it is also corporeal" (Madge & O'Connor, 2005, p. 93). Cyberspace borders and other crossings (e.g., bodies, land, and national and international boundaries) do not escape power; rather, power inscribes them. Informed by power relations, bodies that perform different kinds of seductive crossings participate in negotiation, contestation, and fantasy fulfillments. Similarly, the professional crossings that we make as writers and professors help make possible our production as cosmopolitan subjects, or subjects who are scared of the materialities of corporeal bodies and their effects:

> What assumptions are we perpetuating through this celebration of lack of embodiment in cyberspace.... Exulting the denial of the body reinforces the current gendered, race and classed division of labour.... Tied to this hatred of the flesh is the marginalization of women and other groups who are associated with the body. (Travers, 2003, p. 229)

The epistemic and ontological assumptions initially celebrated become disrupted through the materialization of the intimacies that emerge out of these exchanges. These exchanges bring into bold relief our desires and fantasies of seduction: bodies delineating borders "come to matter in markedly different ways according to the ways in which power marks off, seals, and contains some bodies, making them bodies subjected to interrogation and to capture through projects of 'knowledge'" (White, 2005, p. 8). The authors are all for love, romance, and the euphoria that comes out of making intimate connections. The Internet promises to be a bridge, a romantic nexus, the conveyor of electronic attachment but delivers a mere moratorium on the serious engagement and negotiation of salient differences, eventually necessary between would-be partners. While a terribly appealing fantasy, the transcendence of social locations and asymmetries of power is a dangerous illusion being sold to willing buyers every day via the information highway. There are risks in "closing a deal" that has been brokered in fantasyland, and it is hoped that potential partners who choose to initiate transborder relationships through technology will seek to ground their lofty, virtual expectations and desires in a conscious, corporeal, real-time engagement with a subject who has his own story to tell, a person who is struggling to produce an alternative subjectivity, not a wish-fulfilling "Other."

Notes

1. The Global South and the Global North are not themselves unified and homogeneous spaces and bodies. On the contrary, they are themselves marked by asymmetries such as class, racial, sexual, corporeal, etc.
2. First World here refers to the capitalist, industrial bloc of countries (i.e., North America, Western Europe, Japan, and Australia) aligned with the United States after World War II with an emphasis on common political and economic interests. The Second World refers to the former communist-socialist states (formerly the Eastern bloc and those Republics under the influence of the Soviet Union). Third World here refers to the "developing" countries of Africa, Asia, Latin America, etc.
3. Specific examples of such revolutions include the Civil Rights Movements, the Women's Movements, and the Non-Aligned Movement.
4. We suggest here that nationality and racism are interconnected, albeit with many tensions. Geographies and historical legacies of colonization (e.g., slavery, theft of one's land, genocide) inform whether some bodies are to be sold as objects, others are to be hypersexualized, who is to be the purchaser or the protector of "good" women, etc. For instance, in the contemporary moment, particular lands like the Caribbean are seen as natural and mysterious spaces for exploitation and conquest through sex tourism (Mullings, 2000). Most of those tourists seem to be White and from North America.
5. It is important to note here that this recoding or resignification of female bodies of "Russian" women as sexy and "desirable" emerged after the Cold War was over and the former Soviet Union as well as Eastern European socialist economies moved to restructure themselves within the context of global capitalism.
6. White mythologies refers to the "whitewashing" of systems and practices and derives from the French where *white* also has the cognates *to bleach*, *whitewash*, or *exonerate*. Derrida's term refers to the couching of descriptions or narratives in such a way as to remove or render invisible key or crucial aspects of the phenomenon in question.
7. "Whiteness" is a social construct and an axis of power with structural causes and consequences. Conscious and deliberate actions have institutionalized group identity in the United States (and the rest of the world), not just through the discrimination of cultural stories, but also through the systemic efforts from colonial times to the present to create economic advantages through a possessive investment in whiteness for (European and) European Americans ... Desire for slave labor encouraged European settlers in North America to view, first, Native Americans and, later, African Americans as racially inferior people suited by "nature" for the humiliating subordination of

involuntary servitude … From the start, European settlers in North America established structures encouraging a possessive investment in whiteness. The colonial and early national legal systems authorized attacks on Native Americans and encouraged the appropriation of their lands. They legitimated racialized chattel slavery, limited naturalized citizenship to "white" immigrants, identified Asian immigrants as expressly unwelcome (through legislation aimed at immigrants from China in 1882, from India in 1917, from Japan in 1924, and from the Philippines in 1934), and provided pretexts for restricting the voting, exploiting the labor, and seizing the property of Asian Americans, Mexican Americans, Native Americans, and African Americans…. The possessive investment in whiteness is not a simple matter of black and white; all racialized minority groups have suffered from it, albeit to different degrees and different ways. The African slave trade began in earnest only after large-scale Native American slavery proved impractical in North America. (Lipsitz, 1998, p. 2) Of course, what is significant here is to recognize that these Eurocentric epistemologies and logics (Said, 1978) were very much part and parcel of the constitution of what comes to be known as Euro-U.S. empire/imperialism.

References

3G-Introductions marriage agency (n.d.). "3G: Galina's graceful girls: Ukrainian & Russian women marriage agency." Retrieved August 31, 2008 from http://www.3g-introductions.com

Agathangelou, A.M. (2001). Unpublished interviews with Athenian sex workers.

Agathangelou, A. M. (2002). Sexing "democracy" in international relations: Migrant sex and domestic workers in Cyprus, Greece, and Turkey. In G. Chowdhry & S. Nair (Eds.), *Power, postcolonialism and international relations* (pp. 142–169). New York: Routledge.

Agathangelou, A. M. (2004). *The global political economy of sex: Desire, violence and insecurity in Mediterranean nation-states.* New York: Palgrave.

Agathangelou, A. M. (2006). Colonising desires: Bodies for sale, exploitation and (in) security in desire industries. *Cyprus Review, 18*, 37–73.

Agathangelou, A. M., & Ling, L. H. M. (2003). Desire industries: Sex trafficking, UN peacekeeping, and the neo-liberal world order. *Brown Journal of World Affairs, 10*(1), 133–148.

Alapack, R., Blichfeldt, M. F., & Elden, A. (2005). Flirting on the internet and the hickey: A hermeneutic. *CyberPsychology and Behavior, 8*, 52–61.

Alexander, J. M. (2006). *Pedagogies of crossing: Meditations on feminism, sexual politics, memory, and the sacred.* Durham: Duke University Press.

Anastasia Web (n.d.). "Anastasia is the industry leader in matchmaking tours!" Retrieved August 31, 2008 from http://www.russianbrides.com/tours.asp

Anastasia Web (n.d.). "Dating agency Russian brides: Single Russian women online dating website and flowers delivery." Retrieved August 31, 2008 from http://www.russianbrides.com

Aretxaga, B. (2001). The sexual games of the body politic: Fantasy and state violence in Northern Ireland. *Culture, Medicine and Psychiatry: An International Journal of Comparative Cross Cultural Research, 25,* 1–27.

Balibar, E. (2002). *Politics and the other scene.* London: Verso.

Baudrillard, J. (1990). *Seduction* (B. Singer, Trans.). New York: St. Martin's Press. (Original work published 1979)

Best, S., & Kellner, D. (2005). Debord, cybersituations, and the Internet. Retrieved on October 15, 2006, from http://www.uta.edu/huma/illuminations/best6.htm

Best, S. & Kellner, D. (n.d.). "Debord and the Postmodern turn: New stages of the Spectacle" (para. 13). Retrieved August 31, 2008 from http://www.uta.edu/huma/illuminations/kell17.htm

Biemann, U. (2000). *Writing desire.* New York: Women Making Movies.

Biemann, U. (2003). Border videographies: A gendered reading of globalization processes. Retrieved March 16, 2007, from http://www.jgcinema.org/pages/view.php?cat=materiali&id=105&id_film=56&id_dossier=0)

China-Jiouzhaigou.com. (n.d.). "Chinese dating, hot girl." Retrieved August 31, 2008 from www.china-jiouzhaigou.com/default.aspx?name_query=Beijing&M96G4Wu0X8YUG=uUeD1s

Chittenden, V. (n.d.). "TED case studies case: 487: Russian mail order Brides." Retrieved August 29, 2008 from http://www.american.edu/TED/bride.htm

Cunneen, C., & Stubbs, J. (2000). Male violence, male fantasy, and the commodification of women through the Internet. *International Review of Victimology, 7,* 5–28.

Curtis, B. (2003). Foucault on governmentality and population: The impossible discovery. *Canadian Journal of Sociology, 27*(4), 505–533.

CyberDating.net. (n.d.) Retrieved February 14, 2006, from http://www.cyberdating.net/links/IN.html

Dating-world.net. (n.d.). "Introduction and dating service." Retrieved August 31, 2008 from http://www.dating-world.net/index.htm

Deleuze, G. (1990). Society of control. Retrieved January 15, 2007, from http://www.nadir.org/nadir/archiv/netzkritik/societyofcontrol.html

Derrida, J. (1982). White mythology: Metaphor in the text of philosophy (A. Bass, Trans.). In *Margins of philosophy.* Chicago: The University of Chicago Press.

Elbe, S. (2004, March). *The futility of protest? Biopower and biopolitics in the securitization of HIV/AIDS.* Paper presented at the 45th Annual ISA Convention, Montreal, Quebec, Canada.

Filipina.com. (n.d.). Retrieved August 31, 2008 from http://www.filipina.com/eflp_nosoj.php?pid=61470&D=437561&C=0&domain=filipina.com&V=10143&K=&K2=&K=filipina

A Foreign Affair. (n.d.). "Introduction and tours." Retrieved August 31, 2008 from http://www.loveme.com

Foucault, M. (1976). Disciplinary power and subjection. In C. Gordon (Ed.), *Power/knowledge: Selected interviews and other writings, 1972–1977* (pp. 229–242). New York: Pantheon.

Foucault, M. (1997). The birth of biopolitics. In P. Rabinow (Ed.), *Michel Foucault, ethics: Subjectivity and truth* (pp. 73–79). New York: The New Press.

Gonzalez, V., & Rodriguez, R. (2006). Asian American auto/biographies: The gendered limits of consumer citizenship in import subcultures. In T. Tu & M. Nguyen (Eds.), *Alien encounters: Popular culture and Asian America*. Durham, North Carolina: Duke University Press.

Grewal, I. (1998). On the new global feminism and the family of nations: Dilemmas of transnational feminist practice. In E. Shohat (Ed.), *Talking visions: Multicultural feminism in a transnational age* (pp. 501–530). Cambridge, MA: MIT Press.

Hardey, M. (2004). Mediated relationships: Authenticity and the possibility of romance. *Information, Communication, and Society, 7*, 207–222.

Harrison, A. (Ed.). (2006). *Globalization and poverty. National bureau of economic research conference report*. Chicago: University of Chicago Press.

Hartman, S. V. (1996). Seduction and the ruses of power. *Callaloo, 19*(2), 537–560.

Holloway, S., & Valentine, G. (2001). Making an argument: Writing up in human geography projects. *Journal of Geography in Higher Education, 25*(1), 127–132.

Ingram, P. (2001). Racializing Babylon: Settler whiteness and the "new racism." *New Literary History, 32* (1), 157–176.

Ingram, G.B., Bouthillette, A.M. & Retter, Y. (Eds.). (1997) *Queers in space: Communities/public spaces/sites of resistance*. Seattle: Bay Press.

Kruger, L. J. (Ed.). (2000). *Computers in the delivery of special education and related services: Developing collaborative and individualized learning environments*. New York: Haworth Press.

Latham, R., & Sassen, S. (2005). Digital formations: Constructing an object of study. In R. Latham and S. Sassen (Eds.), *Digital formations: Information technology and new architectures in the global realm* (pp. 1–51). Princeton, NJ: Princeton Press.

Latin Wives, Inc. (n.d.) "Latin wives: Meet the most beautiful Latin women in the world." Retrieved August 31, 2008 from http://www.latinwives.com

Madge, C., & O'Connor, H. (2006). Parenting gone wired: Empowerment of new mothers on the internet? *Social & Cultural Geography, 7*, 199.

Maleno, H., & Muñoz, A. (2003). [Review of the motion picture Frontera Sur]. Retrieved June 21, 2006, from http://www.geobodies.org/fronterasur/Alex_video.html

Moldova Cupid. (n.d.). Retrieved June 30, 2007 from http://www.moldovacupid.com

Mullings, B. (2000). Fantasy tours: exploring the global consumption of Caribbean sex tourisms. In Gottdiener, M. (Ed.), *New forms of consumption: Consumers, culture, and commodification* (pp. 227–250). Lanham, MD: Rowman and Littlefield.

Nodia, G. (n.d.). Humanism and freedom. In P. Peachey, J. Kromkowski, & G. F. McLean (Eds.), *Cultural heritage and contemporary life. Series I: Culture and values, 6.* Retrieved June 7, 2007, from http://www.crvp.org/book/Series01/I-6/contents.htm

Razack, S. (2004). *Dark threats and white knights: The Somalia affair, peacekeeping and the new imperialism.* Toronto: University of Toronto Press.

Reed, H. (1996). Close encounters in the liminal zone: Experiments in imaginal communication part I. *Journal of Analytical Psychology, 41*(1), 81–116.

Said, E. (1979). *Orientalism.* New York: Vintage Books.

Sassen, S. (2002). Digitization: Its variability as a variable in the reshaping of cross-border relations. Retrieved August 15, 2006, from http://www.csrc.lse.ac.uk/events/SSIT2/sassen.pdf

Sayer, K. (2002). Cyberspace as a psychological space. *Yeni Symposium, 40,* 60–67.

Spanos, W. V. (1998). Althusser's "problematic" in the context of the Vietnam War: Towards a spectral politics. *Rethinking Marxism, 10,* 1–21.

Spanos, W. V. (2003). A rumor of war: 9/11 and the forgetting of the Vietnam War. *Boundary, 30,* 29–66.

Sussman, N. M., & Tyson, D. H. (2000). Sex and power: Gender differences in computer-mediated interactions. *Computers in Human Behavior, 16,* 381–394.

Szeman, I. (2002). Remote sensing: An interview with Ursula Biemann. *Review of Education, Pedagogy, and Cultural Studies, 24,* 91–109.

Thrift, N., & Dewsbury, J. D. (2000). Dead geographies—and how to make them live. *Environment and Planning D: Society and Space, 18,* 411–432.

Travers, A. (2003). Parallel subaltern feminist counterpublics in cyberspace. *Sociological Perspectives, 46,* 223–237.

Turner, V. (1967). *The forest of symbols: Aspects of Ndembu ritual.* Ithaca, NY: Cornell University Press.

Ukrainian & Russian Women Marriage Agency. (n.d.). Retrieved February 14, 2006, from http://www.athenaagency.com

Vannini, P. (n.d.). Adorno's legacy: On critical theory, cultural studies, and the global political economy of Britney Spears Inc. Retrieved February 24, 2006, from http://www.gseis.ucla.edu/faculty/kellner/Illumina%20Folder/adornolegacy.htm

White, M. A. (2005). *Bordering loss and forgetting: Re-securing "Canada" post 9-11.* Unpublished master's thesis, York University, Graduate Program in Women's Studies, Toronto, Canada.

A Volga Girl. (n.d.). Retrieved August 31, 2008 from http://www.volgagirl.com

Your Tango Wire Dating. (n.d.). "Your interracial dating site: Discover your interracial love connection." Retrieved August 31, 2008 from http://www.your-
  tangowiredating.com/html/your-interracial-dating-site.html
Yurchisin, J., Watchravesringkan, K., & McCabe, D. (2005). An exploration of dating in the context of internet dating. *Social Behavior and Personality, 33*(8),
  735–750.

Section III

Particular Cultural Combinations

8

Russian–American Marriages
Cultures and Conflicts

Lynn Visson

Historical Background

Prior to perestroika and the collapse of the Soviet Union, Russian–American contacts in general, and marriages in particular, were a risky business, subject to the fluctuations of the political barometer and whims of bureaucrats on both sides of the ocean. The socialist idealists, children of Russian Jewish émigrés, black American Communists, and ordinary Americans who flocked to Russia in the 1920s and early 1930s wanting to build utopia ended up marrying Russians, as did many of the American journalists posted to Moscow. Getting an exit visa for the Russian spouse was far from easy, and many couples suffered from surveillance, harassment, and years of separation. Moreover, getting an exit visa did not guarantee living happily ever after. Not all of the American spouses were permitted to reside permanently in Russia, and many of those who did were forced to renounce their U.S. citizenship and to live in conditions worlds away from those experienced by Americans living with Russian mates in Russia today. The purges at the end of the 1930s and the postwar freeze in Soviet–American relations discouraged Russian–American marriages, and the law of 1947 forbidding Soviet citizens to marry foreigners formalized this situation, though a few exceptions were made and the law was eventually repealed in 1953.

World War II resulted in a mass displacement of Russians, many of whom went to America. Misconceptions and stereotypes about the "enemy," however, were rife on both sides of the ocean during the Cold War period. The Russian Jewish emigration that began in the 1970s also led to numerous Russian–American marriages. In the 1960s and 1970s the gradual opening up of Russian society led to a wave of student, cultural, and business exchanges resulting in more mixed marriages. With the collapse of the Soviet Union and the easing of travel restrictions, ever more Russians and Americans have found love and marriage on opposite sides of the Atlantic. American and Russian diplomats, journalists, performers, teachers, students, scientists, athletes, businessmen, and tourists have acquired spouses from each others' countries. Many of the American partners had a deep interest in Russia, and some had roots there or in Eastern Europe; quite a few spoke the language. The rapid development of cultural and commercial ties has also fostered the growth of a large group of American expatriates who have dated and married Russians.

What attracted these Russians and Americans to each other and contributed to the decision to spend their lives with a person from a totally different culture? Many couples, such as the American dancer Isadora Duncan and the Russian poet Sergei Esenin, or the businessman Armand Hammer and his Russian wife Olga, claimed that they were instantly attracted to their future partner, as though hit by lightning. In the 1930s Zara Witkin, an American engineer who had passionate romances with a Russian screen actress and several other Russian women, wrote to his mother that: "The deep, vital, emotional understanding of life of Russian women, and their warm, natural character results in a stronger, more joyous, more interesting relationship than is known in Anglo-Saxon society" (Witkin, 1991, pp. 302–303). Margaret Wettlin, a young American idealist from Philadelphia who went to Russia in 1932, wrote of her husband, the theater director Andrei Efremov, that "It was a compulsion with him, a desire to punctuate life's prose with exclamation marks" (Wettlin, 1992, p. 72).

Some highly practical factors, however, have also played a role in the attraction between Russians and Americans. For Russians, a relationship with an American has always meant access to both privilege and passports. In the 1960s and 1970s Americans were treated as millionaires by Russians who wanted food from the hard currency shops, jazz records, Western books, panty hose, shortwave radios, tape recorders—the list was endless.

The revolution of 1917, civil war, collectivization, famine, and World War II led to a demographic skew in which Russian women considerably outnumbered men. Because compulsory military service and access to classified information made it difficult for Russian men to obtain exit visas, it was the women who tended to be more aggressive in starting relationships with foreigners when Russia began opening up in the 1960s. In the 1980s there was no dearth of Russians looking for visitors with whom to practice their English and perhaps form a stronger bond, and in the 1990s Russian girls and older women, too, flocked to sign up with international dating services and catalogues, openly advertising in the newspapers for American husbands. A new, enormous source for Russian–American marriages evolved through agency catalogues, Internet matchmaking services, and list servers for would-be spouses.

While marriages between American men and Russian women had been taking place for decades, emigration and perestroika led to an increasing number of unions of Russian men and American women. The reasons for mutual attraction, the kinds of people who sought a Russian or American spouse, the range of problems and conflicts confronting couples living in both the United States and Russia including relationships with friends, family, and child-raising, are all questions arising in the study of Russian–American marriages.

American Men Seek Russian Brides

Over the last 10 years there has been a fantastic boom in agencies and services that bring together lonely American men and stunning young Russian women. The successes and failures of dozens of couples who met through agencies have been splashed across the pages of serious newspapers and popular magazines and featured in television specials ranging from serious investigative studies to lurid exercises in sensationalism.

This boom in Russian–American dating services and in Internet-based agencies was a result both of post-perestroika freedom and a reaction to the drastic financial difficulties caused by the economic collapse, which has reduced almost half the Russian population to dire straits. Poverty, malnutrition, and poor health care endemic across the country have been especially hard on women and made the lure of the West particularly strong.

In a 1999 survey, over 42% of the Russian population declared that their material situation was bad or very bad. Women account for more than 70% of Russians who are unemployed (Goscilo, 1999). Rampant alcoholism and poor health care have resulted in a life expectancy of 57.4–59 years for men and 71 for women; since 1989 the suicide rate in Russia has risen by 60% (*Itogi*, October 10, 2002; *Kommersant*, June 24, 2000, online). Some 6 of every 10 marriages end in divorce, and Russian men do not willingly take on a wife with young children (Wines, 2000).

In this somber climate of social and economic decline, Russian women are complaining with increasing bitterness of the failure of Russian men to support their wives and children. Marriage to a foreigner, and the emigration that comes along with it, appears to provide Russian women with a way to get a responsible, sober husband and improve a terrible material situation.

"Russian men are drunkards, not physically fit, not very good sexually ... while Western men seem to be leaner, more responsible and fit," commented the head of the St. Petersburg Center for Gender Issues. American men are seen as particularly sensitive, sober, and caring (Bekker, 2000). The American men's ingenuous charm and politeness make Russian women, both those who met them through the Internet and through regular channels, feel that these Yankees are "real men" rather than "mama's boys" or "drunken boors." And the American willingness to help around the house is a magnet for women in a country where most men will not lift a finger to wash a dish or help with a child.

In the United States the custom of "mail-order brides" goes back to frontier days when men out West corresponded with women back east in the hope that they would come out to join them. Within the last 10 years more than 75,000 Russian women are believed to have come to the United States on so-called fiancée visas, a 90-day visa during the course of which period the couple is required to marry or the woman must return to her home country. An equal number are believed to have entered on other types of visas but with the same purpose (Konygina, 2003; Smotrov, 2003). According to agency claims, the majority of Russian women seeking husbands abroad are between 18 and 30, almost all with higher education; about half are divorcees and about a third have a child. In the United States, most of the men who sign up for tours to Russia sponsored by agencies such as European Connections are between 30 and 55 (the bulk of them are about 41 or 42), both bachelors and divorced, nearly a third with a child. On one trip the oldest participant was 74 and the youngest 27. This pool of potential husbands is likely to keep growing; according to the U.S. Census Bureau, from 1980 to 2000, the percentage of 35- to 44-year-old bachelors almost tripled (Coleman, 1999; Jeffrey, 2001). Since the average age of Russian women is 29, there is approximately a 13-year age difference for many couples.

Many Web sites and agencies offer a mail-order bride industry, politely known as international correspondence services, which provide brochures containing photos and descriptions of the women and supply their regular and e-mail addresses. Russian women pay a small fee to a local Russian agency for these listings, while American men pay for the address for each woman they select. Most agencies have a minimum age requirement of 18 for girls who wish to sign up, but older women, too, are seeking American spouses. Some agencies have special catalogues and listings for women over 50.

About 600 marriage Internet agencies in the United States and about 400–500 in Russia are servicing the would-be American spouses with candidates from the former Soviet Union (Filatova, 2002; Konygina, 2003; Smotrov, 2003). The large agencies, such as European Connections, Anastasia, Foreign Relations, A Foreign Affair, Russian Connections, Scanna International, and Elite Matchmaking vie with each other and with a host of other Web sites for clients. Their glossy brochures feature slick videos and colorful catalogues with photos and bios of hundreds of girls. The larger firms also sponsor tours to Russia so that the American men can meet the girls with whom they have been corresponding, as well as a host of new women, and offer searches by height, weight, hair and eye color, as well as age and interests. Most of the agencies provide for contact by fax, e-mail, and phone before the American leaves for Russia; the Immigration and Naturalization Service requires all international couples applying for fiancée visas to have met the potential spouse at least once (Scholes, 1998). One of the biggest of these agencies, European Connections, claims a catalogue readership of over 70,000 men and a file of some 7,000 Russian women (Art Steckel, Director, European Connections, telephone interview, July 9, 1998).

These women, who run the gamut from those who have "been around," to naïve eager beavers from the provinces, to desperate older women, are taking a calculated decision—involving huge risks—to give up their country, family, and friends in the search for a better life abroad for themselves and often for their children.

In researching Russian–American marriages, I have interviewed, talked to, and corresponded with more than 100 Americans who sought to marry Russian women and the girls seeking to become their brides. For the most part, the men are educated WASP professionals in their 30s and 40s. Many are computer and software experts earning more than $20,000 a year who have spent a great deal of time and energy "making it" in their fields and woke up one day to decide it was time to "have a family" (Visson, 2001b). Quite a few of those who have been previously married do not want to try again with an American woman, for reasons that are now explored.

When American men visit Russia, a week-long tour includes "socials," huge parties during which the 40-odd goggle-eyed clients may meet between 600 and 800 Russian women (including those with whom they have corresponded, faces they have picked out of catalogues, and brand new girls they do not know). The bill may run anywhere from $3,000 to $10,000. Many of the travelers, however, are overjoyed by these gatherings.

> "Walking into a room full of women in various stages of desperation to get out of their home country," said one American participant, "with a female/male ratio of 40:1—possibly carrying a diamond ring and looking like a famine victim walking into a buffet—sounds a bit like the Russian roulette scene from *The Deer Hunter*. It's Disneyland, guys, nothing more" [Steve]. (Anonymous, 2000)

What is the success rate for these agency-brokered marriages? Since there are no general statistics covering all the agencies engaged in this enterprise, it is extremely difficult to come to definite conclusions. The only available figures come from the agencies, which are naturally interested in claiming as high a success rate as possible. And since the firms are a relatively recent phenomenon, most of the couples have not been married for all that long. Art Steckel, the codirector of European Connections, claims that 75% of the 2,000 men who have gone on his agency's tour since 1992 invite a girl to the United States on a fiancée visa, that half of these men marry women (A. Steckel, telephone interview, July 9, 1998). While it is difficult to generalize, roughly some 10–40% of the Russian female clients of these agencies and dating services seem ultimately to have married Americans. Although articles in the Russian press have recently been claiming that after 2 years of marriage—when the Russian woman can receive her green card and get off immigration parole status—some 90% of these marriages end in wife-initiated divorce, there are no hard statistics to back these assertions (Filatova, 2002; Konygina, 2003).

The boom in Internet and marriage agency marriages between Russian women and American men has resulted in many Americans automatically associating all Russian–American marriages with such unions. Yet today hundreds of Americans and Russians are still meeting through normal channels such as work, leisure activities, mutual friends, travel, and international conferences and are living happily in the United States and in Russia. No matter how they met, all of these couples are confronted by the same cultural differences and traits of national character.

American Men and Russian Women

Regardless of where they meet, what is it that attracts American men to Russian women? The answer repeatedly boils down to one word: "femininity." There seems to be a widespread feeling among the men in question that the feminist movement has gone too far in depriving American women of those qualities that make them most attractive to men. Dozens of American men and Russian women I interviewed said the following: Russian women are beautiful, well groomed and well dressed, bright, educated, want to be wives and mothers, enjoy being women, and make a man feel that he is at the center of the universe.

"Russian women are simply better at being women than American women," said one American man seeking a Russian wife (Coleman, 1999, p. 15). "American women are reputed to be the worst possible mates on this planet," wrote another (Coleman, 1999, p. 12). "What seems to unite the men," wrote a reporter from the *Philadelphia Inquirer* (Drake, 1998, p. F1), who had gone to Russia with a European Connections tour, "was a strong conviction that American women were materialistic and had been corrupted by feminism. They saw themselves as victims." What they wanted was "femininity," not "feminism." Many of these men had had former wives or girlfriends who neglected their personal appearance, put their own interests and careers above those of the man, and complained that his earnings were insufficient.

Russian women who do not want to work, are eager to be housewives and mothers, and are free from the desire for total equality with men that characterizes so many American women are extremely attractive to such American men. Despite the changes wrought by perestroika, Russian women do not generally accept the notion of full gender equality or the need for women to do—or to have the opportunity to do—everything men do. The concept of feminism in Russia is quite different from the American idea of equality of opportunity, access to resources, and protection under the law across sex. "In Russian, the word feministka is pejorative, meaning a bossy man-hater," commented the Russian journalist Elena Khanga (1991, p. A19). A young woman television station director declared that "When I think of feminists, I think of a big-size, masculine lady trying to fight someone and I don't ever want to be that way" (Schillinger, 1995, p. 40). And the well-known Russian writer Tatyana Tolstaya commented that while American feminists were fighting for the right to work in coal mines, their Russian counterparts were fighting for the right not to do so (Gray, 1989).

The negative reactions of Americans and Russians to certain types of behavior in their own cultures foster their attraction to each other. Harvey Balzer, the director of Georgetown University's Russian Area Program, commented that "American men are somewhat sick of emancipated women, and Russian women are somewhat sick of domestic dictators. You've got this funny situation where the American man is looking for an unliberated woman, and the Russian woman is looking for a slightly more liberated man" (Sullivan, 1994, p. A10).

Or, as one American posted to an online list server, "It's not about the short skirts or pretty faces. It comes down to one simple thing: practically all Russian women say, 'I want a man. I need a man.' Practically all American women will not. Of course Russian women are more feminine!" (Robert) (Anonymous, 2001). Another commented, "A feminine woman does not regard men as 'potential oppressors of womankind.' A feminine woman is comfortable around men. She does not consider that traditional gestures such as opening doors, offering to help her with heavy things, etc. are anything else but expressions of solicitude and respect." (Stelios) (Anonymous, 2001).

Fueled by illusions and failed expectations, however, disappointment can set in quickly. All too often the Russian girls fail to understand that a $20,000 car and a $100,000 house are by no means proof that the man is a millionaire. "I thought he lived in a beautiful house," said one young woman of her husband. "It was a mobile home." The man's "business" may turn out to be a single computer in the basement. An American man is taking a considerable risk when he decides to marry someone who does not speak English well; is isolated from her family, friends, and profession; and may be from a completely different social background. Gradually, the realization can dawn that the two do not share basic values or are from totally different worlds and social environments. And many American men have discovered that under that feminine, well-groomed exterior lies an iron will. "Russian women can be very, very stubborn, and very, very demanding," wrote one man (Coleman, 1999, p. 155). They are "soft beautiful velvet over sharp steel," another commented (Anonymous, 2003).

American men are often surprised by Russian women's penchant for strong emotions and strong opinions. "She doesn't just have a headache—her head is splitting," said one American husband. "The slightest problem immediately becomes a tragedy," said another. "She's always interrupting me, straightening my tie, telling me what to wear." The women may be feminine, but they are strong-minded—sometimes too much so for some American men. "The less macho guys, the ones beaten down by feminism are too weak for these Russian women," said one American who had a stormy relationship with his Russian fiancée. These women may be much more stubborn and strong-minded than their husbands, for they are used to weak men—often raised without fathers—who were catered to by their mothers and expected the same kind of smothering attention from their wives.

Disappointments and Disasters

Russian women may discover that, despite material benefits, life in the United States can be filled with disappointment, loneliness, and isolation. Most young Russian women do not know how to drive, a key to basic survival in much of America, particularly in the suburbs. Without a car she may risk going crazy from loneliness in a "gilded cage" equipped with a state-of-the-art freezer, dishwasher, washing machine, VCR, and other appliances she may not have enjoyed in Russia. But there she was free to wander the streets on her own.

And she is often living with a man she barely knows and who has a completely different mindset. "The material conditions were very nice, but everyone is lonely," remarked a 25-year-old Russian woman who left her American husband and went back to Russia. "Americans are good husbands and caring fathers, they don't play the field and don't drink. But it's hard to live with them because of their different mentality" (Merkulova, 1999, p. 3). Many women complained that their American husbands were emotionally distant, shallow, interested only in money, had limited cultural horizons, and knew little or nothing about Russia or the other countries of the former Soviet Union. They were also surprised by the apparent "superficiality" of their husbands' male friendships and by their "casual" or "loose" relationships with parents, siblings, and other relatives as compared to the traditionally close Russian ties with family and friends.

An American husband may suddenly find himself thrust into a series of roles, including being an "all provider," tour guide, and language teacher, as well as a husband and often stepfather. One man sent the following post to the Russian Women's List, an Internet server with more than 1,200 members:

It seems that many men go to Russia looking for a combination Carol Brady/ June Cleaver/Joan Collins, but are surprised when they bring a woman here and she tries to adapt to the new culture. Yes, you will be spending more time with her. You will not be able to go golfing every weekend. You will be spending a lot more money than you do now. You will be expected to change your life style. You will be compromising [BJakman]. (Anonymous, 2000)

The worst-case scenarios go beyond disappointment and dashed expectations to include cases of spousal abuse, with the woman winding up abused, alone, and frightened in a country where she has no one on whom to fall back. Though there are no specific statistics for Russian–American marriages that end in this way, given the huge numbers of these couples, there appear to be relatively few such relationships.

Some of the more lurid cases, however, such as that of 63-year-old Maple Hughes, whose marriage to a Ukrainian girl some 40 years his junior and his move to Odessa with her ended with his sudden death in mysterious circumstances, allegedly at the hands of his Russian wife and her young Russian lover, have received wide media coverage. There was an American from Seattle who married three women, a California wife-beater who was shot by the police when he threatened them, and Anastasia Solovieva King from Kyrgyzstan, brutally murdered by her American husband (Palchikoff, 2003).

In recent years human rights organizations such as the Global Survival Network have been actively trying to protect foreign brides, including Russians, from fraud and abuse. A 1996 law requires agencies to inform women they recruit about the consequences of marriage fraud and domestic violence or risk $20,000 fines. This innovation, however, can be used for dishonest purposes. Since battered immigrant women can petition for permanent residency on their own, without their husbands, a woman can falsely claim spousal abuse, abandon her husband, obtain a green card, and set off on her own in search of a "better" spouse.

While the matchmaking firms vaunt success stories, they do not have the means to properly screen their male clients for criminal records or mental illness. A Russian woman's criminal record is indicated on her record of workplaces (*trudovaia knizhka*), but current U.S. fiancée visa regulations require only foreign-born applicants, not the American sponsor, to provide criminal history information to the INS (Scholes, 1998). Unfortunately, it is the isolated instances of violence that receive broad media coverage; the hundreds of happy marriages do not make for exciting news.

American Husbands and Russian Wives

A few stories of couples who met and married through dating agencies or the Internet may provide a closer look at the problems they have faced and how they have coped.

> "Thursday is our fourth anniversary," wrote one man about his Internet bride. "Still ecstatically happy, very much interested and comfortable with each other, in all aspects from the most intimate to the most public. From socializing to being just the two of us, it just doesn't get any better than this (Stelios). (Anonymous, 2003)

A 35-year-old kindergarten teacher in Kharkov with a 14-year-old daughter from an unhappy first marriage, Masha decided to post her photo and bio on the Internet. When Paul began to write, she was won over. "He was so kind. I didn't need much English to understand that." Paul was a 40-year-old math teacher in an Indiana suburb, also divorced and with a daughter, but he did not see the child often; and when he arrived in Kharkov he was much taken with Masha and delighted to find in Masha's daughter, Dasha, the studious, talented child he had never had. Once Masha and Dasha had arrived in Indiana, however, the couple's problems began. Lonely and depressed, Masha took out her moods on him, and her poor English led to misunderstandings. She admits that, "I was used to the old Russian idea of the wife. You know—tears, screams and wave the rolling pin around as you smash the plates on the floor." She felt guilty about arriving with no money and being dependent on him for everything. The only way she could express her feelings and frustrations was through emotional outbursts.

Yet she was pleased with Paul's attentiveness and patience. Masha's Russian husband used to get drunk every night. "When we arrived at Paul's house and he got himself a glass of orange juice and poured in some vodka, I thought, 'Oh my God, I've done it again.' I'd never seen a man have just one drink and stop. But he was so considerate of my feelings about alcohol, and my panic over it, that he gave up his daily cocktail. That really touched me." Both are sure they will stay together. "I know," she says, "that he loves me more than I deserve."

Edward, 48, a divorced software specialist, decided he wanted a Russian woman in her 30s, with strong values, preferably with a child. He set about studying Russian and made several trips to Russia until he met Irina, a native of St. Petersburg, who was the right age, strong-minded, with a Ph.D. in chemistry, somewhat shaky English, and a little boy.

They got married and John is quite content with Irina's kind of strength. "There's quite a difference between a suburban American woman who prides herself on being aggressive and a Russian woman who is polite, well-mannered—and truly assertive when she needs to be," he said. "She sees our relationship as a partnership, not as a power struggle."

Of course, it was not all easy going. "Anyone who says the first year of marriage to a Russian woman isn't difficult is lying through his teeth," he commented. In the beginning Irina was going stir-crazy in their Denver home while John put in long hours at work. But then she learned how to drive, acquired a better knowledge of English, arranged for daycare for little Vanya, and took a job as a restaurant hostess—at which she did so well that she was promoted to manager. Today she is looking for a laboratory job in her specialty, chemistry.

The experiences of the Russian–American couples who have met and married through the agencies and the Internet run the gamut from debacle to bliss. For a woman who leaves family and friends and is dependent for money, support, and warmth on a stranger in a strange land; for a man who after some 5 days of meetings convinces himself that a younger woman living in poverty is in love with him, the hazards are immense. Nor do the 90 days granted by the visa provide much time for making a final decision to marry.

It is hard enough in one's own culture to make the right choice of the person with whom to spend one's life and raise a family. In a foreign country, without a common language, and without knowledge of the culture and all the cues and gestures that provide insight into an individual's background, education, and social status, such a decision becomes even more difficult.

There are, however, dozens of Americans who have been living for years with their Russian wives whom they met through shared interests and normal channels. Many couples met on U.S.–USSR academic exchanges. Harris and Svetlana Sussman met when she was an administrator and translator at a conference he attended in St. Petersburg; Olga Zatsepina and Julio Rodriguez met through university conferences in Moscow. Maryna, a translator, met her publisher husband Joseph through a correspondence and a shared love for history. "We continue sharing our love for books, arts and words and enjoying the happy companionship of each other in daily life" (e-mail to author, November 1, 2003), she notes. One Slavist who came to Moscow decided to stay there and marry a Russian. As the title of a Russian newspaper article stated, "He doesn't need an American wife" (Karelina, 2000, p. 24).

Russian Husbands and American Wives

It is clear why American men are attracted to Russian women, but aside from the promise of a comfortable life in the United States, what do Russian men see in American women? A recent joke in a Russian magazine stated that "Heaven is an American salary, a Russian wife, an English house and Chinese food. A Chinese house, English food, an American wife and a Russian salary—that's hell" (*Itogi*, December 23, 2003, p. 3). Yet quite a few Russian men have opted for American spouses. For one thing, they are looking for women who are open, straightforward, independent, do not treat them as children, have plenty of energy, and are still going strong at the end of the workday, characteristics that they associate with American women. "She knows how to amuse herself in her spare time," said Helen's husband Pavel. "She doesn't constantly need me for company." The Russians appreciated the directness of their spouses and their involvement in all aspects of their lives. "Gina isn't just my wife—she's also my best friend," said Alex, a young Russian artist.

On the other hand, several of the Russian men I interviewed complained about their wives' lack of attention to good grooming, that they would neglect their hair and nails or fail to sew a missing button on a coat. There were also complaints regarding "American individualism." "Joan says 'I' a lot more than she says 'we,'" said one young husband. "Even though all of her behavior shows that she loves me, sometimes I feel as though I'm a part—although a big part—of her 'personal development plan.'" For Russians raised during the Soviet era when the "collective spirit" dominated the entire society, such "individualism" is hard to fathom.

American women who are partnered with Russian men see them as handsome, romantic, strong, and self-confident. Unscathed by American feminism, the men still open doors, hold coats, pay a woman compliments, pick up her check in a restaurant, and feel that it is their role to take care of the "weaker sex" (Baskina, 1994). Russian men are viewed as more sexually, intellectually, and emotionally confident, not "looking for their identity" or trying to decide which sex they prefer to sleep with. "I had dated American men who were 30 and did not have even half his maturity," Anne wrote of her 23-year-old Russian husband. "He is so grown up and smart it is unbelievable; I guess that may be a cultural difference between Russian and American men" (e-mail to author, September 30, 2002). One young American woman was pleased that her Russian husband did not indulge in the "psychobabble" about feelings and relationships so widespread among Americans. "He constantly shows me that he loves me, and he's very sensitive to my feelings," she wrote. "Was I just being 'American' when I expected him to give a list of reasons? He didn't even seem to know that I was expecting it" (e-mail to author, September 30, 2002). Many American women observed that Russian men showed their love and feelings, rather than discussing them the way Americans did. They also appreciated the way Russians made love without the constant chatter that characterizes so many Americans' behavior in bed. "One simple word—passion," said Julie, describing her Russian husband. "These men are free from psychobabble, they're stronger than American men, and yet they have a more feminine side. They know what they want. They put up with what life gives."

On the other hand, Russian men are not accustomed to doing housework, dishes, or helping out with children. "Misha had never washed a dish before he married me," said Laura. "Why? Because his mother did everything for him. Now he's finally starting to participate in doing household chores." Quite a few Russian husbands find that shouldering a fair share of responsibilities at home comes with an independent American wife who, as opposed to Russian women, does not run the household single-handed the way a "bossy Russian woman," namely, mama, did or go to the opposite extreme of "clinging" to her husband like a helpless little girl without taking a single initiative of her own.

Whether male or female, Russian partners' sense of self as part of a collective of family and friends is still generally much stronger than that of the American spouses, a sense fostered both by Russian tradition and by the "collective spirit" imposed from above by the Soviet authorities for decades. During the years when people were forced to rely on each other for all kinds of scarce consumer good and services and joined together to cope with an all-powerful totalitarian system, the network of family, friends, and acquaintances was of vital importance for survival. "What I like so much about Moscow," said a young American woman who has been living there with her Russian husband for several years, "is that I feel a part of a group. I know all the neighbors; there's always someone to talk to or to watch our son. And I've never had the kind of friends in America I have here."

Different Types of Couples

While even those partners in Russian–American mixed marriages who have a good knowledge of both Russian and English encounter numerous problems in the course of their adaptation to their spouse and to his or her country, many of the couples living in Russia have had an easier time than their counterparts in America. The American expatriates tend to be less nostalgic for home and have more realistic expectations of life in Russia than is the case for Russians living in America. In the preperestroika years they were also generally better informed about Russian life than were the Russian spouses about life in America. And in such marriages there was no question of the American marrying only to obtain a Russian passport or citizenship.

Like all partners in intercultural marriages, Russian–American couples tend to fall into several broad categories (Klimek, 1979; Romano, 1988; Tseng, McDermott, Maretzki, & Jones, 1977). There are those unable to find a place in their own society, seeking a niche elsewhere and a mate who is unaware of the extent of their alienation. Other individuals feel that they have found their roots in another society. Some Americans whose Russian roots go back several generations, as well as children of Russian immigrants who never truly adapted to American society, have chosen to marry Russians. "It was just like my grandmother's kitchen," an American Jewish girl with Russian grandparents said of the home of her Russian émigré fiancé (Aspaklaria, 1985, p. C14; Brady, 1996, p. 39). Even people who do not have roots in a country may fall in love with its culture—or, more specifically, with a representative of that culture.

Shy, physically unattractive people, social misfits, and products of unhappy or broken homes may also be attracted to foreign spouses. Lee Harvey Oswald and Marina Prusakova were both raised without fathers and had difficult childhoods. A relatively homely U.S. citizen quickly discovers that an American passport makes him vastly more popular in Russia than in the United States. Intercultural couples often feel they are unique and different from their compatriots; hooking up with a foreign partner may demonstrate rejection of the values of parents, peers, and American society.

When dealing with a foreign culture, it is often extremely difficult—even for people with a good knowledge of the language—to correctly understand verbal cues, cultural symbols, intonation, and body language. A wrong reading can lead to disaster. One young American woman described her Russian husband to a girlfriend as "a lyric poet with a sensitive soul." She had been utterly won over by moonlit walks along the Neva riverbanks and his guitar renditions of popular ballads. The "poet," however, turned out to be a smalltime black marketeer. The marriage lasted 6 months.

Causes of Conflict

It is all too easy to write off a partner's behavior as the product of a culture, explained away as "he's Russian," or "she's American." Factors such as social status, education, religion, and urban vs. rural upbringing often play as important a role as nationality. And many personal traits may have very little to do with national character, traditions, or customs. Distinguishing personal from cultural behavioral factors can be agonizingly difficult for the partners. "I never know if Pavel is doing something because he's Pavel or because he's Russian," Helen complained. "Is he always late because he's a perfectionist and never finishes anything on time, or because millions of Russians used to rebel against an authoritarian system by showing up late for anything and everything?"

Many areas provide fertile ground for cross-cultural conflict, and attitudes toward money are a major one. Some Russian women who had lived in dire economic straits arrive in the United States expecting diamond rings and a mink coat, while others immediately transfer their frugal habits to their new American life. "In Russia she had to live on less than $100 a month," said Sam of his new Russian wife. He had been used to running up large debts and maxing out credit cards. "We have compromised. I have become better at managing money, and she's gotten a little looser" (e-mail to author, February 5, 2000). Most Russians have never seen a checkbook, as cash is used for almost all daily transactions and paying bills. Unfamiliar with the concept of a budget, many Russians do not understand the reasons for having a savings account. In Russia, if you had money, you spent it. The collapse of the Russian banking system at the end of the 1990s did not foster faith in savings institutions. And Russian women are shocked by the American custom of going Dutch in restaurants. "I wrote Bill off the first time he suggested splitting a check," said one young woman. To a Russian, if a man does not want to foot the bill that means only one thing—that he is stingy, a cardinal sin in Russian thinking (Levintov, 2003).

Friends and Family

Attitudes toward friends and family are another area in which the two cultures differ. Almost all Russians married to Americans say they miss their friends and the kind of close friendships they had in Russia. "Mark calls Jack his friend," Svetlana said, "but all they do is play golf once a month. In Russia a friend is someone you talk to. And talk and talk and talk." American spouses living in Russia often say they have trouble with the kind of all-consuming demands on one's time required by Russian friendship—the willingness to drop everything if a friend needs a sympathetic ear.

In Russia it is considered quite normal if a grown man calls his mother every day. But, as one American put it, "I love my mother, but if I called her every day she'd think I was in real trouble" (Visson, 2001a, p. 45). Russian parent–children ties are frequently far closer and last farther into adulthood than is the case in America. "My husband's parents immediately treated me as though I'd always been part of the family," remarked Jane, who is married to a Russian artist (e-mail to author, April 23, 2001). Many American women complain of a Russian mother-in-law who is an "active party" to their cross-cultural marriages and whose word on how to bring up children may be taken as final (Visson, 2001a). "I was really alarmed that Igor's mother simply took it for granted that she would be taking care of our son, Adam. There was absolutely no discussion of hiring a nyanya (nurse)," said Helen, a young woman living with her family in Moscow. "It was assumed that it was the grandmother's God-given right and duty to raise him" (Visson, 2001a, p. 46).

Child-raising is a minefield for potential conflict, for here cultural misunderstandings abound and passions run high. Both Russians and Americans tend to imitate—or to react against—the way their parents raised them. Attempts by the foreign spouse to impose different values or disciplines on the child can be deeply resented, particularly when stepchildren are involved. American children are taught to share and to compromise; Russian boys from an early age are taught to defend themselves and hit back. A Russian child is swaddled in layers of clothing because of the icy winters; American children are used to running around barefoot and without hats in the warmer climates that prevail in much of the United States.

While Russians tend to cling to children as long as possible, trying to protect them from the real or perceived dangers of the outside world, Americans raise their children to leave home and be independent, often at the age of 18 when they go off to college. The Russian family reveals the full extent of that society's deep-rooted collective spirit. "I find the Russians much more capable of being team players than most Americans could ever be," said Edward. "I see it in my wife's family and in many other Russian families. The Russians all rely on each other" (Visson, 2001a, p. 48). The American emphasis is on independence, on the child's achieving his own space, friends, and lifestyle, while for the Russians, as one American put it, "Safety means the home; the idea is not to shove the children outside the nest but to keep them there" (Visson, 2001a, p. 48).

And then there is the problem of language and culture. It is hard enough to speak a foreign language 24 hours a day with a husband or wife—let alone with one's own child. Will the children speak Russian, English, or both? Will they turn out bicultural as well as bilingual? To see that they do so, many couples make a conscious effort to spend time in both countries. Anna, a Russian bibliographer married to an American university professor, commented that their 5-year-old son, who spoke both languages, was clearly making a distinction between Russian and English. Commenting on several dogs barking outside, the boy remarked that "some dogs bark in English and other dogs bark in Russian" (Visson, 2001a, p. 50). To keep up with Russian language and culture, one mixed couple take their daughter every summer to visit family and friends back home. "Dasha's always a bit quiet the first few days after she returns to the United States, said her Russian mother, Asele. "But then she says, 'Let's speak English because Barney does'" (Visson, 2001a, p. 50). Most couples find, however, that the language and culture of the country in which they reside tends to dominate the child's linguistic fluency and overall way of thinking.

"I think that being brought up in an atmosphere of divergent cultures will make my daughter a better person in the long run," said Ellen, who is married to an American and living in Moscow. "She's used to people disagreeing, to seeing that each culture has good and bad points, and to taking the good from them" (Visson, 2001a, p. 52). The ability to live and love in both cultures, a knowledge of both languages and cultures, respect for each other, and a well developed sense of humor seem to be among the keys to success for the rapidly growing number of Russian–American marriages.

References

Anonymous. (2003). Messages posted to St. John's Russian Women's List (RWL) electronic mailing list. Archived at http://www.maelstrom.stjohns.edu/archives/russian-women-l.html

Anonymous (BJakman). (2000). Message posted to St. John's Russian Women's List (RWL) electronic mailing list, archived at http://maelstrom.stjohns.edu/archives/russian-women-l.html

Anonymous (Robert). (2001). Message posted to St. John's Russian Women's List (RWL) electronic mailing list, archived at http://maelstrom.stjohns.edu/archives/russian-women-l.html

Anonymous (Stelios). (2001). Message posted to St. John's Russian Women's List (RWL) electronic mailing list, archived at http://maelstrom.stjohns.edu/archives/russian-women-l.html

Anonymous (Stelios). (2003). Message posted to St. John's Russian Women's List (RWL) electronic mailing list, archived at http://maelstrom.stjohns.edu/archives/russian-women-l.html

Anonymous (Steve). (2000). Message posted to St. John's Russian Women's List (RWL) electronic mailing list, archived at http://maelstrom.stjohns.edu/archives/russian- women-l.html

Aspaklaria, S. (1985, January 8). U.S.-Soviet couples: The emotional cost continues to surprise. *The New York Times*, p. C14.

Baskina, A. (1994, September 7). Amerikanskie zhenshchiny [American Women]. *Izvestiia*, p. 7.

Bekker, V. (2000, February 18). Lonesome men seek out local love. *St. Petersburg Times*, p. 5.

Brady, L. S. (1996, January 14). Vows: Laura Mason, Alexander Khutoretsky: Weddings. *The New York Times*, p. 39.

Coleman, F. (1999). *To Russia for love: The American man's best option*. Oklahoma City, Oklahoma: Red Star Publications.

Drake, D. (1998, December 1). Time to choose, in To Russia for love: An 8-part Serial. *The Philadelphia Inquirer*, p. F1.

Filatova, N. (2002, September 24). Uzh zamuzh za rubezh [So women are getting married abroad]. *Itogi*, p. 42.

Goscilo, H. (1999). Porn on the cob: Some hard core issues. In M. Levitt & L. A. Toporkov (Eds.), *Eros and pornography in Russian culture* (pp. 553–572). Moscow: Ladomir.

Gray, F. D. (1989). *Soviet women: Walking the tightrope*. New York: Doubleday.

Jeffrey, N. A. (2001, December 7). Marriage: The woman shortage. *The Wall Street Journal*, p. W.1.

Karelina, M. (2000, November 25–26). Emu ne nuzhna amerikanskaia zhena [He doesn't need an American wife]. *Novoye Russkoye Slovo*, p. 24.

Khanga, E. (1991, November 25). No Matryoshkas need apply. *The New York Times*, p. A19.

Klimek, D. (1979). *Beneath mate selection and marriage: The unconscious motives behind human pairing*. New York: Van Nostrand Rheinhold.

Kommersant. (2000, June 24). http://www.kommersant.ru cited in Johnson's Russia List for 6/24/2000. Retrieved June 26, 2000, from http://www.cdi.org/russia/johnson/default/cfm/archive

Konygina, N. (2003, January 23). Zamuzh za inostrantsev vykhodiat ne iz-za deneg [Women don't marry foreigners for money], *Izvestiia*, p. 3.

Levintov, A. (2003, January 16). Brak bez sviazi [Marriage without connections]. *Izvestiia*, p. 12.

Merkulova, A. (1999). Zamuzh za inostrantsa? [Marriage to a foreigner?]. *Argumenty i fakty*, June 10, 1999, p. 3.

Palchikoff, K. (2001, February 4). "The U.S. is no dream for these brides." *The Seattle Times*. http://community.seattletimes.nwsource.com/archive/?date=20010204&slug=bride04m0

Romano, D. (1988). *Intercultural marriage: Promises and pitfalls*. Yarmouth, ME: Intercultural Press.

Schillinger, L. (1995, August 1). The Yupskies are coming. *New York Magazine*, pp. 34–40.

Scholes, R. (1998). *The mail-order bride industry and its impact on U.S. immigration*. Washington, DC: Immigration and Naturalization Service.

Smotrov, A. (2003). Russian brides invade America. RIA Novosti. Retrieved December 24, 2003, from http://www.en.rian.ru

Sullivan, K. (1994, May 24). A U.S.-Russian formula for true romance. *The Washington Post*, p. A10.

Tseng, W., McDermott, J. F., Jr., Maretzki, T. W., & Jones, G. (Eds.). (1977). *Adjustment in intercultural marriage*. Honolulu, HI: University of Hawaii.

Visson, L. (2001a, September/October). Bringing up Vanya Smith. *Russian Life*, 43–51.

Visson, L. (2001b). *Wedded strangers: The challenges of Russian-American marriages* (Expanded ed.). New York: Hippocrene Books.

Wettlin, M. (1992). *Fifty Russian winters: An American woman's life in the Soviet Union*. New York: Pharos Books.

Wines, M. (2000, January 28). For all Russia, biological clock is running out. *The New York Times*. Retrieved January 28, 2000, from Johnson's Russia List, http://www.cdi.org/russia/johnson/default/cfm/archive

Witkin, Z. (1991). *An American engineer in Stalin's Russia: The memoirs of Zara Witkin, 1932–1934*. Berkeley, CA: University of California Press.

9

Constructions of Difference Among Latino/Latina Immigrant and Non-Hispanic White Couples

Roxana Llerena-Quinn and Gonzalo Bacigalupe

There's something [uncle Elver] doesn't like about the news of a Peruvian husband: God made those people different. Not like us Anglican folk …

Being a yanqui doesn't make you better, - Tia Chaba sniffed. The norteamericanos have nothing over us. … (Arana, 2001, pp. 37, 123)

Though it took place more than 50 years ago, this dialogue still resonates with the dilemmas of intermarriage in today's industrialized world. Riding on a train, I [RLQ] overhear a middle-aged Spanish speaking woman telling another sitting next to her that she should discourage her son from dating an American woman. "They have another culture. They don't believe in family like we do." What differences are implied in this statement? What is the prevailing discourse about these differences and what dynamics result from them? Given the persistent trend of high rates of intermarriage among Latinos, are there alternative discourses of resiliency that can be learned from those who dare to go *contra la corriente*, against the current (Andrews, 2003; Bacigalupe, 2003)? In this chapter, we explore emergent themes in Latino–Anglo intermarriage regarding perceived intercultural differences. Intercultural differences are explored by looking at specific factors such as courtship patterns; ideas about family, language, and communications styles; and how couples make meaning about their differences. The values attributed to intercultural differences are often negotiated against the backdrop of the dominant culture and the current social and political contexts from which these differences emerge.

Many of the themes in this chapter were elicited in an exploratory fashion with a group of 20 individuals, some of whom were couples from a nonclinical, middle- and working-class population. More women than men (3 to 1 ratio) volunteered for individual interviews, and all the women were Latinas. The focus of the exploration was limited to heterosexual, first-generation Latino immigrants because of an expectation that the first generation would be the most different from non-Hispanic Whites. We invite readers to witness this piece of writing as an evolving inquiry. Our hope is to advance the integration of ideas and to create metaphors that support and allow emancipatory forms of living, moving beyond current stereotypical metaphors that construct intercultural couplehood as a problem requiring a solution.

Marrying a Latino or Latina in the United States

Since 1960 the number of interracial couples in the United States has increased more than tenfold to 1.6 million, including marriages involving Latinos (Harrison & Bennett, 1995; Waters, 2000). Though intermarriage has always existed, current growth patterns are attributed to the Civil Rights Movement, which promoted greater social interaction among all races and to the repeal of antimiscegenation laws in 1967 (Root, 2001). Such unions now account for about 4% of U.S. marriages, a share that is expected to increase in coming years (Fletcher, 1998; Smith & Edmonston, 1997; Waters, 2000). Despite this growth and the increased acceptance of intermarriage, there is evidence that negative attitudes toward mixed marriages still persist and that they are more pervasive among some groups (Rosenblatt, Karis, & Powell, 1995). A *Washington Post* poll taken during the summer of 1998 revealed that nearly one in four Americans still finds marriages between Blacks and Whites "unacceptable." Other polls have found people more tolerant of White marriages to Latinos and Asian Americans, a feeling shared by some Latinos and Asian Americans, who say they encounter far less resistance to relationships with Whites than to those with Blacks (Fletcher, 1998). These rates may be explained by the fact that nearly half of all Latinos self-identified as "White" in the 2000 Census (Guzman, 2001), possibly reducing the perceived social distance.[1] Paradoxically, in other U.S. public opinion polls, Latinos are ranked among the least favored of all new Americans (Cornelius, 2002). In sum, current responses toward mixed marriages continue to be ambivalent in the U.S. society across racial and ethnic groups.

Our society supports men and women who partner with those who are similar to themselves. The principle of homogamy, as the prevailing discourse about couples, fails to provide space for discussion of the unique challenges and issues heterogamous couples must face and negotiate in both private and public spaces (Killian, 2003). This invisibility adds a layer of burden for these couples, but most unfortunate is the missed opportunity to explore the possibilities embedded in their potentially "revolutionary" efforts. Interracial and interethnic couples provide a vehicle for reexamining old assumptions about differences and for learning how relationships can be transformed by the differences themselves, allowing for "peaceful transfers of power" (Root, 2001, p. 28).

Historically, most of the literature on interracial and/or interethnic studies has focused on Black–White relationships with little attention paid to Latinos and Latinas with non-Hispanic Whites in the United States (Bacigalupe, 2003; Wieling, 2003). The dearth of studies examining Latino intermarriage is surprising in light of the significantly higher rate of intermarriage compared to Whites and Blacks. While 93% of non-Hispanic Whites and Blacks marry within their group, only 70% of Asians and Hispanics do (Harrison & Bennet, 1995; Waters, 2000). Conservative estimates have projected that by the year 2050, 21% of the population will be of multiple ancestries: Asians and Latinos will be the most mixed, at 35 and 45% multiple ancestries, respectively (Smith & Edmonston, 1997; Waters, 2000). Latinos' high rate of intermarriage has a long history that precedes their arrival to the United States, and many Latino immigrants come from countries with mixed-race traditions. Some analysts suggest that these factors may make Latinos more open to interracial marriage, particularly with Whites (Fletcher, 1998; Jacobs & Labov, 2002).

In the United States, rates of intermarriage vary by geographical region. In Los Angeles County, for example, one quarter of the U.S.-born Latinos have married interracially, and more than two out of three intermarriages include a Latino partner (Hayes-Bautista & Rodriguez, 1996). But the psychological research and clinical literature has not kept pace with this statistical growth. Furthermore, the heterogeneity of the Latino population provides a fertile ground for exploring themes and dilemmas that arise from the way differences are constructed and negotiated by couples living in bicultural, often unequal contexts.

Latinos in the United States: Who Are They?

According to a demographic report by the Pew Hispanic Center (2005), Latinos are the nation's largest minority group. The 2000 Census marked the Hispanic population at 35.3 million people, an increase of 58% over 1990. Since then, growth has continued at a brisk pace. The total Hispanic population in 2004 was 40.4 million. That is a jump of more than 14% in just 4 years. Meanwhile, the non-Hispanic population was up by barely 2%. The Latino population is expected to continue to grow from one in seven to one in four by the year 2050 (Guzman, 2001; Ramirez, 2000). In just two generations, the United States will have the second largest number of Latinos in the world, after Mexico (Suarez-Orozco & Paez, 2002).

Locating our Latino identity within the constraints of social research is complex and difficult. We are the representation of hybridization, a form of hybrid identity that existed long before postmodernism's attempt to describe the slippery naming of identities. Far from being a homogenous group, Latinos represent many races and nationalities whose roots extend from the Americas, to Europe, Asia, and Africa. We represent many religions and many languages that reflect our histories of colonization, imperial expansions, and immigration, while having Spanish as the common predominant language.

Latino history of intermarriage dates back to colonial times. The level of mixing and *mestizajes* depends on the ethnic and racial composition of the country of origin, and these levels vary from country to country. Latinos' historical legacies and the high level of *mestizajes* sponsor both colonial and emancipatory discourses, providing the rich backdrop against which Latinos negotiate new sets of social arrangements through intermarriage in this country.

Some Latinos, the *Americanos*, have been here before there was the United States, or before the United States came to them, while others are still arriving (Suarez-Orozco & Paez, 2002). Fifty-eight percent are from a Mexican origin, 14.3% are from Central and South American backgrounds, while 8.6 and 3.7%, respectively, come from Puerto Rico and Cuba. About 6.5% describe themselves as other Hispanic and two of five Latinos are foreign born (Ramirez & de la Cruz, 2002).

Latinos account for better than half of all new immigrants to the United States each year. Once in the United States, Spanish continues to be the main language, although many are bilingual. Unlike other immigrant groups, Latinos are holding onto their language and culture with passing generations (Kao, 1999; Portes & Rumbaut, 2001). As a result of English immersion laws and assimilation policies, a much smaller group speaks only English (Kao, 1999). The heterogeneous nature of the population defies generalizations, and the very term *Latino* has meaning only in reference to the U.S. experience. Outside the United States, we speak of

Mexicans, Cubans, Colombians, Salvadorians, Puerto Ricans, and so forth. The term *Latino* glosses over the contradictions, tensions, and fissures that often separate us. We have varied histories, cultural sensibilities, and current social predicaments. The vectors of race and color, gender, socioeconomic status, language, immigrant status, and mode of incorporation into the United States shape our experiences (Suarez-Orozco & Paez, 2002). These diverse experiences, political preferences, and consciousness are reflected in the names we call ourselves: Dominicans, Mexicans, Mexican American, Chicano, Xicano, Puerto Rican, Neyorican, Boricua, Rican, Hispanics, or Americanos, to list a few (Comaz-Diaz, 2001).

Then, what do Latinos have in common? Unlike other immigrant groups—Europeans, Asians, Africans—Latinos share a common language, whether or not they still speak it. Most Latinos also share the experience of immigration and a history of unequal association between their homelands and the United States—a country that has influenced and sometimes dictated political behaviors in Latin America. In the United States the experience of Latinos has been obscured by the binary "Black–White logic" that has driven racial relations in this country. For example, in an attempt at identifying Latinos in the United States, until the 2000 Census, Hispanics were classified as another "racial group," a method of collecting information about a heterogeneous population that obscured the racial diversity and diverse experiences of Latinos in the United States (Suarez-Orozco & Paez, 2002; Torres-Saillant, 2002). The term *Latino*, for example, does not differentiate the experience of a Mayan, undocumented, monolingual worker from that of a third-generation Cuban medical student (Suarez-Orozco & Paez, 2002).

After the 2000 Census, the term *Hispanic* or *Latino* has been defined as an ethnic group or as a person of Cuban, Mexican, Puerto Rican, South or Central American, or other Spanish culture or origin, regardless of race. "Ethnicity refers to a group's common ancestry through which individuals evolved shared values and customs" (McGoldrick, 2002, p. 1). These values and customs are transmitted through generations by family and reinforced or invalidated by the surrounding community. Either way, ethnicity becomes a powerful influence in determining identity (McGoldrick, 2002). To understand the Latino identity or identities, one needs to deconstruct the multiplicity of social identities, contexts, and histories that shape our cultural experiences in the United States. For those who are interculturally partnered, this is a task that is negotiated in both the private and public realms of the couple's lives, where the visible (i.e., race or language) and invisible differences (i.e., class experiences, citizenship privileges) that delineate their identities impact the relational context.

Constructions of Difference in Relational Contexts

The experience of difference makes visible to us aspects of our identities that might otherwise have gone unexamined. When this happens, the unmarked piece of identity suddenly becomes relevant and important (Jones, 1997). This new awareness brings about an "awakening" process by which our identities also can evolve as we negotiate differences between our inside and outside worlds. Power and privilege also permeate the construction of identity (Deaux, 1993; Espiritu, 1994; Reynold & Pope, 1991). Depending on how power is applied to difference, the experience of difference can be self-expanding or self-constricting. A diminishing, subtracting process can adversely affect relationships. Although all couples negotiate power, intercultural couples further negotiate power differentials imposed by the social context. The manner in which intercultural couples perceive and negotiate the differences can bring about potential liberatory or oppressive consequences for individual partners or the relationship.

In eliciting discourses of difference that emerge in relational contexts, we asked ourselves and others, "Do partners perceive intercultural difference as constitutive of their relationship?" If so, "Where do they locate the difference?" Does a couple locate differences in the realm of country of origin or in ethnic, racial, language, and other markers related to intercultural relationships? If so, what meaning is made about these differences? Moving beyond the couple itself, we asked if these differences are perceived by others. What is the role of the network, the extended family, the neighborhood, and others in perceiving difference? How might these constructions by others play a role in the couple's relationship?

Using previous work that examines various constructions of difference, we explored discourses of difference among intercultural couples (Llerena-Quinn, 2001). A very basic stance is the one that denies intercultural difference or minimizes its significance on the individual or the couple. Any existing difference doesn't really make a difference. Another stance recognizes that differences exist but perceives them as existing in the different "other." This stance espouses the "superiority" of the dominant culture, and difference is seen as a source of deficit. We are in America and we need to do things the American way! Assimilation to the values of the dominant discourse is seen as the goal. Another ethnocentric stance often complements the ones already described. One partner assumes that the spouse is the "Other" and, as such, is the one with a culture. One member of the couple becomes the omniscient observer, the "neutral" anthropologist without a culture, while the other is transformed into the "exotic native." Difference is located in the "cultural other" and not in the "regular" dominant self. Although the partner from the dominant culture may have benign good intentions, adopting a benevolent, paternalistic stance reflects unexamined assumptions about culture, power, self, and other. Relationally, all of these stances render invisible the needs and experiences of the less dominant partner. Although these stances can have an oppressive effect on the relationship, an ongoing and continuous negotiation of dialectical differences can bring about evolutionary and emancipatory shifts.

The profit business motive stance is beyond the scope of this chapter but needs to be mentioned. Although ultimately one needs to question the conditions that give rise to these arrangements, legal, social, or other status motives may also sustain or form the basis of an intercultural relationship. Not unlike older man–younger woman, rich man–trophy wife arrangements, the most well-known case is of couples that marry to be able to obtain documentation to work legally in the United States. Immigration laws play a tremendous role in the constitution of couples. The introduction of timelines that are foreign to the feelings and familial circumstances of the couple distort expectations about marriage and commitment. How does a partner know that the other is not exploiting the relational commitment? What are the rules that the couple ends up establishing vis-à-vis their legal situation?

A more fruitful relational stance is found in those couples that are explicit about the mutual value of interacting across the cultural divide and are able to continuously negotiate their evolving cultural identities. These relationships are ones in which languages are mixed, hybridization is legitimate, and the reinventing of difference as a plus appears throughout the relationship. These couples are aware of the self-expanding and self-enhancing value of their different cultural affiliations. For example, after over 20 years of marriage, Jack, a third-generation French Canadian, still describes his wife Celia's tightly knit Cuban immigrant family as "vibrant" and "alive." Celia's family, in his eyes, has all that his family lost through assimilation. Jack has embraced their "lively energy" and supports his children's identification with their Cuban heritage. He supports his children's bilingualism, even though it has been hard for him to learn a second language. He believes knowing two languages is an asset that benefits the children now and in the future. Celia, on the other hand, describes her marriage as "liberating." She enjoys the independence she has learned from Jack. She comes from a family where grown children talk to their parents everyday. Her own father visited and talked to his mother every day until she died. Celia, although close to her Cuban family, does not feel she has to talk to them everyday. Each partner brought different skills and resources into the marriage that expanded their own resources and choices.

In the next section we introduce central factors and metaphors that provide the background against which we will explore life cycle themes. One has to do with how a "clan," "tribe," or "family" is defined in different "nations" and cultures and the other with how different nations negotiate these differences. The joining of clans and nations are metaphors that help us understand some of the issues emerging among intercultural couples.

Differing Clans and Conceptions of Family: Nuclear vs. Extended Family

Definitions of *family* vary in terms of who is included and how fixed the boundaries are around those relationships. The literature about Latinos has emphasized the notion of familism, the overarching priority that the family as a group has over the individual. Latino families, however, fall along a continuum between individualism and collectivism; however, a general tendency exists toward embracing the group over the individual and strong connection to the extended family. Latino spouses report differences in forms of connection and interaction between their families and the families of their spouses. Many report a strong family orientation, which at times is misunderstood by their partners, who might confuse enmeshment with the mutuality and closeness that characterize families that strongly prioritize responsibility to family. Previously unfamiliar with the Latino culture, Greg decided that after the wedding he and Carmen would not live near her Cuban family in Miami. He feared engulfment by both the extended family and the strong presence of a larger Latino community in Miami. On the other hand, Latino families who have had less contact with people outside their communities also tend to stereotype non-Hispanic White families. A Dominican mother voiced opposition to the news of her daughter's engagement to an American man because she feared that he would erect an impenetrable boundary between mother and daughter and that her Latino family would lose her to the new nuclear family. Fear of cutoffs can become a threat to the integrity of continuing bonds with the family of origin. The non-Latino partner may need to adjust to the process of being inducted as a new member of the Latino extended family. In the case of transnational families, whenever possible, visits to the country of origin and visits by the family abroad may facilitate the process. One must be aware that Latino family visits to the United States may last longer than those by U.S. families and even though this may be a potential source of tension, this also creates the opportunity for the strengthening of cross-cultural bonds.

Immigration: The Couple as the United Nations

The theme of immigration is central in understanding intermarriage between first-generation immigrant Latinos and non-Hispanic Whites. The metaphor of the couple as representatives of nations helps us understand these immigrant experiences (Bacigalupe, 2003). The questions that follow were created in a clinical context but offer a compelling metaphor of couples facing the challenges of intercultural conundrums. We could ask couples questions like the following: In what country was the Latino partner born? What are the sociopolitical issues in the global/local contexts associated with membership in this nation? What are the relational histories of that nation and the United States? How does the couple relationship mirror the present tensions about immigration in the U.S. society?

Similar to narrative therapy techniques, in my (GB) work with couples, these questions have served to normalize and name the impact of experiences of immigration in the couple history. Marta, a Cuban-born political science professor, came alone to the United States when she was 13. She was sent to the United States by her parents to "save her" from the revolution only to grow up a devoted admirer of Fidel Castro. Paul was attracted to Marta and her history, but he wanted her to be less opinionated around his friends to avoid ostracism. Marta took Paul's remarks as an affront that commanded her to assimilate or risk a social embargo, which she experienced as disrespect and met with further resistance. As they carefully unpacked the meaning of the concept of respect for each of them and how their requests to each other were emerging from wanting to deepen their respect, they both became very interested in understanding what informed their different expectations and thus finding distinct ways of "violating" their own values about what intimacy, respect, and the "right thing to do" meant in a marital relationship. What may have been the source of injury and resentment has become for some couples a source of pride and strength as well as an invitation for each member to be attentive to the ways in which dominant social discourses impact their own relationship.

Research is not definitive about how acculturation benefits or inhibits the well-being of those immigrating. We know even less about that process within the relational context. The age of immigration and length of residence of the Latino partner in the United States have an impact on acculturation. Latinos who immigrate before the age of 12 experience less acculturative stress and have better understanding of the nuances of American culture than their older family members in the United States or in the country of origin (Mena, Padilla, & Maldonado, 1987; Padilla, Alvarez, & Lindholm, 1986; Padilla, Wagatsuma, & Lindholm, 1985). However, acculturation is not the same thing as ethnic identity, and a Latino partner who is well acculturated in the United States may still perceive and experience discrimination, value, or take action based on machismo, or experience cultural homelessness, any of which may not be understood by the U.S. partner, especially if they seem contradictory to other aspects of the partner's identity. For Latinos whose families are still in the country of origin, the marriage may also represent a loss via a weakening of the connection to the country of origin as well as to the extended family. When both partners have opportunities for involvement with the Latino partner's culture of origin and with the host culture, the process of becoming acquainted with each other's worlds is facilitated and the sense of loss of community can be minimized.

Emerging Themes in the Life Cycle: The Discovery of New Meanings of Difference

Intercultural couples often minimize the importance of their differences until something in the life cycle disrupts the misconception that differences do not matter or informs one or both parties about the importance of difference to their identities. The catalyst can be a common couple event such as coming to terms with gender role fantasies that the partners had about each other, the meanings they attribute to different communication styles, or expectations about the way children should be raised.

Intercultural couples have to address challenges and milestones common to all couples as they move through the life cycle. Their cultural backgrounds determine the intensity of the challenge and the resources that each partner will have available to resolve them. In this section, we discuss some of the emergent themes we have observed in Latino–non-Hispanic White couples.

Courtship Differences and Family Responses to Dating

Although all Latinos do not follow the same courtship practices in the United States or in their countries of origin, several couples identified themes about differences between American and Latino dating patterns.

Differences between Traditional Latino Courtships and More Liberal American Dating Practices

Many Latino partners from immigrant families tend to adhere to more traditional dating patterns than American partners, who tend to be more casual about dating. For example, a Dominican attorney, reared in a predominantly Latino community in the United States since age 9, reported that the courtship with her Irish American husband was difficult because of the protocol and behavior code expected by her family. Her fiancée had to make significant adjustments to adhere to the traditional standards of Catholic Latino middle-class values, which included no premarital sex and more formality. This was difficult for both since the courtship lasted over 4 years. However, Francis's capacity to appreciate Marissa's dilemma with her extended family allowed him to, for the most part, respect the traditional dating patterns. However, not all couples follow this traditional protocol. A few Latina women, especially those who had moved away from traditional families to attend college, reported feeling "freer" and more comfortable dating American men than Latino men. They felt less scrutiny about their behavior by American partners, compared to more traditional Latino males, on whom they projected parental standards.

Personal and Family Fears Based on Stereotypes

A frequently reported stereotype by Latina women is that American men have a sexual curiosity to find out what it is like to date a Latina or Asian woman, but they are not as interested in finding out who the woman is on the "inside." Extended families and friends reinforce the stereotype:

Latina mothers warn their daughters that American men don't marry Latina girls. When marriage was proposed, a Dominican woman said her mother asked her if she was pregnant, as if this could be the only reason for the proposal!

Ambivalence about intercultural dating also can come from the American side of the family. Tania, a Colombian reporter for a Latino newspaper, said that initially her in-laws disapproved of her relationship with their son, Robert. They wanted him to marry someone from a "good family," which meant someone from the same social class. But marked class differences separated this couple. While her father's job in a factory and her mother's employment as a seamstress had supported Tania's college education, Robert came from an upper-middle-class, highly educated family, largely unaware of their class privileges. Paradoxically, Tania and Robert identified their shared commitment toward social justice as a central aspect of their relational bond. Yet, blind spots emerged from their diverse social class backgrounds at the most unexpected places, producing discomfort in Tania. As one example, Tania, who never went out to dinner with her parents, much less to expensive restaurants, experienced inner conflict as she watched large amounts of money spent on one restaurant meal. In her family, whatever extra money was left over was shared with relatives in Colombia, and what was spent on just one restaurant meal could have made a tremendous difference to a family in her home country. Most disturbing was how her future in-laws treated the servers; i.e., complaining about the food or returning a meal if it was not to their liking. Empathizing with the servers, who resembled her own family members, Tania did not enjoy these shared moments with her fiancée's family, who were polite but largely unaware of their class privilege. What if the non-White partner was low income and the Latino partner was from a wealthy family? Would the dynamics reverse? Or would the ethnic/outsider lens provide new class insights for the Latino partner? In this case, the triple marginalization of being a Latina from a family whose income was lower than that of the White male partner impacted the relational dynamics. Tania's ability to name the marginalized discourse allowed Robert, who already was committed to social justice, to explore his blind spots and those of his parents. Furthermore, he was able to appreciate Tania's personal emotional connection to the suffering of the poor and her resistance to wasting material resources he took for granted. In later visits, Robert took initiative in talking to his family about the strengths and realities of people who work very hard but are not wealthy and do not have access to resources that he enjoys.

However, talking to one's parents is not possible for all couples. Changing Richard's parents' minds about his wife Gabriela was not possible. Richard's parents, although proud of their daughter-in-law, see her as an "exception," not as the rule of her group. Both Richard and Gabriela have opted to no longer try and convince his parents otherwise. They are profoundly aware of the subtle and not-so-subtle ethnocentrism that colors his parents' perceptions as well as others in the dominant culture. Richard, a well-educated journalist and writer, finds that his marriage to Gabriela provides redemption for his American identity in that he feels "less American." Through various trips to Chile, he has looked at his world through a "foreigner lens" and this has added new insights about his American identity. To avoid the social constraints of her gender and class in her country, Gabriela, a writer, had, until she met Richard, chosen not to marry. She did not want to marry and settle with children as her parents expected of her after she completed her education. Rather, Gabriela wanted to devote her life to giving voice to those without a voice through her work and writing. Constantly on the move, Gabriela's father had described her as *indomable* (untameable). Richard and Gabriela find that their marriage has provided the place where they both feel they can expand into being more of themselves.

The perception of class can easily be misconstrued in intercultural couple relationships. Class status can be over- and underestimated by the American partner and family. In addition to being unfamiliar with the immigrant context or the social context in the country of origin of the Latino partner, many White Americans, under the influence of the myth of equality, lack explicit conscious social class awareness. Class meanings are misunderstood when read through ethnocentric lenses. When John, a White U.S. fiancé, first visited his working class fiancée's family in Peru, he thought they were very poor compared to his American standards. Then she took him to see what "poor" means in Peru. Moved by these differences, John became an active fundraiser for the children in the community they visited. Conversely, another Peruvian woman reported that her husband's family thought she came from a wealthy family because she had attended private schools and she grew up surrounded with domestic workers, common practices among middle-class families in South American countries.

Along with class differences, race and religion can foster ambivalence over intercultural dating. For some Latinos, marrying a person of lighter skin color is considered a move up the social ladder. The phrase *mejorando la raza*, improving the race, is invoked to signal approval of a light-skinned partner—a bias shared by U.S. partners' families. A Venezuelan physician said her husband's family accepted her because she was White but was unsure if they would have if she had been Black. For them, the issue was not race or ethnicity but religion. Because of the value they placed on their Jewish heritage, his parents were concerned about how the children would be raised. Having a "good education" and career seemed to positively compensate for many differences. Her awareness of subtle biases around race, class, and religion led her to questions her own biases around race and to explore with her husband more egalitarian stances around difference in general. For them, embracing both their religions provided a more equalitarian solution. Interestingly, each of their two children is showing a preference of one faith over the other while being accepting of both. Couples confronting similar issues negotiated these differences in multiple ways, sometimes through conversion, other times by embracing both faiths.

Marriage: The Newlyweds

By the time couples decide to wed, they have encountered some of the differences that they will have to live with during their life together. For some, it may mean accepting the possibility of not returning to their country of origin and losing the close support of the extended family. For others it may mean a closer exploration of each others' worlds within the U.S. context, while negotiating the boundaries they will erect around their own distinct worlds. And for others yet, it might be embracing both cultures and placing a boundary that includes both of them, their families, and their cultures. The redefinition of individual boundaries vis-à-vis the cultural self may include a decision about the name(s) one or both will take after the wedding and where they will marry or live. Some couples married in the bride's country of origin, while others had ceremonies in both countries, unless the Latino family was all in the United States. The choices open windows to new worlds for the couple, their families, and their friends. The outcome of these negotiations reflects the potential for intercultural couples to create an emergent relational resilience in which both members of the couple incorporate aspects of each other's cultural backgrounds rather than a simplistic assimilation.

Early in the marriage or courtship, each partner may have fantasies about the gender role of the other. However, just because gender roles are culturally ascribed does not mean they are the individual partner's preferred roles or that these roles won't change in response to changes in context. For example, take the assumption that a Latina spouse will cook wonderful meals and cater to her husband's needs while he is the provider. When he also expects her to work outside the home to help with the household expenses, she may be less able to single-handedly keep up with household chores and lavish meals. Many couples are challenging the dominant gender role assumptions from both their cultures. Unlike her female cousins who "do it all," Maritza felt liberated from the oppressive aspects of gender with Michael, who did not expect her to cook all his meals and who helped with the laundry. Maritza's brother Juan, on the other hand, married Judy, a free-spirited artist whose independence initially attracted him. Judy is less concerned with the day-to-day details of running a home, which was not an issue for him until the children arrived. Now Juan is beginning to voice a longing for the ways in which he was raised, wishing Judy was more like the women in his family. The ongoing dialectic around prescribed social and gender roles allows couples to stretch beyond original identities and to explore new ones, at times even daring to challenge the imposed constraints of the current social system.

Becoming a New Unit: The Ongoing Negotiation of Cultural and Family Boundaries

The couple and their extended families continue to explore each others' worlds after the marriage, and this includes being introduced to new foods, languages, and traditions. Some partners learn how to speak Spanish if they did not before. For many Latinas, extensive contact with their families of origin continues after marriage. Contact takes place in the form of phone calls, visits, giving advice and opinions, and support in constructing the new home. Many Latinas reported talking to their mothers daily, sometimes more than once a day. The contact was perceived as wanted and supportive yet at times was also perceived as stressful. A Latina woman noted that when her mother visits for a few days, she rearranges her whole house and reorganizes her cabinets. Immigrant Latinos who are more used to extended family networks may not react as strongly to the loss of privacy during family visits as the partner who comes from a nuclear family background. Stress over the loss of privacy was greater in situations where families visited for extended periods, as in the case of transnational visits. Latina women often felt caught between two worlds, trying to please the family of origin by continuing the old world traditions and adapting to their partners' new world. Latina women often reported that their mothers had an investment in teaching them to be good wives and to cook well in order to please their husbands. However, many of the wives also felt that their husbands had different expectations of them than their families of origin. These women enjoyed the more independent and egalitarian characteristics of their husbands, which were very different from their fathers when they were growing up. For working couples, negotiating the two worlds was particularly difficult during transnational visits because of how long they lasted. Language differences made it more difficult to enjoy the whole process whether the visits were in the United States or the country of origin. Couples and families who were bilingual fared better. Couples who could afford it opted to go on trips to their parents and relatives away from their present house as a way of reducing the potential stress associated with house visits.

Communication and Interaction Styles

Industrialized societies value individual rights and privacy and their communication and interactional styles reflect those values. Similarly, Latinos' communication and interactional styles reflect the values of more traditional and collectivistic family structures. Intercultural couples are often surprised by each other's and their family members' communication styles. While one communication style may seem "enmeshed" to one partner, another may seem "disengaged" to the other. Nora's Cuban family openly expressed their opinions and approved or disagreed with each other overtly. Richard, from a WASP background, felt overwhelmed with all the display of emotion, which looked to him like a "fight." He could not understand how Nora's family could intensely disagree, raise their voices, and then go onto the next thing as if nothing had happened. He, instead, like his family, was reserved and polite, never expressing strong opinions, much less criticism. His respect for the privacy of others resulted in infrequent contact with his siblings and extended family, except for very special occasions. To Nora, this style looked "cold" and "disconnected," and she found it hard to read messages that were not openly stated. The couple had to become versed in reading behavior through the lens of two different cultures and as a result created a more understanding relationship.

Language

One significant aspect of communication is access to one's primary language. To understand the meaning of language in a relationship, one must understand the role language plays in intimacy and in the power dynamics inside and outside the home. Language is intimately connected to one's sense of identity and the experience of emotion. It is also the ticket that allows travel into each other's worlds. Jonathan did not speak Spanish, and each time they visited Rosa's family in Mexico, he felt excluded because of language. Everyone seemed to have a good time together, so he decided to learn the language. Acquiring the language had a positive impact in connecting more intimately with Rosa and with her family. For Margarita, reunions with her family or with Spanish-speaking friends from her country of origin were a struggle because her husband Bob did not speak the language. It was hard to have a normal conversation as she had to translate for both sides, and in the process, she lost her own voice. Language can become an especially serious problem when the immigrant partner does not speak English and her only access to the new context in the United States is through her spouse.

Language difference is not always a problem, however. Michael, who comes from a working-class background, does not feel comfortable with the academic conversations of his wife's Latino colleagues. At these times, he does not mind being excluded from the conversation, hiding his class background behind a language difference. He does not feel cut off from his in-laws, because they speak English.

Raising Children

Intercultural differences that did not cause difficulty in the couple relationship can surface as a problem when the children are born. Partners may have different views on child-rearing or the attributes they value in the person they are raising, often conforming to their own cultural values and identities. Differences can emerge regarding the naming of children, what languages they will speak, and what child-rearing practices they will use. Suddenly, the values that sustained their parents may become of increased importance and find a place within their own value systems. Although all relationships involve a certain degree of traveling into the unknown, immigrant partners may experience the differences as a replication of the immigration experience, only this time within the intimacy of the home. These feelings can be further exacerbated later on when the children grow up more "American" than the immigrant parent, making him a minority within the home. Jack and Celia never had problems due to their cultural differences until it came to raising their son. Jack felt that Celia over-protected the son and was not raising him to be an independent man—the very quality Celia most loved in Jack!

Continued involvement with the extended Latino family, whether abroad or in the United States, helps to decrease feelings of alienation within the family, expanding identity possibilities for the children and providing support to the immigrant parent. This involvement, although often valued, especially in relation to childcare, at times can be perceived as overinvolvement. This fact was accepted with humor by Richard and Nora, who said that each time her mother visits she rearranges the house and they can't find anything. The annoyance was compensated by the grandmother's willingness to assist in childcare whenever and for as long as needed. As the grandchildren become older and reach their teens, Latino parents can find themselves in the middle of "culture wars" between the American grandchildren and less acculturated grandparents who are critical of the parents for not having raised their children according to a traditional cultural standard. Interesting intergenerational and inter-cultural alliances can take place at this time, when Latino partners have realigned their positions with their American spouses to mediate these conflicts. In general, there is a consensus among those we talked with that their Latino families are quite involved before the marriage and remain involved with the couple and the grandchildren after marriage. Latinos are less likely than White Americans to place children out of the home or place the elderly in nursing homes and thus family can be a source of support when needed. But families can be a source of stress when the immigrant family members need to fulfill this demand in the U.S. context where the extended family may not be available as a support network.

Conclusion

What constitutes a significant difference among intercultural couples is complex and evolving. Intercultural couples must negotiate the developmental and relational processes all couples and families face. But in addition, they must respond to the challenges colored by the idiosyncrasies of each partner's cultural context and identity as well as that of the dominant context in which they live. Many factors impact the construction of identity. For Latinos, the strength and quality of one's ethnic identity, the perception and experience of discrimination, and the number of years in the United States are among the contributing factors. For non-Hispanic White partners, the extent to which they notice the role of power, privilege, and outsider experiences in constructing identities influences how they see themselves and their partners. For the couple and their families, these factors dictate what is and is not considered "normal" and just. The couple's awareness of these factors and how each responds to them will facilitate or impede their adjustment throughout the life cycle. The capacity of the partners to travel into each other's worlds and appreciate each other's experiences and how these may not be equal or neutral facilitates connection and growth. Diversity can only thrive in a globally interdependent world when people have multiple and complementary identities and belong not only to a local community and a country but also to humanity at large (Llerena-Quinn, 2001). Addressing imbalances in power helps to reduce threats and risks to the relationship. Root (2001) sees in these relationships a quiet revolution, a revolution of love that can change how we relate to each other, embracing our differences and providing a solution to our race, gender, and ethnic inequalities.

Note

1. Many Latinos are racially mixed or *mestizos*. Though many mestizos identify as White, skin color still determines how they are perceived (Shorris, 1992).

References

Andrews, J. (Writer), & I. Andrews & Clark Explorations (Producer). (2003). *Crossing borders: Bridging home: An interview with Gonzalo Bacigalupe* [Motion picture]. United States: MastersWorks, Inc.

Arana, M. (2001). *American Chica: Two worlds, one childhood*. New York: Dial Press.

Bacigalupe, G. (2003). Intercultural therapy with Latino immigrants and White partners: Crossing borders coupling. In V. Thomas, T. Karis, & J. Wetchler (Eds.), *Clinical issues with interracial couples: Theories and research* (pp. 131–149). New York: Haworth Press.

Comas-Diaz, L. (2001). Hispanics, Latinos, or Americanos: The evolution of identity. *Cultural Diversity and Ethnic Minority Psychology, 7*(2), 115–120.

Cornelius, W. A. (2002). Ambivalent reception: Mass public responses to the "new" Latino immigration to the United States. In M. M. Suarez-Orozco & M. M. Paez (Eds.), *Latinos: Remaking America* (pp. 165–189). Berkeley, CA: University of California Press.

Deaux, K. (1993). *Social psychology in the 90's* (6th ed.). Pacific Grove, CA: Brooks/ Cole.

Espiritu, Y. L. (1994). The intersection of race, ethnicity, and class: The multiple identities of second-generation Filipinos. *Identities, 1*(2–3), 249–273.

Fletcher, M. A. (1998, December 28). American's racial and ethnic divides: Interracial marriages eroding barriers. *Washington Post.* Retrieved September 18, 2004, from http://www.washingtonpost.com/wp-srv/national/ daily/dec98/melt29.htm

Guzman, B. (2001). The Hispanic population. *Census 2000 Brief C2KBR/01-3.* Washington, DC.

Harrison, R., & Bennett, C. (1995). Racial and ethnic diversity. In R. Farley (Ed.), *State of the union: America in the 1990's: Social trends* (Vol. 2, pp. 141–210). New York: Russell Sage Foundation Press.

Hayes-Bautista, D. E., & Rodriguez, G. (1996, May 5). L.A. county answer for racial tensions: Intermarriage. *Los Angeles Times,* p. M6.

Jacobs, J. A., & Labov, T. G. (2002). Gender differentials among sixteen race and ethnic groups. *Sociological Forum, 17*(4), 62–46.

Jones, S. R. (1997). Voices of identity and difference: A qualitative exploration of the multiple dimensions of identity development in women college students. *Journal of College Student Development, 38*(4), 376–386.

Kao, G. (1999). Psychological well-being and educational achievement among immigrant youth. In D. J. Hernandez (Ed.), *Children of immigrants: Health, adjustment, and public assistance* (pp. 410–477). Washington, DC: National Academy Press.

Killian, K. D. (2003). Homogamy outlaws: Interracial couples' strategic responses to racism and to partner differences. *Journal of Couple & Relationship Therapy, 2*(2/3), 3–21.

Llerena-Quinn, R. (2001). How do assumptions of difference and power affect how and what we teach? *AFTA Newsletter, 82,* 22–26.

McGoldrick, M. (2002). *Culture: A challenge to concepts of normality.* Retrieved October 22, 2002, from, http://www.MulticulturalFamily.org

Mena, F. J., Padilla, A. M., & Maldonado, M. (1987). Acculturative stress and specific coping strategies among immigrant and later generation college students. *Hispanic Journal of Behavioral Science, 9,* 207–225.

Padilla, A. M., Alvarez, M., & Lindholm, K. J. (1986). Generational status and personality factors as predictors of stress in students. *Hispanic Journal of Behavioral Sciences, 8,* 275–288.

Padilla, A., Wagatsuma, Y., & Lindholm, K. (1985). Acculturation and personality as predictors of stress in Japanese and Japanese Americans. *Journal of Social Psychology, 125*, 295–305.

Pew Hispanic Center. (2005). *Hispanics: People in motion.* Washington, DC: Author.

Portes, A., & Rumbaut, R. G. (2001). *Legacies: The story of the immigrant second generation.* Berkeley, CA: University of California Press.

Ramirez, R. R. (2000). *The Hispanic population in the United States: Population characteristics (Current Population Reports P20-527).* Washington, DC: U.S. Census Bureau.

Ramirez, R. R., & de la Cruz, G. P. (2003). *The Hispanic population in the United States: March 2002. Population characteristics.* Washington, DC: Bureau of the Census.

Reynolds, A. L., & Pope, R. L. (1991). The complexities of diversity: Exploring multiple oppressions. *Journal of Counseling and Development, 70*(1), 174–180.

Root, M. P. P. (2001). *Love's revolution: Interracial marriage.* Philadelphia: Temple University Press.

Rosenblatt, P. C., Karis, T. A., & Powell, R. D. (1995). *Multiracial couples: Black and White voices.* Thousand Oaks, CA: Sage.

Shorris, E. (1992). *Latinos: A biography of the people.* New York: W. W. Norton.

Smith, J. P., & Edmonston, B. (1997). *The new Americans: Economic, demographic and fiscal effects of immigration.* Washington, DC: National Academy Press.

Suarez-Orozco, M. M., & Paez, M. M. (2002). Introduction: The research agenda. In M. M. Suarez-Orozco & M. M. Paez (Eds.), *Latinos: Remaking America* (pp. 1–37). Berkeley, CA: University of California Press.

Torres-Saillant, S. (2002). Problematic paradigms: Racial diversity and corporate identity in the Latino community. In M. M. Suarez-Orozco & M. M. Paez (Eds.), *Latinos: Remaking America* (pp. 435–455). Berkeley, CA: University of California Press.

Waters, M. C. (2000). Immigration, intermarriage, and the challenges of measuring racial/ethnic identities. *American Journal of Public Health, 90*(11), 1735–1737.

Wieling, E. (2003). Latino/a and White marriages: A pilot study investigating the experiences of interethnic couples in the United States. *Journal of Couple & Relationship Therapy, 2*(2/3), 41–55.

10

Asian Indians in Intercultural Marriages
Intersections of Acculturation, Gender, and Exogamy

Mudita Rastogi

Asian Indians in the United States include people who trace their ancestry to the Indian subcontinent and were either born and raised in the United States or have immigrated here directly from India or from other countries. The 2000 census figures reveal that the number of Asian Indian people in the United States is about 1.7 million (U.S. Census Bureau, n.d.). This chapter focuses on intercultural marriages of two types: (a) Both the wife and the husband identify as Asian Indian but differ in their levels of acculturation; and (b) where one partner is of Asian Indian heritage and the other is not. Members of the Asian Indian community in the United States range widely in their level of acculturation. This chapter will detail how acculturation impacts an individual's values, family structure, relational expectations, and gender schema (Jain & Belsky, 1997) and the effects these have on the couple's relationship. I will also discuss the possible challenges faced by couples where one partner comes from outside the Asian Indian community. I will provide case vignettes to illustrate these issues based on my research and clinical and community work. All names and some identifying information have been changed to protect confidentiality. Interspersed in this chapter are also pointers for mental health professionals. I have not discussed same-sex or cohabiting heterosexual intercultural couples within the Asian Indian community as there is no body of literature describing these relationships. I will revisit this issue at the end of the chapter.

History and Demographics

The first Asian Indians arrived in the United States in 1750 but their numbers were small until the 1960s (Sheth, 1995). The majority of the Asian Indians migrated to the United States after the Immigration Act of 1965, which lifted the nation-based immigration quotas (Ramisetty-Mikler, 1993). Das and Kemp (1997) state that the majority of Indians who came in the 1960s and the 1970s held advanced educational degrees and those who came in the 1980s and 1990s were a mix of students, professionals, and the relatives of those who had arrived in the early years.

Some of the characteristics of the Asian Indian community include an overall higher level of education than the general population and a proficiency in the English language compared to many other new immigrant groups (Sheth, 1995). Both of these have been cited as reasons why Asian Indians have been professionally successful in the United States. Their reported median family income in 1999 was over $70,000 compared with approximately $53,000 for Whites (U.S. Census Bureau, n.d.). However, Min (1995) argues that the myth of the "model minority" is misleading. Min points out that the Asian Indian median family income is high because the family has more employed members that contribute to the family income. Asian Indians are also paid lower than what their educational achievement might command compared to their White counterparts. Secondly, Asian Indians are concentrated in areas where the cost of living is higher (e.g., large metropolitan areas on the East and West Coasts and Chicago) compared to other parts of the United States. Therefore, a higher family income does not mean a higher standard of living. Thirdly, there is quite a range in the income of Asian Indian families. For example, 7.2% of the Asian Indian population in the United States lives in poverty and this number is comparable to Whites (Sheth, 1995).

Over 90% of Asian Indians live in families that consist of at least one married couple. Only 4.5% live in female-headed households. Asian Indians have the lowest divorce rate (2%) for any group in the United States (Sheth, 1995). This may be because of the stigma associated with divorce (Rastogi & Wampler, 1998). Asian Indians practice a variety of religions including Hinduism (the most common), Islam, Christianity, Sikhism, Jainism, Buddhism, Zoroastrianism, and Judaism (Wolpert, 1991). There are also significant within-group differences in language, ethnicity, subculture, and traditions. The caste system is acknowledged in covert ways although most families do not openly discuss it and may even protest that they do not believe in the caste system. It rears its head almost certainly when the issue of marriage comes up. At best the families of the bride and groom cannot help but notice the caste of their future in-laws. At worst families will arrange marriages only within their own subcaste. Indian last names frequently reveal the caste one belongs to and sometimes the geographical region of one's origin and one's ancestral religion. (For details on the caste system, see Dirks, 1989 and Marriott 1968a, 1968b.)

Statistics on Intermarriage

Data show that Asian Indians in the United States are among the most likely of all Asian American ethnic groups to marry among themselves (Qian, Blair, & Ruf, 2001; Sheth, 1995). Analyses by Qian et al. (2001) show that only one out of every 180 marriages in the Asian Indian community is exogamous. For Whites in the United States, this number is one out of 34. Of the Asian Indian marriages outside of their ethnic group, the vast majority of them are with White partners; extremely few marriages take place between Asian Indians and other non-White people. The interracial partners are highly likely to be college educated and most partners have the same level of education, or else the man has a higher level of education (Qian et al., 2001). Finally, these authors also point out that Asian Indians born in the United States are more likely to marry outside of their ethnic group than Asian Indian immigrants.

The authors explain their findings by pointing out that, at this time, the majority of Asian Indians in the United States are foreign born and also that Asian Indians have held on to their cultural traditions over centuries. There is perhaps a third explanation. Asian Indian families have always arranged marriages within their castes and preferably their own subcastes. Many social practices revolved around distinguishing between the in-group and the out-group. For example, an individual might work alongside a person of any caste in a factory but may not go to their house to eat a meal due to notions of "pollution" resulting from interactions across castes (Saberwal, 2004). These strong beliefs may or may not exist in their original form in a family, but their remnants play a role in Asian Indians' evaluations of potential mates. The more similar the bride and the groom's families are in every way, the better the match is considered to be. Therefore, it is not surprising that endogamy is the rule among Asian Indians in the United States.

There is also a different kind of cross-cultural marriage that takes place. It occurs between partners that are at differing levels of acculturation within the Asian Indian community. The factors that impact acculturation and assimilation are discussed later. Partners that vary significantly from each other on these issues face special challenges in their relationships. Empirical data for these unions are not available, although some clinical and theoretical literature does refer to these "intercultural" couples.

Understanding Asian Indian Families

In order to look closer at these intercultural marriages, it is important to understand the organization of traditional Asian Indian families and to identify the dynamics of relationships within the family. While Asian Indians' families are not all the same, the issues described below are frequently considered to be their core features.

Family Structure and Dynamics

The families of the bride and the groom are actively involved in the arrangement of marriages. The future husband and wife may be introduced through family friends, marriage brokers, "matrimonial" advertisements in Indian newspapers, or through special sites on the Internet. For examples of the latter, the reader is referred to the following links: http://www.matrimonials-india.com/ and http://www.shaadi.com/. Among Asian Indians in the United States and in some urban families in India, the prospective bride and groom have final veto power regarding mate selection. Even so, women have fewer vetoes than men do. Other Asian Indian families "allow" their adult children to date but with the understanding that it will lead to a quick decision regarding marriage. Some families, follow a double standard and may not allow their daughters to date at all or allow only male children to go out with non-Asian Indians.

In India, brides frequently move into the home of their in-laws after marriage. Asian Indians in the United States may reside in nuclear families so that women often enjoy more freedom from the conformity expected within extended families (Sheth, 1995). However, they also lose the support that comes from having a large family, especially with regard to child-rearing.

Indians continue to adhere to tradition within the family even when they may have adapted to foreign norms in educational or professional settings (Sodowsky, Kwan, & Pannu, 1995). Women are often the carriers of tradition for the family. Couple relationships of Asian Indians in the United States have seen some movement away from traditional gender roles but these vary based on the age and degree of acculturation of the couple (Agarwal, 1991; Jain & Belsky, 1997). Though more Asian Indian women have sought employment in recent years, they retain primary responsibility for housework and childcare (Almeida, 1996). As in the case of women from many other ethnic groups, their careers remain secondary to their husband's. Communication and conflict in couples follow gendered patterns. For example, Mathur (1994) used ethnographic, in-depth interviews to compare Asian Indian and White couples. Asian Indian husbands were more likely to speak for their wives and reported less awareness of conflicts in the relationship, compared with their White counterparts. However, the Asian Indian couples also expressed certainty that their relationship would last; this was missing in White couples.

Collectivism

Asian Indians accord a great importance to their familial relationships. Family is a major source of support (and sometimes stress) in Asian Indian lives. Family members experience strong intergenerational bonds and are socialized toward a collective orientation (Segal, 1991; Sue & Sue, 1990). Individuals are expected to make sacrifices for the good of the family and the community (Rastogi & Wampler, 1998). Interdependence is fostered through living in extended families and frequent exchanges with kin (Sodowsky & Carey, 1988). Even for Asian Indians living in nuclear families in the United States the sense of connection with the extended family is maintained via visits from family members from India, who might easily stay with them for up to 6 months at a time (the maximum time allowable on a tourist visa to the United States). Additionally, many families prefer to spend most vacations and weekends visiting their relatives and friends with a good deal of frequency. Authors like Rolland (1988) suggest that Asian Indians define themselves in the context of their familial relationships. Therefore, it is more useful to refer to a "familial self" in the Asian Indian context rather than an "individual self" possessing clear boundaries.

Hierarchy

Traditional families follow a hierarchy when it comes to power and privilege. This can be observed in areas involving important decision-making and overt behavior within relationships. Gender and age frequently determine one's power within the family (Das & Kemp, 1997; Durvasula & Mylvaganam, 1994; Rastogi & Wampler, 1998; Segal, 1991). Intergenerational interactions are hierarchical and even adults respect the wisdom of their elders (Rastogi & Wampler, 1999). Couple conflict was traditionally resolved with the intervention of older family members. (Even fairly assimilated Asian Indian couples are hesitant to seek a therapist for this reason.)

As a gender, females are valued less than men (Bumiller, 1990). While some attitudes have changed, and more so in families with higher levels of education, many traditions, actual behaviors, and role expectations continue to favor men. As a therapist I find that the issue of male privilege never fails to be mentioned in couple therapy with Asian Indians. It is most often mentioned with resentment by the female partner. The mother–son bond has traditionally been the strongest of all relationships in the family (Kakar, 1981). In later life this leads to an alliance between adult sons and their mothers. This has two major ramifications: Women often gain power in a family through their adult sons. Second, new brides may find themselves at the bottom of the family hierarchy unless they can get along with their mother-in-law (Rastogi & Wampler, 1998).

Revisiting Acculturation

Transitions related to migration as well as the degree of acculturation act as potent mediating factors in understanding Asian Indian behaviors and relationships (Rastogi, 2007). Acculturation is a long-term process and is defined as adapting to a new culture based on contact with the majority group in the new country. However, our understanding of acculturation has moved away from a one-dimensional construct. One of the best known models of acculturation is the bidirectional approach proposed by Berry (1980). He suggested four different types of acculturation experiences, including assimilation, separation, marginalization, and integration based on whether a person (a) Values his native culture and identity; and (b) wishes to embrace the new culture. In a study of acculturation, Sodowsky and Carey (1988) found that Asian Indians could be classified as traditional, bicultural, and "Americanized." The first group consisted of people who held on to traditional Indian values and practices. The bicultural group embraced parts of both cultures and the Americanized group was highly assimilated into White American culture. The size of the last group was small and, interestingly, its composition was not influenced by one's length of stay in the United States. On measures of acculturative distress, younger people score higher and report more adjustment difficulties than older adults, and people who immigrated at a younger age score lower due to having a bicultural orientation (Sodowsky & Lai, 1997). Higher income and family support were also associated with fewer adjustment problems in the host culture. Mehta's (1998) work supports some of the above findings. To summarize, acculturation is impacted by (a) the amount of contact with and acceptance by the dominant culture; (b) the cultural orientation toward and involvement in the new culture; (c) one's language usage and cultural skills that help function in the new culture; and (d) demographic variables.

Authors such as Sodowsky et al. (1995) suggest that in addition to acculturation, an individual's ethnic identity gives us additional information. Ethnic identity involves defining one's ethnic membership and is central to how people see themselves. Their research shows that for Asian Indians, a strong interest in their own ethnicity was associated with the belief that their family was interested in its Indian heritage. Thus, for this population, their sense of self and identity are very closely related to their family.

Couples of Asian Indian Origin: A Focus on Acculturation and Gender

When viewing acculturative style using the lens of gender, one discovers that acculturation can interact with gender to produce multiple categories useful in classifying couples. The structure of the model proposed here uses the categories of traditional, bicultural, and Americanized based on the work of Sodowsky and Carey (1988). These categories are subdivided further based on whether they describe the husband or the wife, resulting in a matrix of nine cells. Couples falling into each of the nine categories have unique characteristics, strengths, and potential pitfalls. For example, a couple that consists of a bicultural wife and a traditional husband looks very different from a couple where the opposite is true.

I chose to build the matrix using these two variables because the factor of acculturation emerged from the literature as a central organizing construct. Gender, too, is a core factor in determining the experiences of an

TABLE 10.1   A Model for Classifying Asian Indian Couples by Acculturative Style and Gender

Husband	Wife		
	Traditional	Bicultural	Americanized
Traditional	1. Immigrant couple, with similarities in experiences and role expectations.	2. Wife's assimilation raises issues around gender and power.	3. Relationship is a rarity; likely to be an arranged marriage. Needs considerable negotiation.
Bicultural	4. Wife may be a new immigrant. Requires negotiation and dealing with her isolation.	5. Both bicultural with similarities in experiences. One partner may assimilate faster.	6. Requires negotiation around gender issues and relationships with extended family.
Americanized	7. Relationship is a rarity; likely to be an arranged marriage. Needs considerable negotiation.	8. Couple may deal with issues of ethnic identity, child-rearing, and leisure activities.	9. Least likely to be an arranged marriage. Partners often different from each other in areas like religion, caste, etc.

Asian Indian individual. The details of the model were developed out of my clinical and community work experiences with Asian Indian couples and it has yet to be tested empirically. As with all models there may be outliers or cases that do not fit neatly into any one cell. Generalizations help organize data but also run the risk of glossing over "within-cell" differences. Also, in keeping with the focus of this chapter and this book, I discuss in detail only those categories where the partners differ from each other in their levels of acculturation; couples who are similar in their acculturative style (cells 1, 5 and 9) are not discussed in detail. The key points of each couple type are summarized in Table 10.1 and are discussed in detail below.

- Traditional wife, traditional husband. This couple will have many similar experiences and role expectations. Their disagreements are less likely to be attributed to cultural differences. They are often immigrants, in an arranged marriage, and their challenges lie in navigating mainstream culture and raising second generation children in the United States.
- Bicultural wife, traditional husband. Deepak (age 28) moved with his wife Veena (age 25) (from Hyderabad, India) to a large university town in the United States to complete a Ph.D. in Chemistry. Veena befriended their American host family and soon became involved in the local

cultural and social activities. She gained many international friends while he continued to spend all his time at the lab. Over several months, she switched to Western clothing, began cooking more American food, and questioned the couple's gendered division of labor and Deepak's need to make all financial decisions. Deepak's fears over losing his male privilege and the inability to keep up with her changing values caused a great deal of conflict in their marriage. The expectations of the partners around gender and power issues and differential rates of assimilation proved to be challenges.

- Americanized wife, traditional husband. Tina's parents had migrated to the United States when she was 4 years old. She was raised in a predominantly White suburb, within an extended family. Tina's interests and activities were those of the average teenager of her neighborhood. At the age of 20, Tina and her parents went back to their hometown in India for a month-long vacation. She was introduced by her parents to Jatin, a family friend, who was completing his medical training. As planned by the two families, they got to know each other and were engaged at the end of the month. A year later, Tina and Jatin were married in the United States. Tina now lives with Jatin, her two sons, parents in-law, and brother in-law. She struggles with the lack of privacy that she and her husband have and the expectation of having to defer to her mother-in-law on issues ranging from the day's menu to the color of the window treatments. Tina copes with these stresses by socializing with her family of origin almost every weekend and shopping and having lunch with her girlfriends. Her in-laws happily take care of the boys while she is gone. Although her husband is very supportive of her, they maintain somewhat separate social lives as he is not comfortable with her circle of friends. To make this relationship work, both partners make significant compromises. Tina is also appreciative of the help she receives from her in-laws in the area of child-rearing.

- Traditional wife, bicultural husband. Paul had lived in the United States for 10 years. Upon completing his M.B.A. he had worked his way up in a Fortune 500 company. He dated a bit but eventually accepted his parents' invitation to look for an arranged match in India. He met two women, both of whom were known to the family via their priest. Paul chose to marry Shyla, and she accompanied him back to the United States. Once in the United States, Shyla was unable to even get a driver's license, due to the nature of her H4 type "dependent visa." She faced a steep learning curve as she adjusted to her husband's social life, frequent travels, and her own isolation. She had trouble understanding American accents and colloquial terms. She loved to cook Indian food, but Paul had grown used to salads and sandwiches. This further cemented her sense of rejection. They had a baby boy within a year. When they went to see a couple therapist, they were fighting over basic child-rearing issues. Their 5-year-old refused to sleep in his own bed and also threw frequent tantrums. Shyla wanted to raise the child in a lenient manner, as she herself was raised, and Paul was more firm about boundaries. The couple struggled to understand each other's values around multiple issues. One of the strengths of this couple was that despite their problems, both said that they were completely committed to making their marriage work.

- Bicultural wife, bicultural husband. This couple is likely to have many similar experiences and values around culture and assimilation. However, as they embrace both their culture of origin and their new environment, they might acculturate in different ways or assimilate at different rates. Their challenge lies in keeping up with each other and also deciding on the cultural values that they will raise their children with.

- Americanized wife, bicultural husband. Maya (now 32) was born in Canada and raised in the United States. Her parents were physicians and had moved to North America in the 1970s. While growing up, she resented not being allowed to date. In fact, her parents never even talked with her about dating, sexuality, etc. She followed a "Don't ask, don't tell" policy with them as she drank, partied, and strictly dated only non-Indian men. Her closest girlfriends were White American and Maya did not learn to speak her parents' native language. In graduate school she surprised herself by falling in love with Satish, who was from New Delhi. Her parents were secretly delighted, for among other things, Satish came from the same caste as they did. The couple got married and reported a good relationship except in the area of in-laws. In couple therapy, Maya complained of Satish's divided loyalties. As an only child, he was extremely close to his widowed mother. His mother recently came and stayed in their home for 3 months. During that time, Maya resented that Satish would come home from work and go straight to his mother's room and chat with her for a good 30 minutes before even saying "Hi" to Maya. For the rest of the evening, mother and son would talk in Punjabi, a language that Maya comprehended somewhat but could not speak. In his mother's presence, Satish was uncomfortable holding Maya's hand or hugging her. Satish also began talking about taking up a temporary assignment in India so he could be closer to his family. Maya was terrified that she would have to put up with her mother-in-law's visits every year and she was certainly not interested in living in India. The couple worked hard to negotiate their communication, intimacy, and family-of-origin issues. With the therapist's help and her husband's support, Maya found ways to connect with her mother-in-law. In turn, Satish learned to meet Maya's needs better, especially in the presence of his mother.

- Traditional wife, Americanized husband. Aslam had lived in the United States since he was 10 years old. He came from a conservative Muslim family and felt quite disconnected from his parents' beliefs as he identified very much as an "American." When he turned 23, his grandmother and mother began pressuring him to agree to an arranged marriage with a "very nice" Muslim woman who had been raised in India and South Africa. Initially Aslam stalled them as he could not imagine himself getting married to someone he did not know, but they persisted. Then following the death of his mother, he was unable to put off his grandmother any longer. The marriage was arranged quickly as Farah (the future bride) and her family were expected to be in the United States within 2 weeks. When Aslam met Farah it was in the presence of several relatives. Aslam then asked to speak with her on the phone. At the end of the 45-minute conversation, he decided that he could not go through with the marriage. According to Aslam, they had nothing in common. Farah was much too traditional compared to him. His family was devastated and his father was livid, but his friends and siblings supported him. While Aslam regretted his own part in this "mistake," he moved out of his family home and called off the wedding.

   This combination is unlikely by its very definition. The major reason that these unions occur uncommonly is that if one partner is "Americanized," he is unlikely to agree to marry someone with whom he does not share much in common. Should the marriage take place (as with Tina and Jatin) the couple will have to negotiate several challenges to make it work.

- Bicultural wife, Americanized husband. Shanta (39) had lived most of her adult life in the United States. She met her husband Ron (short for Rohinton, age 48) 6 years ago through a mutual friend. Ron was a chef and had two girls, now aged 13 and 11, from a previous marriage with a White American woman. Ron was raised in India but had lived in the United States for 30 years and was highly Americanized. Shanta's family in India was aghast that she was in love with an older divorced man, a single father, from another religion. (Her family was conservative Hindu; his was Zoroastrian.) After they got married (against her family's wishes), Shanta chose not to have any children of her own. While not currently unhappy with her life, Shanta often tells her friends that she and her husband "live in separate universes." She has a strong interest in Eastern religions, yoga, and Indian literature, but none of her family members share these. She is forced to vacation in India every summer solo, as her family is not interested in going there. Shanta feels like the "odd man out" at home. While she loves her husband and says that she had grown a lot through this relationship, Shanta wishes she could share her ethnic heritage with her family. She has a hard time connecting with her stepdaughters as she is unable to relate to their music, clothes, and friends. Ron takes his girls' side in these disagreements by telling her to "be more open to the kids' choices."

In this case, we see differences regarding ethnic identity, religious beliefs, and leisure activities between partners and the possibility of conflict/disconnection with children/adolescents as the main challenges.

- Americanized wife, Americanized husband. Jai and Monika (both 35) are second-generation Asian Indians. They met up on a trip to Guatemala and found that they had many experiences in common. They talked about facing a considerable amount of conflict with their parents during their adolescent years for identifying with the mainstream American culture rather than as South Asians. The couple dated off and on for almost 5 years, lived together for a while, and finally married on an impulse in Las Vegas. Few of their interests, behaviors, or daily routines reflect their families' Asian Indian heritage, and they see themselves as a "regular, modern American couple." They have given their children American names and are considering changing their last name to make it more "easily pronounceable."

This kind of couple is least likely to be an arranged marriage. The partners are often different from each other in terms of religion, caste, etc., and are a lot less likely to be in a racially endogamous marriage. They may struggle with their own sense of belonging and their connections with their family's ethnic heritage vs. the culture they grew up in. Their strengths include adaptability and the ability to be open to a variety of new experiences and people.

Asian Indians in Interracial Relationships

Roger (2003), while noting that interracial marriages are on the rise, questions the entire notion of discrete races. Many Americans are bi/multiracial even when they claim to belong to one race. It is important to remember the arbitrary nature of race as we discuss interracial relationships. As detailed earlier, data show that Asian Indians most likely marry within their own ethnic group, and if they do marry outside of the community, it is likely to be to a White person (Qian et al., 2001). Suro (1999) found that more Asian women marry outside of their race than do men. The challenges faced by these couples are likely to be greater than those that comprise partners with different levels of acculturation but from within the same ethnic group. Drawing from the literature on Indian families' structure and dynamics, Table 10.2 juxtaposes Asian Indians

TABLE 10. 2 Comparing Asian Indians and Middle-Class White Americans on Areas That Impact Couples

#	Areas	Asian Indians	Middle-class White Americans
1.	Family structure	Extended, multigenerational	Nuclear family, two generations
2.	Primary relationship focus	Shared between one's children, parents, and spouse	One's spouse, followed by one's children, and then one's parents
3.	Decision-making	Context driven, situational	Rule driven
4.	Interdependence between adult family members	Greater amount tolerated and expected	Independence is valued
5.	Relational orientation	Collective	Individualistic
6.	Tolerance for hierarchy	High	Value egalitarianism
7.	Communication patterns	Indirect	Direct
8.	Parenting style	Likely to be authoritarian	Varied; likely to value authoritative style

and middle-class White Americans on key areas that impact couples. I have presented three vignettes below. The numbers inserted within the vignettes refer to the topics listed in Table 10.2 so that the reader can see how these areas might play out for the couples.

According to MacFadden and Moore (2001) and Risdon (1954), interracial couples face greater social disapproval than those marrying within their race. For example, Seema, a 25-year-old Asian Indian doctoral student, was dating and living with Brian, an African American fellow student, for more than a year. She had kept this relationship a secret from her parents. Her parents had always clearly expected to have a say in who she married. Seema feared that Brian had two strikes against him: he was not Asian Indian and he was African American. When she finally told her parents, her mother wept and her father withdrew in anger. This continued over the entire weekend of her visit and via phone, fax, and e-mail over the next few months. Her parents begged her to reconsider. They told Seema that they would never accept this relationship as it was best to marry within one's own community and religion. They pointed out that the entire Indian community would talk about them, and this would limit the potential marriage options for Seema's younger sister (areas 3, 5, and 8). The stress of this led Seema and Brian to break up. Later, she explained it by saying that she could never have been happy in a relationship that brought her parents so much grief (areas 3 and 5). Even through her anger, part of her wondered if her parents might be right after all (areas 4 and 6).

Interracial marriages also lead the couple to grapple with issues of identity, religion, and language (Tvrtkovic, 2001). Several authors (McFadden & Moore, 2001; Saenz, Hwang, & Anderson, 1995; Tvrtkovic, 2001) note that interracial marriages also bring up challenges around the ethnic identity of one's children, language usage, food preferences, and relationships with the extended family. A study by Saenz et al. (1995) looked at the ethnic identity of children in interracial marriages. They found that the offspring of Asian Indians marrying Whites were more highly likely to identify as White (64.1%), compared with other Asian/White children. McFadden and Moore (2001) discuss many different ways to resolve the above issues in intercultural marriages.

Tanuj and Samantha met on their first day at work and fell in love right away. He was originally from Ahmedabad, a Hindu, and had lived in the United States for 3 years, and she was a nonpracticing Unitarian from New York. They dated for 6 months and were curious about each other's culture and background. Both sets of parents accepted the relationship after some initial apprehensions. The couple had a Hindu wedding in India and a civil ceremony in New York. They then relocated to a small, less diverse town for work reasons. Over the next year, Tanuj found himself deeply missing his parents, a strong Indian presence in the town, and questioning his decision to live in a place that lacked ethnic diversity. For his sake, his parents flew in for the summer and spent 8 weeks with them. The length of their stay tested Samantha's patience as it reduced the couple's privacy considerably (area 1). When the couple was expecting twins, they had a difficult time deciding on baby names. Tanuj wanted his parents to choose the names (area 6) but Samantha did not agree to that. Eventually, they found names that were common to both cultures. When the twins became toddlers, Samantha and Tanuj disagreed on how to discipline the children (area 8). She was a firm believer in providing them with structure. On the other hand, Tanuj and his mother (who was visiting again) were alternately indulgent and strict with the children. The couple had difficulty communicating about their major differences. Samantha was direct and assertive; Tanuj would hint at what he wanted (area 7). With each compromise, Tanuj felt that he was losing a part of himself. Then, when Tanuj's father died suddenly, without Samantha's input on timing, he invited his mother to move in with them. As the oldest son, this was something he felt he had to do (areas 1, 2, 3, and 4). Samantha was shocked. She pointed out that he was a better son than a husband and threatened to move out unless he withdrew the offer to his mother.

In couple therapy, they talked about the challenges and the joys of their intercultural, interracial, and interreligious marriage. It had turned out to be more difficult than they had imagined in their early months together. It was a growth experience and also at times painful. For the first time, they honestly confronted their fears for their children's identity issues and the struggle to integrate Protestant and Hindu beliefs. They also learned ways in which they could accept and respect each other and negotiate differences and agreed to move to a more diverse metropolitan area as soon as possible.

McFadden and Moore (2001) discuss multiple ways in which couples may resolve their cultural differences. While Tanuj and Samantha tried a pluralistic approach as well as integration, the following couple found the solution in one partner adopting the other's culture. Jyoti was 18 when she moved from Mumbai (Bombay) to the United States to begin college. She met John (age 19), a White American from Dallas, at an international student event and they became friends. John was interested in Indian culture, Hinduism, and meditation. Also, having been raised in an alcoholic family, he was very attracted to Jyoti's closeness with her parents and extended family. As their relationship deepened, John took language classes to learn Jyoti's mother tongue, Marathi. He cooked Indian food, read Indian literature, and began to practice Hinduism. By the time they got married 10 years later, he had traveled extensively in India, was a huge fan of Bollywood movies, and could chat with his in-laws in their own language. His family and some friends privately wondered about the extent of his transformation, but Jyoti's family loved John. The latter joked that they had found the perfect Maharashtrian Brahmin (Jyoti's family's caste) groom for their daughter. After their wedding John officially changed his last name to that of his wife's.

Conclusion

This chapter did not discuss South Asian same-sex couples and cohabiting heterosexual couples. This is one major gap in the literature as there was a lack of a body of literature that deals exclusively with these couples in intercultural relationships. Their invisibility is a problem. In order to complete the picture of Asian Indians in the United States, these areas need to be researched and documented. For more information about gays and lesbians that identify as South Asian, please go to the Web site http://www.salganyc.org/ (South Asian Lesbian and Gay Association, n.d.).

The literature and the case vignettes presented in this chapter illustrate that Asians Indians in the United States have unique characteristics as a group that impact their choice of partner and (in most cases) lead them to marry endogamously. Asian Indians marrying interculturally face special challenges and rewards. At times such couples may see mental health professionals to help deal with their conflicts. For resources related to intervention, the therapist is referred to writings by Das and Kemp (1997), Durvasula and Mylvaganam (1994), Rastogi (1999, 2002), and Rastogi and Wampler, (1998, 1999). Maker, Mittal, and Rastogi (2005) provide a comprehensive assessment model for working with Asian Indians in the United States. Also, Table 10.1 and Table 10.2 from this chapter may be used to generate a discussion about the couple's differences and similarities, eventually leading to higher levels of acceptance and understanding that extend across the different ethnic groups.

References

Agarwal, P. (1991). *Passage from India: Post 1965 Indian immigrants and their children: Conflicts, concerns and solutions*. Palos Verdes, CA: Yuvati.

Almeida, R. (1996). Hindu, Christian, and Muslim families. In M. McGoldrick, J. K. Pearce, & J. Giordano (Eds.), *Ethnicity and family therapy* (pp. 395–423). New York: Guilford.

Berry, J.W. (1980). Acculturation as varieties of adaptation. In A.M. Padilla (Ed.), Acculturation: Theory, model, and some new findings. (pp. 9–25). Boulder, CO: Westview.

Bumiller, E. (1990). *May you be the mother of a hundred sons*. New York: Random House.

Das, A. J., & Kemp, S. F. (1997). Between two worlds: Counseling South Asian Americans. *Journal of Multicultural Counseling and Development, 25*, 23–33.

Dirks, N. B. (1989). The original caste: Power, history, and hierarchy. *Contributions to Indian Sociology, 23*(1), 59–77.

Durvasula, R. S., & Mylvaganam, G. A. (1994). Mental health of Asian Indians: Relevant issues and community implications. *Journal of Community Psychology, 22*, 97–108.

Jain, A., & Belsky, J. (1997). Fathering and acculturation: Immigrant Indian families with young children. *Journal of Marriage and the Family, 59*, 873–883.

Kakar, S. (1981). *The inner world: A psychoanalytic study of childhood in India*. New Delhi, India: Oxford University Press.

Maker, A., Mittal, M., & Rastogi, M. (2005). South Asians in the United States: Developing a systemic and empirically-based mental health assessment model. In M. Rastogi & E. Wieling (Eds.), *Voices of color: First person accounts of ethnic minority therapists* (pp. 233–254). Thousand Oaks, CA: Sage.

Marriott, M. (1968a). Caste ranking and food transactions: A matrix analysis. In M. Singer & B. S. Cohn (Eds.), *Structure and change in Indian society* (pp. 133–171). Chicago: Aldine.

Marriott, M. (1968b). Multiple references in Indian caste systems. In J. Silverberg (Ed.), *Social mobility in the caste system in India* (pp. 103–114). The Hague, The Netherlands: Mouton.

Mathur, A. (1994). *Marital conflict and its resolution: A comparative study of American and Indian cultures.* Unpublished master's thesis, University of South Dakota, Vermillion, SD.

McFadden, J., & Moore, J. L., III. (2001). Intercultural marriage and intimacy: Beyond the continental divide. *International Journal of the Advancement of Counseling, 23*, 261–268.

Mehta, S. (1998). Relationship between acculturation and mental health for Asian Indian immigrants in the United States. *Genetic, Social, and General Psychology Monographs, 124,* 61–77.

Min, P. G. (1995). An overview of Asian Americans. In P. G. Min (Ed.), *Asian Americans* (pp. 10–37). Thousand Oaks, CA: Sage.

Qian, Z., Blair, S. L., & Ruf, S. D. (2001). Asian American interracial and interethnic marriages: Differences by education and nativity. *International Migration Review, 35*(2), 557–585.

Ramisetty-Mikler, S. (1993). Asian Indian immigrants in America and sociocultural issues in counseling. *Journal of Multicultural Counseling and Development, 21*, 36–49.

Rastogi, M. (1999). Domestic violence in immigrant Indian families in the U.S. *Family Networker, 2*, 2–3.

Rastogi, M. (2002). Mother-adult daughter questionnaire (MAD): Developing a culturally sensitive instrument. *The Family Journal, 10*(2), 145–155.

Rastogi, M. (2007). Coping with transitions in Asian Indian families: Systemic clinical interventions with immigrants. *Journal of Systemic Therapies, 24*, 55–67.

Rastogi, M., & Wampler, K. S. (1998). Couples and family therapy with Indian families: Some structural and intergenerational considerations. In U. P. Gielen & A. L. Comunian (Eds.), *Family and family therapy in international perspective* (pp. 257–274). Milan: Marinelli Editrice.

Rastogi, M., & Wampler, K. S. (1999). Adult daughters' perceptions of the mother-daughter relationship: A cross-cultural comparison. *Family Relations, 48*, 327–336.

Risdon, R. (1954). A study of interracial marriages based on data for Los Angeles county. *Journal of Sociology and Social Research, 39*, 92–95.

Roger, D. (2003). The progress of love. *Scientific American, 289*(4), 33.

Rolland, A. (1988). *In search of self in India and Japan: Toward a cross-cultural psychology.* Princeton, NJ: Princeton University Press.

Saberwal, S. (2004). Anxieties, identities, complexity, reality. In M. Hasan, (Ed.), *Will secular India survive?* (pp. 93–124). Gurgaon, India: ImprintOne.

Saenz, R., Hwang, S., & Anderson, R. T. (1995). Persistence and change in Asian identity among children of intermarried couples. *Sociological Perspectives, 38*, 175–194.

Segal, U. A. (1991). Cultural variables in Asian Indian families. *The Journal of Contemporary Human Services, 72*, 233–242.

Sheth, M. (1995). Asian American Indians. In P. G. Min (Ed.), *Asian Americans* (pp. 169–198). Thousand Oaks, CA: Sage.

Sodowsky, G. R., & Carey, J. C. (1988). Relationships between acculturation-related demographics and cultural attitudes of an Asian Indian immigrant group. *Journal of Multicultural Counseling and Development, 16*, 117–136.

Sodowsky, G. R., Kwan, K. K., & Pannu, R. (1995). Ethnic identity of Asians in the United States. In J. G. Ponterotto (Ed.), *Handbook of multicultural counseling* (pp. 123–154). Thousand Oaks, CA: Sage.

Sodowsky, G. R., & Ming Lai, E.W. (1997). Asian immigrant variables and structural models of cross-cultural distress. In A. Booth, A. C. Crouter, & N. Landale (Eds.), *Immigration and the Family: Research and Policy on U.S. Immigrants* (pp. 211–234). Mahwah, NJ: Lawrence Erlbaum Associates.

South Asian Lesbian and Gay Association. (n.d.). Retrieved August 20, 2008, from http://www.salganyc.org/

Sue, D. W., & Sue, D. (1990). *Counseling the culturally different* (2nd ed.). New York: Wiley.

Suro, R. (1999). Mixed doubles. *American Demographics, 21*, 56–62.

Tvrtkovic, R. G. (2001, September 10). When Muslims and Christians marry. *America*, pp. 11–14.

U.S. Census Bureau. (n.d.). Census 2000 summary file 4 (SF4)—Sample data. R etrieved April 12, 2004, from http://www.factfinder.census.gov/servlet/DatasetMainPageServlet?_program =DEC&_lang=en&_ts=

Wolpert, S. (1991). *A new history of India.* Oxford, UK: Oxford University Press.

11

Bridges Crossed, Paths Traveled
Muslim Intercultural Couples

Manijeh Daneshpour

Marriage is both a powerful individual experience and an arrangement of considerable social consequence. While a number of historians of marriage and family have explored the significant transformations in the ways that men and women court, marry, and form families (Rose, 2001), a sustained historical examination of marriage across religious lines in America is surprisingly absent.

Even though church officials, rabbis, and Muslim leaders historically have created rules that forbade or severely regulated interfaith marriage, Americans have always married across religious lines. These strictures dissipated somewhat over time, so that by 1920 most Americans seemed to accept mixed faith marriages as a matter of course—even if religious officials still worried about them (Rose, 2001). This is not to say that Americans enthusiastically endorsed or even encouraged such unions but rather that they recognized that people from differing faiths would fall in love and marry each other—and that this search for personal happiness and fulfillment trumped religious affiliation (Rose, 2001).

Individuals who married across religious lines strained, and sometimes explicitly transgressed, accepted norms. They knowingly chose their own destiny rather than complying with prevailing social norms. In this way they both defined and redefined what it meant to be Catholic, Jewish, Protestant, or Muslim. The family, rather than church, mosque, or synagogue, became the agent of religious experience.

Thus, each year, among 2.3 million American unions, thousands of Catholics marry Protestants, Jews marry Christians, and Buddhists, Mormons, Muslims, and Greek Orthodox believers marry someone from another religion. Yet little is written about this phenomenon (Nelson, 2003).

Demographic projections predict a growing trend as the country's expanding ethnic and religious diversity offers more chances for relationship partners to cross paths, cultures, and faiths in new ways. Nelson (2003) notes that this mixing is a norm among the young people she marries, who are so used to cultural and religious variety that they don't even begin to consider a potential for conflict. "When they're young and you talk about conflict in terms of religion and race," she says, "they look at you as if you're Martian" (Nelson, 2003, p. 5).

Reactions to Interfaith Marriage

It is apparent that reaction to interfaith marriages can be strong, and many couples fear great disapproval from their families, ethnic group, and/or society at large. This attitude is largely derived from beliefs about other religious traditions. Many conservative Christian dominations, for example, discourage interfaith marriages based on their understanding that the Bible condemns such marriages. Liberal Christian denominations see the potential for an extra level of conflict within interfaith marriages, but clergy are generally willing to marry such couples. Non-Christian religions vary: Hindus welcome interfaith marriages, Muslims place restrictions on them, and many Jews discourage them (Tvrtkovic, 2001).

Muslim women wishing to marry Christian men face the additional worry of potential ostracism from the faith community, as they are expected to marry only within the faith (Tvrtkovic, 2001). One traditional Muslim authority writes that "Islam considers the husband [to be the] head-of-the-family and therefore requires that a Muslim [woman] cannot marry a non-Muslim because she will [then] be under the authority of a non-Muslim husband" (Tvrtkovic, 2001, p. 12). A non-Muslim male who wishes to marry a Muslim woman could proceed if he first sincerely converted to Islam. If a man married to a Muslim woman converts to another religion, then the marriage is dissolved.

The situation is very different for Muslim men. Mohammad Abbasi Khatib, a lay minister at the Dar-Ul-Islam mosque in Teaneck, New Jersey, explains that: "A Muslim male is permitted to marry a person of the Book—in other words, a Jew or Christian. The only objection to this would be if the woman he was marrying wasn't living up to the requirements of her own religion" (Tvrtkovic, 2001, p. 12). He adds: "What's important to us is that ... someone believes in God and can always be held accountable to something" (p. 13). This would imply that an agnostic, atheist, Buddhist, and some Unitarian Universalist women may not be eligible to marry a Muslim man. Also, if a Muslim man agrees to allow his children to be raised as non-Muslims, then he will be regarded as having abandoned Islam.

Thus, Christian–Muslim couples may wrestle with these concerns: different religious understandings of marriage (sacrament versus sacred contract, divine versus human institution), Islam's greater family involvement in mate selection and marriage, Islam's proscription of dating, potential legal problems in countries with sharia (Islamic law) in force, greater cultural differences when one partner is from an Eastern collectivistic culture and the other is from a Western individualistic cultural context, and difficulty distinguishing the religious from the cultural (Tvrtkovic, 2001). Nevertheless, Christian and Muslim men and women do marry cross-culturally and they do deal with the complexity of these issues.

Religious and Community Resources for Interfaith Couples

While there seem to be numerous books, brochures, courses, and community resources dealing with relationship and community issues for Christian–Jewish couples, perhaps because of their longer history of intermarriage and their greater numbers, there are practically no resources for Christian–Muslim couples in the United States. The few print resources available to pastors, Imams, and couples are either outdated or written for a non-American context.

Lack of resources, combined with the reluctance of many imams and pastors even to broach the subject of interfaith marriages, has left many Christian–Muslim couples at a loss. To whom can they turn for advice about the unique issues they face? Where can imams, priests, and campus ministers go when called upon to counsel the small but growing number of such couples?

This chapter is an attempt to provide a greater understanding of Muslim intercultural couples, with the hope that it will be helpful to the couples themselves and to imams, pastors, and counselors who work with these couples. The term *Muslim intercultural couples* will be used in order to describe those marriages in which one partner is Muslim and from a Muslim country in the East and the other partner is Christian and from the United States or Europe. This chapter will describe some of the dynamics that previously have not been addressed, including what makes these marriages unique and special, the reasons behind couple difficulties, potential challenges for many couples, and suggestions for managing differences and making them work for the relationship instead of against it.

Stages of Marital Transition

No couple lives in a vacuum. Their ups and downs and the social, cultural, and marital adjustment process they go through will be affected by what is going on in the world around them. This includes the attitudes of society toward the marriage they've chosen as well as their own comfort level within the society in which they reside. Their relationship will also reflect the various developmental stages they pass through in the life cycle: newly married, young parents, middle-aged parents with adolescent children or empty nests, and those retired or anticipating retirement. According to Romano (1997), a couple will pass through phases as each moves from being a single individual to being in a partnership. Although the forms, details, and timing vary with each couple and set of circumstances, most Muslim intercultural couples experience three general stages of adjustment.

The Honeymoon Phase

The honeymoon phase is when couples find a new sense of intimacy and connection, and everything new and different is a wonderful enriching gift. Some couples know each other well when they marry and also know a great deal about each other's culture. As a result, they are better prepared for what their joint future holds than those who marry more impulsively and do not have a clear understanding of the serious implications of their cultural and religious differences.

The Setting-In Phase

This phase is when some of a couple's differences may cause major disagreements. Most intercultural couples go through all three phases before they work out which or whose ideas about how they are going to live their lives will win out.

As the novelty of the marriage wears off, and spouses shed some of their politeness and careful behavior, they may begin to share previously unexposed aspects of themselves, both personal, in terms of being comfortable enough to exhibit old habits and manners, and cultural, in terms of cherishing some of the norms, rules, and roles from their culture of origin. These parts were not necessarily hidden but previously may not have been obvious or given much importance. In this phase each partner expects to settle into his own culturally preconceived notion of married life, which may have been largely unconscious or unexamined. Each comes to understand, perhaps regretfully, that their partner's conception of these marital roles (division of labor, decision-making, and social interactions) is different than their own and is going to affect how they fulfill them.

This phase is even more complicated for Muslim intercultural couples than for other couples due to the lack of norms and lack of useful nonbiased information for their relationship formation and maintenance. They are on their own to find information about each other's cultural and religious traditions and to seek similarities and compromises for their differences.

In this phase, couples learn about likes and dislikes; each may want to continue having and doing the things he likes and want the other to share his tastes. Some fortunate ones, who were originally attracted by their similarities of interest as well as viewpoints, find that these shared interests are what keep them going despite their many dissimilarities. But others discover that they are worlds apart. And so there are choices and compromises to be made and, most difficult of all, sometimes even their styles of reaching these compromises may be quite different. It is important to note that, in some cases, people have simply married the wrong partner, not the wrong culture. They may have difficulty accepting or understanding that cultural differences have little or nothing to do with their real problems. Family-of-origin issues, differences in personality in terms of being an introvert or an extrovert, and previous relationship experiences and expectations create major issues that may be largely separate from cultural issues such as patriarchal beliefs regarding gender relations or a value of maintaining strong connections with extended families. In this stage Muslim intercultural couples can misunderstand each other greatly due to the non-Muslim partner's lack of unbiased information about Islamic cultures and the Muslim partner's use of cultural masks to delay or deny the real issues that are more personal than religious or cultural. Cultural masks might be thought of as a strategy in which people defend or justify their beliefs or behavior by referencing their culture, when in fact personality characteristics or family-of-origin experiences are contributing factors. People may hide behind cultural explanations, inappropriately using them to defend themselves. This strategy is possible because of the widely held assumption that the beliefs and practices of a culture different than one's own are somehow off limits for challenging or questioning. As an example, a domineering husband may attempt to convince his partner that his rigid behavior is justified by his cultural or his religious background, even though his belief system and behavior have more to do with his family upbringing and are not necessarily characteristic of his religion or his culture. It is important to note that since couples typically live in the cultural context of one partner, if that partner chooses a cultural mask it is easier to see, understand, and challenge. For couples in the United States, lack of information about the Eastern cultural context makes use of cultural masks more of a possibility for the Muslim partner. A case example may clarify some of these issues:

Mrs. A, an African American woman who converted from Catholicism to Islam several years ago and is married to a Somali man, was referred to me by Mrs. A's friend. Mrs. A reported that she and her current husband had a very short courtship before they got married and she did not know much about his Somali culture. She reported that in the beginning of their marriage, they related to each other very well. They did many things together and shared many interests. However, after their first child was born, she stayed home often while he spent many hours away from home and socialized with his friends and relatives. Over time, he became more distant and she became more frustrated. When she challenged him about not being home more often and not connecting with her as much, he claimed that his behavior was typical and normal in his culture. She believed his explanation and instead of holding him accountable she started resenting his culture for allowing men to become distant and irresponsible after only a few years of marriage. She decided to not participate in any gatherings with his family and friends and he responded by becoming more and more disconnected from her and their child. After discussing some of their marital interactions, it became clear that her lack of information about his cultural background gave him an excuse: he used a cultural mask to get away from family responsibilities. Thus, it was suggested to Mrs. A that she participate in her husband's cultural and family events and get to know his culture and extended family better. She attended gatherings and went more frequently to the local mosque. After talking to Somali women, and observing their relationship with their partners, she realized that not all Somali men distance themselves from their wives after a few years of marriage and especially after they have children. She started challenging him and using his own cultural background to hold him accountable. He resisted at first but then responded by spending more time with her and their child. Their relationship significantly improved.

The Life-Pattern Phase

This phase is when differences are either resolved or accepted, when a pattern of negotiation is determined or the conflicts become habits. What happens at this point in marriage depends entirely on the particular couple. Some end the marriage, while other intercultural couples believe that their marriage actually has a greater potential for success than a monocultural one and work hard until they iron out the problem areas (Romano, 1997). Some resolve their difficulties by "habitually fighting them out, usually from their original starting point, and continue doing so, time after time, until the end of their marriage (or their lives)" (Romano, 1997, p. 29).

Muslim intercultural couples may have relationship issues and differences between partners that are even more complicated and dramatic than those faced by other intercultural couples. This is due to the pervasive lack of knowledge about Islam and Muslims and because differences connect to both cultural and religious aspects of identity that may be unconscious as well as conscious, making them more difficult to resolve. It is important to note here that Christian Americans may lack knowledge about many cultures and religions but information about Islam and Muslims has been particularly lacking. There are many reasons for this, including the unavailability of unbiased literature, due to social and political controversies, and the media's interest in portraying negative images of this group.

In Muslim intercultural couples' relationships, not all differences cause problems and create big challenges. However, because of differences between Eastern and Western cultural contexts, and the differences inherent in Christianity and Islam, Muslim intercultural marriages carry a great potential for multiple mixtures of cultural values, assumptions, beliefs, and religious, ethnic, educational, and cultural backgrounds. In the next section some of these challenges will be described, followed by practical guidelines to help couples face these challenges and a perspective about the unique and rewarding aspect of these couples' relationships.

Challenges for Muslim Intercultural Couples

Belief System and Values

One way to understand couples in conflict is to view the partners as operating from two different value systems that are not in agreement. Couples
with similar values generally have a greater chance of marital compat-
ibility, no matter what their cultural differences may be. The challenge for
Muslim intercultural couples is that they may have similar values in some
domains but not in others, which they may not realize until they are well
into the marriage.

Stewart and Bennett (1991) offer a model for better understanding the
nature of cultural values. They divide cultural values and assumptions
into four components, which they then analyze from a cross-cultural perspective. The first component, the form of activity, compares the Western
orientation toward "doing" with the orientation of many Eastern cultures
in which "being" or "being-in-becoming" or self-growth are the predominant values. Second, the form of relationships to others compares the
Western orientation toward interpersonal equality in relationships with
the status conscious, formal, and longer lasting relationships common to
many Eastern cultures. Third, perception of the world compares the way
different cultures consider humankind's relationship to nature. While
Westerners prefer mastery over nature, many other cultures, including
Eastern cultures, see humans as an integral part of nature. Fourth, perception of the self compares the manner in which people in different societies
see themselves (as individuals or as part of a group) and how that affects
the way they behave (emphasizing a reliance on self-motivation or acting in terms of obligation toward a group). These complex differences in
worldviews or visions of life may be compounded if couples are unaware
of their own fundamental values. The big challenge is that spouses often
do not explicitly know much about their own cultural value orientations,
much less those of their partners.

Gender Relationships

In even the most progressive societies, true equality between the sexes
is more a goal than a reality. It is only the form of male superiority that
differs from culture to culture. In some societies, primarily non-Western

ones, the women's role is to serve the man, which includes physical labor, deferring to his judgments, and following his demands. In Western societies, on the other hand, male dominance takes a more subtle form: the woman is offered certain courtesies that designate her as the weaker sex, and certain customs are followed that demonstrate the man's authority. Traditional examples include who holds the door or pays the restaurant check. While the specific activities vary considerably from culture to culture, there are many activities that are limited to men and others that are the exclusive province of women. However, when two people from cultures that view these roles differently marry and attempt to build a family life together, differences may become a major issue. This is especially true if (a) the societies are culturally far apart, like Eastern and Western cultures; (b) one or both of the spouses adheres strictly to his society's interpretation of gender roles; and (c) the man comes from an Eastern cultural context and the woman from a Western cultural context (Romano, 1997).

No matter what dynamics exist in couples' relationships, in Muslim intercultural families it is important for partners to have a basic agreement about gender roles. This does not necessarily mean agreement about how specific responsibilities are actually divided, but having a general conceptual agreement about roles creates a better process of negotiation for both partners. However, the dynamics become more complicated with Muslim intercultural couples when the man is an Easterner or, more specifically, a Middle-Easterner and the woman is a Westerner. This issue is important to consider since women, regardless of their culture of origin, tend to be more relationship oriented than men and generally try harder to keep their relationships going. When a woman is married to a man whose cultural belief is that her role is to serve him or that she is inferior, she may work hard to maintain the relationship, leading her to give in to him and to give up aspects of herself (Romano, 1997), sometimes in ways that are not in her best interest.

In addition, if a Muslim lives in a non-Muslim country and marries a local Christian woman, he places himself under great pressure. His wife will be living among her people and within her own cultural context. Socially she has no reason to modify her behavior or beliefs in order to be more accommodating to Islamic principles. In fact, all the inevitable compromises may have to be made by her husband, who is an outsider coming into her society. The case is different if she travels to his home country. It is then she who finds herself in a position of having to make compromises in order to adjust to her new environment. The social context of couples is of great importance with respect to gender dynamics.

The male–female role issue is also tied to subtle and often intangible ideas regarding meanings of marriage and intimacy; beliefs about respect, integrity, and mutual support; and questions of power (Heller & Wood, 2000). Muslim multicultural couples need to pay close attention to these underlying issues, which are often not discussed. If they are not, both spouses can feel betrayed, misunderstood, cheated, or rejected and, ultimately, either or both may feel like a failure for not being able to live up to the other's ideals.

Time Orientations

Although no culture is purely present, past, or future oriented, the importance a culture places on temporal frames of reference varies and, as a result, people in different parts of the world move at different paces. In Arab countries, people are generally more relaxed and unhurried, engaging in time-consuming activities and conversations. Interpersonal activities are considered more important than meeting the demands of an external timekeeper. On the other hand, the emphasis in American culture is on productivity and time management. People are generally in a hurry and do not have much time for the interpersonal aspect of life. A good illustration of this difference is that "tomorrow" specifically means the day after today in English, but burka, the comparable Arabic word, refers to a less defined time in the future.

It is interesting to note that individuals, as well as cultures, move to different rhythmic patterns. Individual rhythm is inherent; that is, it "begins in the center of the self" (Hall, 1983, p. 57). Each person has his own sense of time and of place, but each individual has also been trained from the moment of birth to conform to certain cultural rhythms. Each culture has been "choreographed in its own way, with its own beat tempo and rhythm" (Hall, 1983, p. 58). Thus, "while personality is undoubtedly a factor in interpersonal synchrony, culture is also a powerful determinant" (Hall, 1983, p. 59) Though not every individual is in sync with his own culture, people generally orient themselves to the dominant rhythm of their culture of origin. Although couples do, over time, adapt to one another's rhythms or learn to allow for their differences, a spouse from a Western culture can be slowed down only so much, and a spouse from an Eastern culture speeded up just so much, before strain shows. The Eastern partner, for example, may want more time to accomplish tasks and demand greater understanding, while the Western partner believes that too much time has already being wasted, leading to a major issue in their relationship.

Political Views

Politics may seem to be irrelevant to the concept of love and marriage, but in Muslim intercultural marriages politics play a role if (a) the partners or their families adhere to fundamentally different political philosophies or come from historically hostile lands; (b) the couple is forced to live in a different country because of a political situation or because of the beliefs or practices of one of the partners; or (c) one partner comes from a country that is in a state of war.

Politics can seriously intrude into relationships when couples' countries are long-term enemies. The adjustment of the intercultural couple is also affected by the political climate of their chosen country. If this climate includes hostility toward the country of one partner, a violent or repressive government, civil war, racial tension, terrorist activities, or political instability, the marriage may reflect this cultural climate because the couple is not completely separate or isolated from these events. In today's political climates, many Muslim intercultural couples have to renegotiate their loyalties, and their connection or lack thereof, to their own cultural backgrounds when one partner is from a predominantly Muslim country. Many couples who assumed, prior to recent events in the Middle East, that they did not have strong political views have noticed old loyalties arise, creating new challenges that impact their sense of couplehood.

Economics and Financial Issues

In all marriages, monocultural and intercultural, financial issues can be a source of major disagreement. In intercultural marriages, financial problems might seem more numerous and tougher to solve because partners often have culturally based differences regarding such matters as who earns the money, who controls its expenditure, how much should be spent for different activities, and how expenses should be prioritized. For Muslim intercultural couples, different value orientations are involved and different priorities must be considered. Therefore, it may take more money to keep such a marriage going smoothly because of the diverse needs and desires of the partners. Couples should come to understand that both personal and financial resources are integral to the success of their marriages. For example, the Eastern partner may see the need to send some money overseas to provide for extended family, whereas the Western partner may see that as a burden on their financial resources, so understanding the partner's sense of obligation to help his family may bring the couple much closer to each other and strengthen their personal connection.

Extended Family Relationships

Contrary to popular belief, families are not something young men and women shed upon marrying but usually something they acquire more of (Romano, 1997), especially if one partner is from the West and the other is from the East. In a Muslim intercultural marriage, not only does the couple have to deal with culturally diverse in-laws, they may have to understand and absorb new concepts of family that will have a great bearing on how they live their married lives.

In Western cultures, parents normally begin educating their children at an early age to accept personal responsibility for their actions and then push them out of the nest as soon as they can stand on their own two feet. Therefore, as young adults, men and women make their own decisions and expect to live with the good and bad consequences of the choices they make.

In Eastern cultures, on the other hand, parents never really let go of their children. They maintain patriarchal authority and do not expect to be abandoned in their old age. They devote themselves to their children when they are young but continue to have power over their children and expect eternal respect and loyalty from them when they are grown. Therefore, not only do the family ties not decrease, they greatly extend when a son or daughter marries.

These cultural differences make for quite diverse interpretations about how to handle and relate to in-laws. More often than in monocultural marriages, parents may strongly disapprove of the child's choice of a spouse. This initially may pull the couple closer in mutual self-defense, but in the long run parental opposition can precipitate conflict and distrust and severe loyalty struggles. Western culture sees the family of procreation as the most important unit, whereas Eastern cultures see the family of procreation only as an extension of the family of origin. Therefore, while the Western partner demands loyalty to the nuclear family, the Eastern partner sees his loyalty to the whole extended family as more centrally important.

Another complicated factor is that close family involvement can be a double-edged sword. The extended family can be the couple's best ally, offering care and support, or the couple's worst enemy, confusing involvement with interference, invading a couple's privacy, and perhaps instigating arguments and causing problems. Although some couples bond more closely as a reaction against nonsupportive parents, others say that external problems that arise because of one family or the other cause more conflict than any other issue. It is important to note that compared to other multicultural couples, Muslim intercultural couples have the least resources to deal with this particular issue due to lack of adequate and unbiased information available to them both from Eastern and Western cultural contexts. There are misunderstandings and stereotypical views of Christianity in Middle Eastern cultures, as well as a distorted understanding of Islam in Western cultures.

Socioeconomic and Class Status

Similarity in social background is an important ingredient in any marriage, intercultural or not, as it implies similarity in education, attitudes, tastes, and manners. While there are no empirical data on the social class backgrounds of Muslim intercultural couples, there seems to be more crossing of class lines in these relationships than in monocultural ones (Daneshpour, 2003). One possible reason is that the majority of Eastern people who can afford to come to the United States to work or study are from upper-class families. They often have high family and professional status in their own countries but in the United States their professional degrees are often not recognized by the educational system and thus their credentials are not considered valid. In addition, due to their minority and immigrant status, they often do not have the opportunity or the privilege to use their class, professional, and family status to meet and marry people from upper-class backgrounds.

There is the popular belief that if cross-cultural couples belong to the same social class, their marriage will not be more complicated than a monocultural marriage. While this may or may not be true, many Muslim intercultural couples are simply unaware of their class differences. They just don't know enough about their partner's culture to assess his status within it. Often one of the partners has never been to the other's country to see the culture in action. Therefore, one partner has no idea what is and is not acceptable behavior in the other's society and may draw on stereotypical understanding of the culture and interpret questionable behavior as being about culture rather than about class differences. For example, a Middle Eastern partner's refusal to help with chores in the family is usually attributed to his culture's patriarchal beliefs and expectations about women performing these tasks. However, his behavior may be related to having had maids who performed domestic tasks in his household while he was growing up and his behavior may have less to do with his Middle Eastern cultural background than with unexamined social class assumptions.

Spirituality and Religion

Even for couples from the same country, religion may be a major source of conflict. This is true not only because the partners may disagree on where and how to worship or pray as a family but because so much of what people do and believe, their attitudes about right and wrong, and their philosophies of life, stem from what they have learned and not learned from their families' religious backgrounds.

In any marriage, problems can arise when religious beliefs differ or when one partner's behavior conflicts with the other's beliefs. Mutual respect for each other's religion is a must for a compatible marriage, but often it is not enough.

Because Muslims perceive Islam as a way of life, it strongly influences accepted behavior in so many ways that it is difficult to know where religion ends and cultural values begin (Daneshpour, 1998). The problem is much greater if one partner is intensely religious and the other less so. Even people who do not actively practice their religion are often influenced, consciously or unconsciously, by the values and thought patterns of their religious pasts. Sometimes couples think they have resolved the religion issue because they have settled on where to marry and what kind of ceremony to have and have come to some sort of agreement regarding where to worship and how to raise children. But religion runs deeper and can disrupt the relationship if not carefully attended to.

In Muslim countries, religion determines the degree of freedom women have. It regulates such things as gambling, dancing, sexual behavior, and the use of alcohol, and many people bring these belief systems into their relationships regardless of their level of religiosity.

For those Muslim and Christian partners who decide to marry outside their religion, one of three things usually happens: (a) one partner converts to the religion of the other; this takes time and usually happens after several years and is based on many compromises from both partners to redefine their relationship; (b) both partners keep their own faith and try not to interfere in the practices or beliefs of the other; this group needs to do lots of negotiation and differentiation in order to keep the marriage from dissolution; or (c) both partners drift away from their own religion and either join a third religion or refrain from adhering to any formal religion at all. In many cases both partners have already distanced themselves from their cultural heritage, and religious practices are not an issue (Daneshpour, 2003).

With regards to practice of religion, it is important to know that few couples have arguments regarding theology. Nevertheless, religion will impact their decisions regarding how many children to have and the use of birth control; attitudes toward abortion, fidelity, and divorce; whether family funds will be donated to religious institutions; how holidays will be spent; how much time will be devoted to religious ceremonies; which food will be served in the house; how one or both will dress or behave in various circumstances; and what moral code, medical practice, and so on will be adhered to (Daneshpour, 2003).

What is important is that the partners become aware of and able to articulate their underlying beliefs and discuss the practices that are most important in their religious heritage. Without this, successful negotiation on religious matters is unlikely to occur.

Children and the Family's Multicultural Context

Raising children in a Muslim intercultural family is a challenge due to many different issues, including discipline, guidance, nurturance, and identity. Usually without analyzing what they are doing, most people automatically revert to their own childhood to find a model for parenting and for teaching their children survival skills and the unspoken conventions of relationships. Because these couples were raised in different countries and cultures, the parents may have conflicting models. Parents may find themselves at odds in agreeing upon a clear and consistent pattern of roles and rules for their children. Parents in basic agreement regarding their value systems may still find that they emphasize different values while raising their children. The desired end result might be the same, but the route along the way might differ radically.

Parents who clash over child-rearing issues are often really battling over some basic differences in philosophy, values, or beliefs that they as a couple have not managed to resolve; the child merely provides the spark for conflict. But these underlying issues are often difficult to recognize or define, let alone come to grips with; so instead of going to the heart of the matter, the couple fights over the particulars.

Often the majority of differences show up just before the child is born. What religion and what language should be taught? Should family celebrations reflect both cultures and both religions or should the host country win out? Should the child be raised monocultural or bicultural, monolingual or bilingual?

Raising children tests how well a couple has learned to handle challenges in general and to deal with their many differences. It is with children's issues that all other problems surface and must be confronted. Differences don't matter; how they are managed does (Romano, 1997).

Problem-Solving, Language, and Communication

Different people have different styles of communication, and true communication between Muslim intercultural couples requires that they learn not only to understand, accept, and accommodate each other's states of mind but that they realize that problems will not go away simply because partners have become aware of each other's different styles. Generally, overt, explicit, and open communication is positively valued in the Anglo-American cultures (Tamura & Lau, 1992). Family communication focuses on listening skills, speaking skills, self-disclosure, clarity, continuity-tracking, and respect and regard (Olson, 2002). Very good communication consists of congruent, clear messages and open discussion of self, feelings, and relationships.

In contrast, indirect and implicit expression is common among Muslims (Daneshpour, 1998). Indirect means of communication include frequent allusions to proverbs and folk parables. Muslims, like other Easterners, are not encouraged to make their desires explicit to others. Instead, they are expected to be highly sensitive to what other people have in mind, despite the minimal use of verbal interaction (Daneshpour, 1998).

In Eastern cultures, indirect and covert communication can create a strong bond between speaker and listener. This style of communication respects a person's judgment about her understanding of the dialogue's context. A partner loses face, and possibly self-autonomy and independence, when explicitly criticized or ordered by the other. This is an important consideration for multicultural couples because use of "I" statements and explicit messages, methods of communication generally promoted by American therapists, are strongly discouraged in Eastern societies. They are viewed as self-centered and insensitive to the relationship (Daneshpour, 1998).

Although losing face and use of shame are socially important as a means of engendering loyalty to family and culture, they should not be misused in intimate relationships. For example, in a Muslim intercultural relationship it may not be comfortable for the Eastern partner to openly and explicitly raise criticisms or make demands for change, since this could involve discussing issues that would shame the partner directly. Instead of bringing a concern to a therapy session or discussing it directly with the partner at home, the Eastern partner may even choose to discuss concerns with a third party, who then could discuss the issue with the Western partner indirectly. On the other hand, this avoidant approach may frustrate the Western partner if she wants explicit ideas on what her partner does not specifically like about her behavior. In working with an interfaith couple, one therapeutic intervention for this relationship pattern would be to concentrate first on understanding these dynamics, by making this communication pattern more explicit and then having the couple discuss it in session so that they do not attempt to change their behavioral pattern prematurely.

When multicultural couples broaden their understanding by becoming more culturally aware it can help eliminate some of the perplexity and blaming that is often otherwise present. Multicultural couples will find that over time they even benefit from learning and using each other's style and compensating for each other's blind spots. It takes a lot of work, but the results of the effort may be well worth the investment.

Health and Stress

Cultures teach people how to handle stress and/or resolve conflict. Stress can be defined as anything pushing people mentally or physically out of balance, and it can cause problems in the Muslim intercultural relationship. Whatever the cause, each person has ways of responding to stress, depending on age, sex, personality, and cultural or ethnic backgrounds. When dealing with life's problems, people tend to go back to their roots, which give them a sense of comfort and identity. But the ways people choose may be perplexing and upsetting to their partners.

One catalyst for stress may be different cultural beliefs about how to handle illness and suffering. How sick is sick? What is healthy? How can illness be prevented? How should it be reacted to? Who should treat it and how?

People with different cultural backgrounds have different answers to these questions. McGoldrick, Giordano, and Pearce (2005) discuss how people differ across cultures in (a) how they experience pain; (b) what they label as symptoms; (c) how they communicate their pain or symptoms; (d) what their beliefs are about the cause of illness; (e) how they regard helpers; and (f) what treatment they desire or expect.

Even though many Muslim intercultural couples do not realize it at the beginning of their relationship, the way people experience and express pain is greatly influenced by culture. In some cultures, the norm dictates that suffering is done silently, while in others it is expected or allowed to be demonstrative and verbal. Also, what is labeled as a symptom differs cross-culturally (Brislin, 1993). An intercultural couple may need to negotiate about treatment for illnesses, with Easterners often relying on more nontraditional methods and Westerners generally relying more on scientifically proven medical methods.

Guidelines for Better Connections and Happier Relationships

Martial satisfaction and happiness are personal matters involving two people, not necessarily two entire cultures. Nevertheless, there are some issues to which Muslim intercultural couples can attend and thereby make their relationships less challenging and more rewarding.

Commitment to the relationship is a central tenet for all successful relationships, and Muslim intercultural couples are no exception. Once couples negotiate their investment and make a conscious effort about how hard they need to try to make it work, their dedication will carry them through.

Communication and problem-solving are some of the most important ingredients of a successful marriage regardless of what style of communication couples use, be it verbal or nonverbal. In a Muslim intercultural relationship, it is very helpful if partners learn each other's language in order to understand the other partner's culture better. It is also important to understand each other's styles of communicating and problem-solving, as this will assist couples as they negotiate role and rules.

The ability to perceive and be responsive to emotional, physical, and cultural needs means accepting and giving in to some of the partner's wishes; this can potentially include compromises that a partner would not need to make in a monocultural marriage. To outsiders, compromises across cultural lines may look out of balance, but they make the intercultural relationship healthier. For example, covering one's head when going to a mosque may not be a comfortable choice, but doing so makes the Muslim spouse happier and increases his ability to compromise on other issues.

Cherishing each other's culture seems to be very simple, but in reality, partners need to reexamine their own cultural values regarding their partner's cultural background. This is especially true in a Muslim intercultural marriage because Muslims and Islamic cultures in general have never been portrayed positively in the Western media. Christianity and Islam have been presented as polarized religions that cannot be compatible or share common ground. In addition, Westerners generally believe in the superiority of most aspects of their own culture. These issues will create serious challenges, and successful couples are ones that can come to their own opinion about similarities and differences and can cherish good aspects of each other's cultures without giving in to extreme cultural and religious stereotypes.

Adaptability is an essential character trait for Muslim intercultural couples so they can be sensitive to each other's needs and wishes. It can help them negotiate cultural and religious issues and find ways to tolerate the confusion their two different ways of being bring into their daily routines, particularly if they knew little about each other's cultures before knowing each other.

A positive sense of self and strong cultural identity can help Muslim intercultural couples feel more at ease and less defensive. Since Muslim cultures have been portrayed as excessively patriarchal, Muslim male partners may feel threatened and defensive when assumptions are made about women's rights issues in relation to Muslim women. On the other hand, many Easterners view Westerners as extremely individualistic and noncollaborative and the Western partner may feel bombarded by critical judgments and assumptions about her cultural corruption and highly self-centered Western beliefs. These issues can be highly damaging to a person with low self-esteem. It is important that each person in the relationship work on building his self-esteem so that they will be able to maintain a mutual connection in the face of stereotypical assumptions and judgments.

Mutual goals help partners work together toward a common vision, even if there are differences in their methods of achieving them. This is a sensitive matter because it is based on values and belief systems. If partners' educational values, for example, are the same, they will have an easier time negotiating rules related to education for themselves and their children. If they both like traveling and extended families are important, they can use this commonality as a way of getting closer so that they have a foundation for negotiating other less agreed-upon goals.

Prerequisites for Permanent Commitment

Certain actions—like living together and socializing with a partner's family—can facilitate a couple's movement toward permanent commitment. These actions may not be practical or possible for a Muslim intercultural couple, depending on the Muslim partner's country of origin and the level of conservatism of his family of origin. However, getting to know the culture of the partner before committing to a long-term relationship is a responsible decision. Both partners need to socialize with their partner's community; they need to learn the language; they need to learn about the partner's religion and find ways to use resources other than the partner to find out about the religion, especially if there are different interpretations of the religion by different countries and cultural groups. It is important to note that Islam is the religion of more than one billion people across the globe; even though the basic religious doctrines are the same for all Muslims, each culture has adapted them differently. To understand the culture that one is going to become a part of, it is helpful to read books about geography, customs, and people's ways of connecting. It is also a good idea to search for a wide range of resources since viewing a culture from only one perspective means we don't really know the culture. Furthermore, couples can always consider premarital discussion with both Christian and Muslim leaders to better understand their own spiritual development and what issues may come up in their journey to become one.

Muslim Intercultural Couples' Incentives

When partners venture across racial, ethnic, and religious lines to enter into marriage, they are met with many challenges on the other side. Concurrent with this crossing of borders is the arising of the opportunity to increase their knowledge about the "Other" while examining and redefining their own values and ideas. Crossing this line results in exposure to innovative, different, yet valid ways of approaching life and resolving problems. It is at this point that adaptability becomes a key resource.

Muslim intercultural couples have an opportunity to develop an international identity that is both more realistic and more expansive than either partner originally had. In American society, the perspective of the "Other" is a vantage point that is often unfamiliar, as most Americans have been deprived of it in the sheltering arms of a naïve society that does not expect them to learn, explore, and know about others who experience life differently. Conversely, the rest of the world views the American way of life as filled with excitement, vitality, and opportunity. By gaining an international perspective, these mutually exaggerated and false views of the two differing worlds can be brought into better perspective, resulting in better understanding of the lifestyles and struggles existing on both sides. Thus, Muslim intercultural couples can develop an international identity that is perhaps more collectivistic than the dominant American way of life and less hierarchal than traditional Islamic culture.

Another asset for Muslim intercultural couples is the perspective of bicultural children who have the advantage of fusing both worlds in their ongoing negotiation to find their niche in life. The hope is that Muslim intercultural couples can live with paradox and help break walls of dichotomous difference.

Conclusion

Muslim multicultural couples have chosen a path that is certainly less traveled. They have chosen a complicated route in life, one that takes more work, more empathy, more honesty; they ultimately face more challenges. Concurrently, in choosing this path, they prove to the rest of the world that it is possible to create harmony and connection in human life, even in the face of significant differences.

In their pioneering, they have given hope to the possibility of bringing together people from differing backgrounds and of having them understand and love each other, cherish each other's culture, and make it work. They have proven successful in their ability to live together, raise bicultural children, expand their worldviews, and celebrate their differences. They have fused the beauty of two different cultures and patched the imperfections of each with the strengths of the other. This patchwork is desperately needed in the world we live in today. By mending a structure with the strongest patches of all differing cultures, eventually a strong network of intertwining ideals and practices will weave a quilt so strong that the idea of not understanding "the other" will be nonexistent. In the acceptance of intercultural marriages, the first thread of the needle may be worked into this quilt of cultural peace and tranquility in order to create strong bonds and connections that cannot be taken away by differences in our political views or our genders—and not even by our different faiths.

References

Brislin, R. (1993). *Understanding culture's influence on behavior.* Orlando, FL: Harcourt Brace.

Daneshpour, M. (1998). Muslim families and family therapy. *Journal of Marriage and Family Therapy, 24,* 287–300.

Daneshpour, M. (2003). Lives together, worlds apart? The lives of multicultural Muslim couples. In V. Thomas, T. Karis, & J. Wetcher (Eds.), *Clinical issues with interracial couples: Theories and research* (pp. 57–72). New York: Haworth Press.

Hall, E. T. (1983). *The dance of life.* New York: Anchor Books/Doubleday.

Heller, P. E. & Wood, B. (2000). The influence of religious and ethnic differences on marital intimacy: Intermarriage versus intermarriage. *Journal of Marital & Family Therapy, 26,* 241–252.

McGoldrick, M., Giordano, J., & Pearce, J. K. (2005). *Ethnicity and family therapy* (3rd ed.). New York: Guilford.

Nelson, M. Z. (2003). A house divided: Interfaith families cut across lines and make religious institutes edgy. *Publishers Weekly, 250*(12), 8–15.

Olson, D. H. (2002). Circumplex model of marital and family system: Assessing family functioning. In F. Walsh (Ed.), *Normal family process* (3rd ed., pp. 514–549). New York: Guilford.

Romano, D. (1997). *Intercultural marriage: Promises and pitfalls.* Boston: Intercultural Press.

Rosc, A. (2001). *Beloved strangers: Interfaith families in nineteenth century America.* Cambridge, UK: Harvard University Press.

Stewart, E. C., & Bennett, M. J. (1991). *American cultural patterns: A cross-cultural perspective.* Yarmouth, ME: Intercultural Press.

Tamura, T., & Lav, A. (1992). Connectedness versus separateness: Applicability of family therapy to Japanese families. *Family Process, 31*(4), 319–340.

Tvrtkovic, R. G. (2001). When Muslim and Christian marry. *America, 185*(6), 11–16.

12

U.S./Caribbean Couples
Perspectives from Caribbean Psychology and Mainstream Social Psychology

Stanley O. Gaines, Jr. and Marina W. Ramkissoon

A disproportionately high percentage of relationship studies have focused on the experiences of couples in which both partners are from the United States (Goodwin, 1999) and are of European descent (Gaines, Buriel, Liu, & Rios, 1997). Persons from developing countries, such as those comprising the Caribbean, have been grossly underrepresented in the field of personal relationships. In this chapter, we first give an overview of some of the research related to interpersonal relationships that has been conducted in the Caribbean, especially in Jamaica. Despite the possibility of pan-cultural similarities in personal relationship processes, a cross-cultural perspective is important to show differences as well as similarities between Americans and persons of various ethnicities and races from the Caribbean. We also apply social exchange theory to the study of Caribbean relationships in particular, as this theory provides a useful framework for understanding both Black Americans and Caribbeans in relation to European descendants in the United States. Finally, areas for future research are suggested.

The second part of the chapter focuses on research on accommodation in relationships with a Jamaican population. We shall draw largely upon interdependence theory (Thibaut & Kelley, 1959), a social-psychological theory that has been tested widely in research on personal relationships. Using the impact of cultural values on accommodation (Gaines et al., 2005; Gaines, Ramkissoon, & Matthies, 2003) as a point of departure, we shall consider the extent to which American–Caribbean relationships might represent interpersonal challenges for the partners involved.

In the final part of the chapter, we consider the results of an initial study (Jackson & Cothran, 2003) regarding the overall quality of relationships between Black American and Black Caribbean persons. Examining the results of this study we conclude by critiquing this fledgling line of research on U.S./Caribbean relationships.

Interpersonal Relationships in Caribbean Psychology

In the Caribbean, psychology itself is a burgeoning field, with the University of the West Indies (Mona Campus, Jamaica) first offering a bachelor's of science in psychology in the 1990s. Fostered within a multidisciplinary department, psychology's origin was more sociological and social psychological. Interpersonal relationships among Black Jamaicans were investigated indirectly through studies on family and gender, fatherhood and masculinity, and the influence of historical events like slavery and colonialism on how people related to each other. Greater reference was made to conjugal or other union types, mating patterns or habits, visiting relationships, cohabitation, concubinage, parenting, and gender/ sex roles than to psychological issues and concepts. Sociological and economic factors such as race, ethnicity, skin color, and unemployment were emphasized.

Of particular note is the virtual absence of large-scale research on personal relationships that is directly psychological in approach, involving either Caribbean people only (for an exception, see Gaines et al., 2003) or comparisons between them and other demographic groups. In order to extend the study of interpersonal relationships to the Caribbean, it will be necessary to apply theoretical models developed abroad to an analysis of the region's specific cultural, social, demographic, historical, and psychological dimensions.

The Caribbean has to be viewed as a racially and ethnically heterogeneous place, populated mostly by descendants of Africans, Europeans, Chinese, East Indians, and Syrians. Some islands are more demographically unique than others, such as Trinidad, where the population is almost 50% Black and 50% East Indian. Each cultural group adheres, to some extent, to unique values and customs that influence the dynamics of interracial and interethnic relationships within the Caribbean. There are very few studies that investigate these dynamics. Because most of the islands are still heavily influenced by social stratification systems passed down from plantation society, racial and socioeconomic prejudice and discrimination continue to influence people's perceptions of interracial relationships and choice of partner.

The Caribbean is also very much a diaspora and consists of immigrants to many countries, including the United States. These migrant populations, although phenotypically similar to Black Americans, sometimes maintain different value systems and customs that affect their attitudes toward interracial relationships (Waters, 2000). Given this diversity, U.S./Caribbean relationships are understandably complex. The current chapter focuses on Black Jamaicans, at home and abroad, and their relationships with Americans.

Blacks in Jamaica and White Americans

Many Black Jamaicans are still influenced by an "inferiority complex" based on skin color, inherited from the plantation society (Fanon, 1952/1967). The Eurocentric domination, enslavement, and oppression of Blacks by White planters created feelings of inferiority (Ashcroft, Griffiths, & Tiffin, 1995). Black identity (alter) was only viewed in relation to White identity (ego) and therefore Blackness, by definition, was considered inferior by both Blacks and Whites. In Jamaica today, because the population is more than 90% Black, gradations of hue rather than race are used to differentiate the population, and persons who have lighter skin tones are called *browning*. Although socioeconomic class is very significant in Jamaican society, among Blacks, many men and women still consider lighter skin tones more valuable and desirable.

Even the Caribbean gender socialization literature shows the ongoing importance of skin color (Leo-Rhynie, 1993). Jamaican children are brought up to believe that "brown" and "White" playmates are preferable to darker-skinned ones. Further, males and females seek White features in a partner when considering child-bearing outcomes (Fanon, 1952/1967). Many innercity Jamaican women (and men) practice skin bleaching, where chemicals are used to lighten facial skin color, a procedure that has the perceived effect of improving self-esteem and enhancing the person's image to onlookers (Charles, 2003).

Attention to skin color is seen in this excerpt from Fanon (1952/1967), who described the life of Mayotte Capecia, a Black woman from Martinique, who was married to a White man, and who found out that her grandmother was White:

> *Mayotte:* I found that I was proud of it.... I should have guessed it when I looked at her [grandmother] color. I found her prettier than ever, and cleverer and more refined ... (p. 47)

When talking about her marriage, Mayotte highlights how important skin color and status were in forming and maintaining the relationship:

> *Mayotte:* I should have liked to be married, but to a White man. But a woman of color is never altogether respectable in a white man's eyes. (p. 42)

In contemporary Jamaica, similar attitudes are still present, demonstrated by discussions with Black Jamaican males[1]:

> *Interviewer:* How did you react when you found out your cousin (Black Jamaican male) married a White woman?
>
> *Black Jamaican male:* At first it didn't matter, but on seeing her I was turned off. Some Jamaican men cool with having a "Whitee," because they look up to them. It gives them status. It's because they feel inferior to them so they try to make up for it. That's why they go for Black girls with brown skin too. But money nowadays more important than race. Once you have money you cris [okay]. (Ramkissoon, 2004)

It can be inferred that for some Black Jamaican men and women, the motivation for choosing a White American woman may be related to identity enhancement through association with a more valuable social group. This is, however, complicated by the importance of economic status, in that being economically well off tends to make race less important (discussed further in the section on social exchange). Race-related conflicts between Black Jamaicans and White Americans are, therefore, more likely when the American's socioeconomic status is low.

Race-related tensions may also emerge in situations in which racial identity and skin color are most salient. Couple interactions can be based on either or both partners' identification with their racial group or on personal individual characteristics. Heightened awareness of racial group membership and skin color may create challenges to a couple's interpersonal connection. As an example, family and friends' attitudes toward skin color will impact how a couple's union is received, and consciousness about this may influence couple dynamics.

> *Interviewer:* Would you ever get involved with someone from the Caribbean?
>
> *Ed (White Canadian male visitor to Jamaica):* I've been to Jamaica about ten times. I've never been with someone from here but I certainly would. When I was younger I used to feel conscious about what my parents would say. Would they disown me or something? But now I don't care. (Ramkissoon, 2004)

Discussion with a White male American Roman Catholic Priest visiting Jamaica revealed that interracial couples may even make decisions about bearing children based on how they imagine people will receive the relationship:

> *Priest:* They (interracial/intercultural couple) made a decision not to have any children. Too many problems.
> *Interviewer:* What kind of problems?
> *Priest:* Too hard to raise them.
> *Interviewer:* Why?
> *Priest:* Racial prejudice. It's too hard to cope. (Ramkissoon, 2004)

Family life for many Black Jamaicans and Black Americans continues to be influenced by events from the past. While some have argued that Black matrifocal families are still shaped by retentions from an African heritage (Herskovits, 1941), others highlight the influence of slavery and the plantation society on family life for Blacks (Frazier, 1966; Smith, 1957). Whereas many White Americans are accustomed to the nuclear family type, many Black Jamaicans and Black Americans grow up in female-headed households and single-parent families (Barrow, 1996). Although the nuclear family is also held as an ideal by many Black families, there are a significant number of absent fathers, who live in separate residences from their children and visit the household occasionally, especially in the lower socioeconomic classes. Additionally, many of these homes are characterized by fluid household boundaries, gaps in communication between parents and children, and economic hardship (Le Franc, Bailey, & Branche, 1998). It is not uncommon for a woman to have children by several men and to be supported by them economically while living in her mother's home. Marriage for Blacks normally comes late in life (Brown, Anderson, & Chevannes, 1993), and represents a movement toward increased responsibility for the man as provider and less infidelity for both partners. Nuclear families are more prevalent in the higher socioeconomic classes for Blacks (Barrow, 1996).

Additionally, Jamaican men, in particular, hold on to traditional gender role expectations in the family setting. Women are expected to be housewives and childcare givers, even if they are employed outside the home. Black Jamaican women hold the expectation that the man is the provider, even if she has an income.[2] She expects to be cared for and, contradictorily, to be treated as an equal in some spheres of life.

Family of origin differences between a White American partner and a Black Jamaican partner may create conflicts for a couple when starting their own family. A White female American may expect that a Black Jamaican man will marry her if she becomes pregnant, whereas his socialization might lead him to expect to continue a visiting relationship. White American men may also not fulfill the expectation of Black Jamaican women to be "kept," if they are not economically well-off. Middle-class White American women tend to be independent and not comply with strict gender expectations of housewife and childcare giver, which may be problematic for the traditional Black Jamaican man.

Black Caribbean Immigrants and Black Americans

First-generation Black Caribbean migrants to the United States are viewed as successful in their attempts at integration into the economic structure (Waters, 2000). Waters claims that, compared to Black Americans, these immigrants were much more positive about race relations and were perceived to have better work attitudes, greater openness to interracial interaction, and more innocent beliefs about American race relations. These attitudes made them more favorable to White employers than Black American workers and contributed to antagonism with Black Americans who viewed them as "sell outs." First-generation immigrants resisted ethnic assimilation, keeping their racial identities but also maintaining positive relationships with Whites.

Because of changes in accent and culture over time, second-generation Caribbean immigrants, on the other hand, were forced into the category of Black American. Like native Black Americans, they have more negative attitudes toward work and interaction with Whites, a factor that has contributed to their demise economically and socially (Waters, 2000). The realities of racism in America between Blacks and Whites have destroyed much of the optimism of cultural equality and acceptance held by the early immigrants.

Interpersonal relationships between Black Americans and first-generation Black Caribbean migrants are therefore expected to be strained because of differences in attitudes toward work, racism, and Whites. Whereas the Black migrant is less focused on racial inequality, Black Americans' emphasis on it is likely to make them reject persons with seemingly pro-White attitudes. Black Americans may also be less tolerant of attempts at assimilation into the White economy and culture. The intermarriage rates in America for foreign-born Blacks with Whites are actually higher than for native-born Black and White Americans (Smith & Edmonston, 1997). Foreign-born Blacks are likely to feel less pressure to assimilate to White norms while maintaining their ethnicity, until they begin to directly experience racial discrimination.

For Black Caribbean migrants (second generation) who have become racialized as Black Americans, and who have essentially lost their Caribbean ethnicity and traditions, interpersonal relationships with native Black Americans are often characterized by "love and trouble" (Patterson, 1999, p. 4). Orlando Patterson (1999) makes many compelling arguments for the impact of slavery on contemporary Black male–female relationships, both among Black Americans and Black Jamaicans and between these groups. He characterizes them as experiencing a crisis and claims that Black Americans, especially, are characterized by single-mother families, multiple partnering, and relationships with high levels of mistrust, anger, and jealousy.

A few Caribbean studies have documented similar conclusions (Brown et al., 1993; Chevannes, 1992; Henry & Wilson, 1975) showing that Jamaican women are perceived as untrustworthy by their male partners. Patterson's observations echo Edith Clarke's (1957/1970) seminal work on Black Jamaican families. She described casual concubinage, multiple partnering, and an emphasis on male prowess but also observed stable family unions, where cohabitation preceded legal marriages. Rodman's (1971) study of lower-class Blacks in Trinidad suggested economic instability as the main reason for loose conjugal relationships and noted the prevalence of "friending" or less demanding noncohabiting relationships.

Conflict between Black Americans and second-generation Black Jamaican migrants who share similar experiences of racial discrimination might be less because of cultural and national differences and more because of intergenerationally transmitted relationship patterns, some of which seem dysfunctional. Black males, Jamaican and American, are described as emotionally unavailable and with a need to express "manhood" as demonstrated by early initiation into sexual activity, multiple partnering, and child-bearing from an early age (Patterson, 1999). For a White male or female socialized through more stable and trusting families and relationships, the differences in practices and values may cause conflict between him and a Black Jamaican. For instance, breaches of middle-class White American parenting role expectations, such as those described below, would likely cause conflict between a White American man and a Black lower-class Jamaican female:

Child: "My mother works day and night, but it doesn't look like she is using the money she earns to help support me ..." (Le Franc et al., 1998, p. 6)
Child: "Some women, when they get money they don't put food for their children. Dem buy clothes for demselves, dress up and gone leave you

alone hungry ... meanwhile the pickney (i.e., children) are there
hungry and nothing is there ..." (Le Franc et al., 1998, p. 6)

In summary, the literature discussed above demonstrates that the
dynamics of interpersonal relationships between Americans and Jamaicans
are varied and complex, depending on the groups involved. First, self and
identity enhancement may be key factors when considering the effects of
lingering inferiority complexes of Black Jamaicans (in Jamaica) and their
preference for a brown or White partner. Although no data were available,
it is likely that many Black Americans also experience this inferiority complex but may manifest it in different ways. Second, Black Jamaican immigrants to the United States may or may not suffer from such complexes but
appear to be more open to cultural interchanges and relationships with
Whites, until they knowingly face racial discrimination. It should also
be noted that most persons do not marry outside their social class and
that Black Caribbeans in America who marry Whites are generally not
from the lower classes. Third, when it comes to conflicts between second-
generation Black Caribbean migrants and Black Americans (and within
the groups themselves), explanations are drawn from slavery and plantation society in terms of inherited patterns of dysfunctionality in relationships (Patterson, 1999). Patterns of distrust, jealousy, and multiple
partnering, as well as Black men's strong desire to express manhood and
dominance, are linked to their historical lack of power in both the private
and public spheres. It can be argued that this dysfunctionality lives on
today despite improvements in the socioeconomic status of Blacks as a
whole.[3] Whereas all the explanations put forward above are very plausible,
there is a great need for further evidence and theorizing about intercultural and interracial relationships.

Social Exchange in Relationships

As mentioned in earlier sections, although skin color is a significant factor
in determining partner choice and the maintenance of relationships, for
many Black Jamaicans today, economic stability is just as or even more
important. For many, romance appears to be secondary to more practical
and utilitarian considerations for forming and maintaining relationships
among Black Caribbeans at home and abroad. The visiting relationships
discussed above, where Jamaican women are financed by several partners and/or baby fathers, is an example of this utilitarianism. Visiting

relationships involve male partners visiting the woman, who normally lives in her mother's home, and who may or may not have children with the male partner. The male generally expects to be able to have sexual intercourse with the woman in exchange for material goods and money, either for her or for her children. Some women may be in several visitor relationships simultaneously or sequentially depending on her economic needs. Many of these relationships do not end up in legal marriage until the couple is much older (40s) or financially secure. In a study on Black Caribbean families, one Black man gave his opinion on female multiple partnering:

> *Jamaican male:* "The girls nowadays no want one man you know; dem want all twenty man ... because if you see a man can't give them everything, dem a go know that a next man can give them something. And if him don't have it to give them, a next man have to give them." (Le Franc et al., 1998, p. 7)

Along with economic dependence on men comes vulnerability to domestic violence and strict gender role expectations. Although these patterns are more prevalent in the lower socioeconomic classes, they are also quite common for the higher classes and persons with post high school level education.

Dirks and Kern's (1976) analysis of mating pattern data in the British Virgin Islands (BVI) from Methodist baptismal records (1823–1965) and Methodist marriage registry information (1880–1970) supports theories of social exchange and reflects the impact of socioeconomic hardships. They show that mating patterns varied for specified economic periods. Extralegal mating generally followed rules of exchange that allowed for maximization of short-term benefits. Marriage and long-term relationships were not valued if they did not provide immediate benefits or if they would divert funds away from personal needs to items for the home, partner, or offspring. Marriages were reserved as options for maximizing benefits in the long term such as commanding respect in the community and old age security. House building in the BVI also appeared to be a major turning point in one's mating status, as only then was it deemed appropriate for a couple to be legally bound.

Le Franc et al. (1998) discuss the relevance of social exchange theory to interpersonal relationships among lower-class Jamaicans.

> ... [T]he principle of exchange is a very dominant one: thus, loyalty, status, fidelity, the supply of sexual and other domestic "services," and the provision of financial support are all placed in the same equation and traded against each other in a quasimarket relationship. The absence of balance and equilibrium

> often and easily leads to stress, the exercise of the "exit" option, and therefore alterations to the household boundaries. (Le Franc et al., 1998, p. 9)

Hence, satisfaction for a woman comes from finding economic security for herself and her children from one or more men. Men receive sexual satisfaction from multiple partnering as well as bolstered "macho" reputations. Exchanges of emotional support and notions of romance therefore feature less in these relationships. Persons who are not faced with economic hardship on a daily basis can afford to form relationships based more on romance and emotional desires. Furthermore, differences in economic status many affect Caribbean couples as well as U.S./Caribbean couples. However, notions of romance and emotional support may not be held as strongly by Black Jamaican women compared to White American women. Additionally, Black Jamaican males are believed to be emotionally unavailable as a whole. For White American women, who, given their socialization, may have stronger expectations for romance, there may be significant discrepancies in relationship expectations if they are involved with Black Jamaican men. Black Jamaican women, who traditionally have the notion of being kept and who often are solely dependent on men for income, are likely to get involved with richer White American males to fulfill these needs, rather than based on romantic expectations. Further research is needed to substantiate these expected relationship patterns and to tease out the effects of nationality and socioeconomic class on relationship dynamics among Blacks and between Blacks and Whites.

Summary

Although there is little psychological data available on interpersonal relationships in the Caribbean region, the literature does provide fertile cultural and social information for future research. Theories of self and identity that discuss how persons enhance self-esteem and negotiate ethnic and racial identity in the face of discrimination are relevant to the Caribbean experience. Social exchange frameworks are also relevant to understanding the utilitarianism often observed in Black interpersonal relationships. Further, gender socialization and family forms play a part in expectations of partners. Applications of these and other theoretical frameworks, however, must first specify the group of Caribbean persons under study, given their diversity and complexity.

Accommodation in Personal Relationships

Within the field of personal relationships, one of the most influential theories is interdependence theory (Thibaut & Kelley, 1959; for reviews, see Berscheid, 1985; Berscheid & Reis, 1998). According to interdependence theory, human beings possess the capacity to weigh the short-term and long-term benefits and costs of behaving in ways that promote individual and relational goals. When individuals are confronted with the choice between behaving in ways that promote individual goals over the short term and behaving in ways that promote relational goals over the long term, individuals often opt to act in ways that promote relational goals over the long term. The concept of interdependence includes, but is not limited to, individuals' willingness to forgo achieving short-term individual goals for the sake of achieving long-term relational goals.

One of the most intensively studied aspects of interdependence in personal relationships is accommodation, or individuals' willingness to forgo reciprocating partners' anger or criticism, for the sake of maintaining their personal relationships (Rusbult, Verette, Whitney, Slovik, & Lipkus, 1991; for a review, see Berscheid & Reis, 1998). Four distinct yet interrelated behaviors comprise accommodation: (a) exit, or an overt, destructive response to partners' anger or criticism; (b) voice, or an overt, constructive response to partners' anger or criticism; (c) loyalty, or a covert, constructive response to partners' anger or criticism; and (d) neglect, or a covert, destructive response to partners' anger or criticism. To the extent that individuals respond to partners' anger or criticism with voice and loyalty, and to the extent that individuals refrain from responding to partners' anger or criticism with exit and neglect, individuals engage in accommodation toward their partners.

Within mainstream journals in the fields of social psychology and personal relationships, a variety of individual differences in accommodation have been documented. For example, individual differences in attachment styles (e.g., Gaines et al., 1997; Scharfe & Bartholomew, 1995) and gender-related personality traits (e.g., Rusbult et al., 1991) have been identified as significant predictors of accommodation in romantic relationships. With the exception of attachment styles (e.g., Gaines, et al., 1999; Gaines & Henderson, 2002), specific individual difference influences on accommodation rarely have been examined in mainstream or non-mainstream journals.

*Cultural Values as Individual Difference Influences
on Accommodation*

One set of individual difference variables whose influences on accommodation have been confined to studies published outside mainstream social psychology and personal relationship journals is cultural values, or organized sets of beliefs that are communicated from societal agents to individuals (Gaines, Buriel, Liu, & Rios, 1997). Since the early 1980s, cultural psychologists' conceptualizations of cultural values have progressed from unidimensional and bipolar (e.g., Hofstede, 1980) to bidimensional (e.g., Triandis, 1990) to multidimensional (e.g., Schwartz, 1994). Cultural psychologists generally have devoted greater attention to developing taxonomies of cultural values than to documenting the effects of cultural values on social behavior (for a review, see Triandis, 1995).

For the purposes of this chapter, we will adopt the taxonomy of cultural values that Gaines, Buriel, Liu, & Rios (1997) proposed as having special relevance to the study of personal relationship processes: (a) individualism, or an orientation toward the welfare of oneself; (b) collectivism, or an orientation toward the welfare of one's larger community; (c) familism, or an orientation toward the welfare of one's family, both immediate and extended; (d) romanticism, or an orientation toward the welfare of one's romantic relationship dyad or pair; and (e) spiritualism, or an orientation toward the welfare of all living entities, both natural and supernatural. Gaines, Buriel, Liu, & Rios (1997) was interested primarily in cultural values as predictors of interpersonal resource exchange (i.e., the reciprocity of affectionate and respectful behaviors) in personal relationships. However, just as one might expect cultural values to be reflected in the reciprocity that characterizes interpersonal resource exchange, so too might one expect cultural values to be reflected in the lack of reciprocity that characterizes accommodation.

In Figure 12.1, we present a model of hypothetical effects of cultural values on accommodation, following Gaines et al. (2005). In the model, individuals' personal orientations are measured positively by the "me-orientation" of individualism; individuals' social orientation is measured positively by the "we-orientations" of collectivism, familism, romanticism, and spiritualism; and individuals' accommodation is measured positively by voice and loyalty, and negatively by exit and neglect. According to the model, individuals' social orientations will be a significant positive predictor of accommodation, whereas individuals' personal orientations will be a significant negative predictor of accommodation. The predictions within

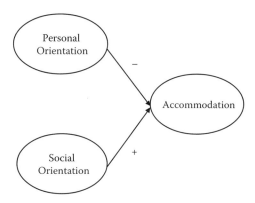

Figure 12.1   Hypothesized impact of cultural values on accomodation across all nations.

the model are based on two assumptions: individuals' orientations toward persons in addition to themselves promotes individuals' striving to fulfill long-term relational goals; and individuals' orientations toward themselves (without necessarily considering the social and emotional needs of persons in addition to themselves) promotes individuals' striving to fulfill short-term individual goals.

Within-Couple Differences in the Impact of Cultural Values on Accommodation Among U.S./Caribbean Couples

So far, we have focused on potential problems in interracial relationships in which one partner is Black (whether American or Caribbean) and the other partner is White (specifically, White American). Next, we shall consider potential problems in international relationships in which one partner is Black American and the other partner is Black Caribbean. The model presented in Figure 12.1 does not identify individuals' nationalities as moderators of links between cultural values and accommodation in personal relationships. Nevertheless, results of published studies using American heterosexuals (Gaines et al., 2005) and Jamaican heterosexuals (Gaines et al., 2003) suggest that nationality may indeed moderate the effects of cultural values on accommodation. As predicted, in the United States (Gaines et al., 2005), individuals' social orientations were significant positive predictors of accommodation but, contrary to predictions, individuals' personal orientations were unrelated to accommodation. In Jamaica (Gaines et al., 2003), as predicted, individuals' personal orientations were significant negative predictors of accommodation but, contrary to predictions, individuals' social orientations were unrelated to accommodation.

Taking the results of Gaines et al. (2005) at face value, we would anticipate that among heterosexual couples with one American partner and one Caribbean partner, considerable potential exists regarding partners' misinterpretation of the agendas that underlie each other's attempts at accommodation (see Snyder & Cantor, 1998). In anticipating the potential for partners' misinterpretations of each other's agendas, we are assuming that regardless of race or nationality, individuals generally seek to understand why their relationship partners have chosen to act in a particular manner (consistent with attribution theories in social psychology; for a review, see Fiske & Taylor, 1991). However, we are also assuming that the specific conclusions that individuals reach regarding their relationship partners' reasons for behaving in a particular manner are influenced by their cultural background (see Fiske, Kitayama, Markus, & Nisbett, 1998). We acknowledge that, like interracial relationships, international relationships are not randomly distributed throughout the partners' respective populations; any findings about general tendencies in those populations may not apply to international couples, who may represent the extreme ends of the continuum. For example, even if Americans in general differ from Caribbeans in the cultural value of romanticism, persons in U.S./Caribbean relationships may not differ from each other regarding romanticism; shared romanticism might be a prerequisite for relationship development in general and for international relationship development in particular (for a similar argument regarding shared romanticism among partners in U.S. interracial relationships, see Gaines et al., 1999).[4]

Among U.S./Caribbean couples, partners might draw on societal stereotypes and misattribute each other's accommodation.[5] We are assuming that, even though accommodation in itself is desirable in personal relationships, partners' correct interpretations of the reasons for each other's behavior is desirable, whereas partners' incorrect interpretation of the reasons for each other's behavior is undesirable in personal relationships (see Fiske & Taylor, 1991, for a discussion of the negative consequences that can result from errors in attribution processes). An American partner may, for example, misattribute a Caribbean partner's accommodation to Jamaicans' emphasis on group-level success and thus assume that the Caribbean partner is pursuing the agenda of maintaining the relationship when in fact the Caribbean partner is pursuing the agenda of protecting self-esteem (see Gaines et al., 2003). Likewise, a Caribbean partner may misattribute an American partner's accommodation to Americans' emphasis on individual-level success and thus assume that the American partner is pursuing the agenda of protecting self-esteem when in fact the American partner is pursuing the agenda of maintaining the relationship. These attributions might not accurately reflect the relative importance of personal and social orientations in partners' accommodations. Psychotherapy might be required in order for partners to attain genuine understanding of the agendas that are reflected in each other's attempts at accommodation (see Baptiste, 1984).

It is possible that "me-oriented" Americans are less likely than "me-oriented" Caribbeans to realize when others do not share their world view. Perhaps more than persons of any other nationality, Americans have a tendency to project their cultural values—especially individualism—onto others. In contrast, Caribbeans may be well aware that Americans do not share Caribbeans' cultural values. Such a tendency would be consistent with the view that the United States promotes cultural hegemony throughout the world (Sardar & Davies, 2003).[6]

Before we prematurely conclude that conflict is inevitable in U.S./ Caribbean relationships, let us consider the results of unpublished research on cultural values and accommodation in the United Kingdom (Gaines, Larbie, Sereke-Melake, Pereira, & Patel, 2004). Consistent with hypotheses, among British heterosexuals, individuals' social orientations were significant positive predictors of accommodation and individuals' personal orientations were significant negative predictors of accommodation. In fact, as Figure 12.2 indicates, results of a multigroup structural equation

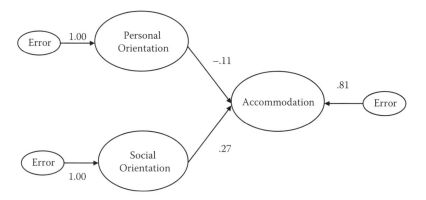

Figure 12.2 Actual impact of cultural values on accomodation across the United States, Jamaica, and the United Kingdom.

analysis (see Joreskog & Sorbom, 1996) reveal that, after controlling statistically for differences in measurement error across the three nations, both of the original predictions concerning cultural values and accommodation are supported empirically in the United States, Jamaica, and the U.K. Perhaps American and Caribbean partners are not inherently prone to misattributing the agendas behind each other's accommodation efforts after all.

Finally, even when conflict does occur in U.S./Caribbean relationships, regardless of the specific cultural value(s) that partners manifest, it is possible that when one partner is angry or critical toward the other partner, the other person has the capacity to defuse the conflict by deciding not to seek retribution. As Rusbult and her colleagues (1991) have noted, all relationships are marked by some expressions of anger and criticism by one partner toward the other partner. We do not wish to pathologize U.S./Caribbean relationships per se. Rather, we ask whether American and Caribbean relationship partners view each other's underlying values accurately.

Potential Influences of Socioeconomic Status, Race, and Nationality on the Impact of Cultural Values on Accommodation among U.S./Caribbean Couples

So far, apart from nationality, we have not considered the role of demographic variables in moderating the impact of cultural values on accommodation. However, certain demographic variables are so confounded with the aforementioned U.S./Jamaica dichotomy that it is worth disentangling those variables and exploring their possible impact on links between cultural values and accommodation. For example, the reliance on data from university-educated participants in the studies by Gaines et al. (2005) obscures the fact that, on average, Jamaicans are dramatically different from Americans in terms of socioeconomic status (SES) (i.e., Jamaicans are much more likely to be classified as lower-SES, and much less likely to be classified as middle-SES, than are Americans; see Jones & Zoppel, 1979). It is possible that the impact of cultural values on accommodation as reported by Gaines et al. (2005) is more characteristic of middle-SES individuals than of lower-SES individuals. If a middle-SES American is paired with a lower-SES Jamaican in a romantic relationship, then the potential for SES to moderate the impact of cultural values on accommodation and to foster conflict should not be discounted.

Another possible moderator of links between cultural values and accommodation is an individual's racial group membership. Persons of European descent comprise approximately 70% of all Americans, whereas persons of African descent comprise more than 90% of all Jamaicans. In the study of American heterosexuals by Gaines et al. (2005), race was not examined as a moderator of links between cultural values and accommodation. Even in the study of Jamaican heterosexuals by Gaines et al. (2003), racial distinctions (which did not moderate the impact of cultural values on accommodation) were limited to distinctions between (a) persons for whom both parents were of African descent; and (b) persons for whom at least one parent was not of African descent. If a White American is paired with a Black Jamaican, then the potential of race to moderate links between cultural values and accommodation and to foster conflict should not be underestimated.

Returning to nationality as a possible moderator of links between cultural values and accommodation, we cannot assume that Jamaican participants represent Caribbean persons as a whole. Among Caribbean nations, one finds considerable diversity regarding predominant languages, religions, and other products of culture (Baptiste, Hardy, & Lewis, 1997). Even if U.S./Jamaican differences are not sufficient to moderate the impact of cultural values on accommodation, it is not clear whether U.S./Haitian or U.S./Cuban differences are similarly weak in relational terms. If an American is paired with a person from any Caribbean nation other than Jamaica, then the potential of nationality to moderate links between cultural values and accommodation and to foster conflict should not be ignored.

Finally, a variety of interaction effects may occur among SES, race, and nationality as moderators of links between cultural values and accommodation. For example, among Caribbean nations, the islands of Trinidad and Tobago are unique in terms of SES (e.g., Trinidad and Tobago are among the wealthiest islands in the West Indies) and in terms of racial composition (Baptiste et al., 1997). How, if at all, would a pairing between a middle-SES American of African descent and a middle-SES Trinidadian of Asian descent differ from a pairing between a middle-SES American of European descent and a lower-SES Haitian of African descent regarding the impact of cultural values on accommodation or on the potential for conflict? Researchers in the field of personal relationships have not begun to address such questions.

Summary

Initial studies by Gaines (Gaines et al., 2004; Gaines et al., 2005) and his colleagues suggested that, using an interdependence perspective, American and Jamaican persons might act upon different cultural values when responding to partners' anger or criticism (i.e., among American persons, collectivism is a significant positive influence on accommodation; among Caribbean persons, individualism is a significant negative influence on accommodation). Subsequent research by Gaines and colleagues indicates that, when data from British persons are included and results are compared across American, Jamaican, and British persons, individualism generally is a significant negative influence on accommodation in all three nations, and collectivism generally is a significant positive influence on accommodation. Nevertheless, it is possible that socioeconomic status, race, and/or nationality mediate the impact of cultural values on accommodation, depending upon the nation in question.

Beyond Exchange and Interdependence Theories: Results of Initial Research on U.S./Caribbean Relationships

Moving beyond the boundaries of exchange and interdependence theories, at least one study (Jackson & Cothran, 2003) has examined relationships between Black American and Black Caribbean (specifically, Black West Indian) persons.[7] Jackson and Cothran (2003) did not provide results regarding personal relationship processes involving Black American and Black Caribbean persons. However, they did offer results regarding Black American and Black Caribbean persons' general attitudes toward U.S./Caribbean relationships.

On the one hand, a clear majority of Black American and Black Caribbean persons reported that they had contact with each other at some time in the past. On the other hand, a majority of Black American and Black Caribbean persons reported that the quality of their relationships with each other was low, and just under half of Black American and Black Caribbean persons reported that communication with each other was negative. Moreover, Black American and Black Caribbean persons held a variety of negative stereotypes toward each other.

Although the results of the Jackson and Cothran (2003) study concerning Black American/Black Caribbean relationships were disappointing, Black American/Black African relationships fared even worse.

Black African/Black Caribbean relationships fared somewhat better than Black American/Black Caribbean or Black American/Black African relationships with regard to positivity versus negativity of intergroup opinions. The poor relationships observed by Jackson and Cothran (2003) support the work on migrant experiences discussed above (Waters, 2000), where Black Caribbeans appear to be more open-minded towards Whites until they experience racism openly and are therefore spurned by Black Americans. Jackson and Cothran (2003) contend that this negativity is the result of Western enslavement and corresponding miseducation of Blacks throughout the African diaspora; even when Blacks do not accept racial stereotypes when directed toward them personally, they may nonetheless internalize and apply those same racial stereotypes to fellow Blacks, especially when the other Blacks belong to national outgroups. This explanation is similar to the self-negation arguments of Fanon (1952/1967). It remains to be seen whether corrective education will suffice to improve Blacks' attitudes and relationships with fellow Blacks across national lines.

Despite the insight that Jackson and Cothran (2003) offer with regard to relationships among Black Africans, Black Americans, and Black Caribbeans, the aforementioned lack of data from both members of the relationships in question cannot be overlooked. As we pointed out earlier in this chapter, the assumption of random distribution of international relationships across partners' respective national groups has not been tested. Also, the Jackson and Cothran (2003) study was atheoretical and no hypotheses or research questions were stated. Clearly, more research on Black American/Black Caribbean relationships is needed, especially research that not only is theory based but also is concerned with the cognitive, affective, and behavioral dynamics that drive Black American/Black Caribbean relationships in particular, and U.S./Caribbean relationships more generally.

Conclusion

We noted that the field of personal relationships rarely has dealt with relationships involving persons from Caribbean nations. Based on the limited evidence at hand, we do not have reason to believe that U.S./Caribbean relationships are inherently problematic. Possible interaction effects among SES, race, and nationality make it difficult for us to conclude definitively that U.S./Caribbean relationships are indistinguishable cognitively, affectively, or behaviorally from other relationships. The one study that we were able to find regarding U.S./Caribbean relationships provides a sobering assessment of the quality of Black American/Black Caribbean relationships. We urge researchers in the field of personal relationships to greatly accelerate efforts to study the social and psychological experiences of couples from which at least one partner is from a Caribbean nation. Theoretical frameworks and concepts worth considering for the future work include social and personal identities, self-esteem enhancement strategies, social exchange, and social perception processes. Finally, as Gaines et al. (1997) pointed out, scholars in the field of personal relationships need to begin taking ethnicity into account more explicitly and more consistently than they have done so far.

Notes

1. There are no known published Caribbean studies that focus on U.S./Caribbean couples specifically. Anecdotal evidence was gathered for the current book chapter from discussions with two Black Jamaican males, two White male tourists visiting Jamaica, and a Black female Jamaican clinical psychologist whose clientele include American/Caribbean married professionals.
2. Evidence of these expectations comes from discussions with a clinical psychologist who provides therapy for American/Caribbean couples.
3. The current chapter uses evidence provided by Patterson (1999) and others on dysfunctionality in Black relationships and families to demonstrate trends among groups rather than to contribute to stereotyping of Blacks.
4. We are indebted to the editors of this volume for raising the issue of random distribution across populations.
5. We do not know of any research directly bearing upon the effects of societal stereotypes, as distinct from information that is more specific to their unique relationships and particular partners, on misattributions. However, we note the results of a study (Johnson & Cothran, 2003) that found substantial stereotyping among Black Americans, Black Africans, and Black Caribbean persons toward each other.
6. We are indebted to the editors for raising the issue of Americans' individualism as possibly obscuring an awareness that other persons may not share their viewpoints.
7. Jackson and Cothran (2003) indicated that by *West Indians* they were referring primarily to persons from Jamaica, Trinidad and Tobago, and Guyana. Jackson and Cothran did not make further distinctions among these West Indian groups.

References

Ashcroft, B., Griffiths, G., & Tiffin, H. (1995). *The post-colonial studies reader.* London: Routledge.

Baptiste, D. A., Jr. (1984). Marital and family therapy with racially/culturally inter-married stepfamilies: Issues and guidelines. *Family Relations, 33*, 373–380.

Baptiste, D. A., Jr., Hardy, K. V., & Lewis, L. (1997). Family therapy with English Caribbean immigrant families in the United States: Issues of emigration, immigration, culture, and race. *Contemporary Family Therapy, 19*, 337–359.

Barrow, C. (1996). *Family in the Caribbean: Themes and perspectives.* Kingston, Jamaica: Ian Randle Publishers.

Berscheid, E. (1985). Interpersonal attraction. In G. Lindzey & E. Aronson (Eds.), *Handbook of social psychology* (Vol. 2, 3rd ed., pp. 413–484). New York: Random House.

Berscheid, E., & Reis, H. T. (1998). Attraction and close relationships. In D. T. Gilbert, S. T. Fiske, & G. Lindzey (Eds.), *The handbook of social psychology* (Vol. 2, pp. 193–281). New York: McGraw-Hill.

Brown, J., Anderson, P., & Chevannes, B. (1993). *Report on the contribution of Caribbean men to the family: A Jamaican pilot study.* The Caribbean Child Development Centre, School of Continuing Studies, University of the West Indies.

Charles, C. (2003). Skin bleaching and the deconstruction of Blackness. *Ideaz, 2*(1), 42–54.

Chevannes, B. (1992). Sex behavior of Jamaicans: A literature review. *Social and Economic Studies, 42*(1), 1–45.

Clarke, E. (1970). *My mother who fathered me.* London: George Allen and Unwin. (Original work published 1957)

Dirks, R., & Kerns, V. (1976). Mating patterns and adaptive change in Rum Bay, 1923–1970. *Social and Economic Studies, 25*(1), 34–54.

Fanon, F. (1967). *Black skins, white masks* (C. L. Markmann, Trans.). New York: Grove Press. (Original work published 1952)

Fiske, A., Kitayama, S., Markus, H. R., & Nisbett, R. E. (1998). The cultural matrix of social psychology. In D. Gilbert, S. Fiske & G. Lindzey (Eds.), *The handbook of social psychology* (4th ed., pp. 915–981). New York: McGraw-Hill.

Fiske, S. T., & Taylor, S. E. (1991). *Social cognition* (2nd ed.). New York: McGraw-Hill.

Frazier, F. (1966). *The Negro family in the United States.* Chicago: University of Chicago Press.

Gaines, S. O., Jr., Buriel, R., Liu, J. H., & Rios, D. I. (1997). *Culture, ethnicity, and personal relationship processes.* New York: Routledge.

Gaines, S. O., Jr., & Henderson, M. C. (2002). Impact of attachment style on responses to accommodative dilemmas among same-sex couples. *Personal Relationships, 9*, 89–93.

Gaines, S. O., Jr., Henderson, M. C., Kim, M., Gilstrap, S., Yi, J., Rusbult, C. E., Hardin, D. P., Gaertner, L. A. (2005). Cultural value orientations, internalized homophobia, and accommodation in romantic relationships. *Journal of Homosexuality, 50,* 97–117.

Gaines, S. O., Jr., Granrose, C. S., Rios, D. I., Garcia, B. F., Page, M. S., Farris, K. R., & Bledsoe, K. L. (1999). Patterns of attachment and responses to accommodative dilemmas among interethnic/interracial couples. *Journal of Social and Personal Relationships, 16,* 277–287.

Gaines, S. O., Jr., Larbie, J., Sereke-Melake, Z., Pereira, L., & Patel, S. (2004, July). *Revisiting cultural values as predictors of accommodation in heterosexual relationships: Evidence from the United Kingdom.* Paper presented at the conference of the International Association for Relationship Research, Madison, WI.

Gaines, S. O., Jr., Ramkissoon, M., & Matthies, B. K. (2003). Cultural value orientations and accommodation among heterosexual relationships in Jamaica. *Journal of Black Psychology, 29,* 165–186.

Gaines, S. O., Jr., Reis, H. T., Summers, S., Rusbult, C. E., Cox, C. L., Wexler, M. O., et al. (1997). Impact of attachment style on reactions to accommodative dilemmas in close relationships. *Personal Relationships, 4,* 93–113.

Gaines, S. O., Jr., Rios, D. I., Granrose, C. S., Bledsoe, K. L., Farris, K. R., Page Youn, M. S., et al. (1999). Romanticism and interpersonal resource exchange among African American/Anglo and other interracial couples. *Journal of Black Psychology, 25,* 461–489.

Goodwin, R. (1999). *Personal relationships across cultures.* London: Routledge.

Henry, F., & Wilson, P. (1975). Status of women in Caribbean societies: An overview of their social, economic and sexual roles. *Social and Economic Studies, 24*(2), 165–198.

Herskovits, M. (1941). *The myth of the Negro past.* Boston: Beacon Press.

Hofstede, G. (1980). *Culture's consequences: International differences in work-related values.* Beverly Hills, CA: Sage.

Jackson, J. V., & Cothran, M. E. (2003). Black versus Black: The relationships among African, African American, and African Caribbean persons. *Journal of Black Studies, 33,* 576–604.

Jones, E. E., & Zoppel, C. L. (1979). Personality differences among Blacks in Jamaica and the United States. *Journal of Cross-Cultural Psychology, 10,* 435–456.

Joreskog, K., & Sorbom, D. (1996). *LISREL 8: User's reference guide.* Chicago: Scientific Software Inc.

Le Franc, E., Bailey, W., & Branche, C. (1998). The family unit: An elusive dream? *Caribbean Dialogue, 4*(1), 1–9.

Leo-Rhynie, E. (1993). *The Jamaican family: Continuity and change.* Jamaica: Grace Kennedy Foundation.

Lewin, K. (1951). *Field theory in social science.* New York: Harper.

Patterson, O. (1999). *Rituals of blood: Consequences of slavery in two American centuries.* New York: Basic Civitas.

Ramkissoon, M. (2004). [interviews on inter-racial relationships]. Unpublished raw data.

Rodman, H. (1971). *Lower class families: The culture of poverty in Negro Trinidad.* London: Oxford University Press.

Rusbult, C. E., Verette, J., Whitney, G. A., Slovik, L. F., & Lipkus, I. (1991). Accommodation processes in close relationships: Theory and preliminary evidence. *Journal of Personality and Social Psychology, 60,* 53–78.

Sardar, Z., & Davies, M. W. (2003). *Why do people hate America?* London: Icon Books.

Scharfe, E., & Bartholomew, K. (1995). Accommodation and attachment representations in young couples. *Journal of Social and Personal Relationships, 12,* 389–401.

Schwartz, S. H. (1994). Are there universal aspects in the structure and content of human values? *Journal of Social Issues, 50,* 19–45.

Smith, J. P., & Edmonston, B. (1997). *The new Americans.* Washington, D.C.: National Academy Press.

Smith, M. G. (1957). The African heritage in the Caribbean. In V. Rubin (Ed.), *Caribbean studies: A symposium* (pp. 67–75). Kingston, Jamaica: Jamaica Institute of Social and Economic Research, University College of the West Indies.

Snyder, M., & Cantor, N. (1998). Understanding personality and social behavior: A functionalist strategy. In D. T. Gilbert, S. T. Fiske, & G. Lindzey (Eds.), *The handbook of social psychology* (Vol. 1, 4th ed., pp. 635–679). Boston: McGraw-Hill.

Thibaut, J. W., & Kelley, H. H. (1959). *The social psychology of groups.* New York: Wiley.

Triandis, H. C. (1990). Cross-cultural studies of individualism and collectivism. In J. J. Berman (Ed.), *Nebraska symposium on motivation: Cross-cultural perspectives* (Vol. 37, pp. 41–133). Lincoln, NE: University of Nebraska Press.

Triandis, H. C. (1995). *Individualism and collectivism.* Boulder, CO: Westview Press.

Waters, M. (2000). *Black identities: West Indian immigrant dreams and American realities.* Cambridge, MA: Harvard University Press.

Author Note

The authors are indebted to Terri A. Karis and Kyle D. Killian for their constructive comments on earlier versions of this chapter. Please address all correspondence to Stanley O. Gaines, Jr., School of Social Sciences, Brunel University, Uxbridge, Middlesex UB8 3PH, United Kingdom (phone 011-44-189-527-4000, extension 65485; fax 011-44-189-526-9724; e-mail

Stanley.Gaines@brunel.ac.uk); or Marina W. Ramkissoon, Department of Sociology, Psychology, and Social Work, University of the West Indies, Mona Campus, Mona, Kingston 7, Jamaica (phone 1-876-512-3341; fax 1-876-977-9031; e-mail marina.ramkissoon@uwimona.edu.jm).

Index

electronic attachments, internet marital trade and, 111–140
Elite Matchmaking, 151
e-mail, 116, 120
English immersion laws, 170
English language, 55
as global language, 60, 66
Japanese women and, 60
Esenin, Sergei, 148
ethnic identities, assymetrical, 100
ethnicity, White Americans and, 100
ethnocentrism, 10
European Connections (marriage Internet agency), 151, 152, 153
exogamy
Asian Indians in intercultural marriages and, 189–206
exogamy, Asian Indians in intercultural marriages and, 189–206

F

face, 37
facework, 37
Falicov, Celia Jaes, xvii
families
Asian Indian, 192–194
conceptions of, 174
definitions of, 174
Latino, 174
Latino/Latina immigrant and non-Hispanic White couples, 177–179
multicultural context of, 221
Muslim intercultural couples and, 221
nuclear, 174
responses to dating, 177–179
structure and dynamics, 192
families, extended, 174, 218
Muslim intercultural couples, 218
families of origin, intercultural couple relations and, 8
family boundaries, Latino/Latina immigrant and non-Hispanic White couples, 181
fears, Latino/Latina immigrant and non-Hispanic White couples and, 177
Fellini, Federico, xxi
feminism
Russians and, 149
Western, 73
Fiddler on the Roof, 131
Filipino women, 11
Australia and, 130, 132–133
internet sites and, 133

Find a Husband After 35 Using What I Learned at Harvard Business School (by Rachel Greenwald), 78
First World, 118, 130, 139 n. 2
foreign language, desireability and, 58
Foreign Relations, marriage Internet agency, 151
Foucault, Michel, 54, 123
biopower and, 113
French Kiss (movie), 58
French language, 58

G

Gaines, Stanley O., 229–250
gender relations
Asian Indians in intercultural marriages and, 189–206
in cultures of origin, 9
Muslim intercultural couples, 214–215
Georgetown University, Russian Area Program, 153
German language, 55
Global North, 116, 119, 130, 132, 139 n. 1
Global South, 114, 116, 119, 132, 139 n. 1
Global Survival Network, 156
"Goodwife.com: The Foreign Bride" (web site), 128
Grearson, Jessie, 71–88
Greenwald, Rachel, 78
Guess Who's Coming to Dinner (movie), 111

H

Hammer, Armand, 148
Harris, Sydney, xvii
health, Muslim intercultural couples and, 223
Heidegger, Martin, 123
Helene International Marriage Agency (web page), 114
hierarchy, Asian Indian families, 194
Hinduism, 190
history and demographics, Asian Indians in intercultural marriages, 190
homogamy, xix
Hughes, Maple, 155
huppah, 25–28
Huppah as a window shade, 27

I

"I Can't Love You in Your Language" (psychoanalytic report by PRado de Oliveira, 1988), 66